RED

CAT,

WHITE

CAT

RED CAT, WHITE CAT

China and the Contradictions of "Market Socialism"

ROBERT WEIL

MONTHLY REVIEW PRESS
NEW YORK

Library of Congress Cataloging-in-Publication Data

Weil, Robert, 1940-
    Red cat, white cat : China and the contradictions of "market
socialism" / Robert Weil.
        p.   cm.
    Includes bibliographical references and index.
    ISBN 0-85345-967-3 (cloth : alk. paper). — ISBN 0-85345-968-1 (paper)
    1. China—Economic policy—1976- 2.China—Economic
conditions—1976- 3. Mixed economy—China. I. Title.
HC427.92   IN PROCESS
338.951'009'049—dc20   95-34266
                                                  CIP

Monthly Review Press
122 West 27th Street
New York NY 10001

Manufactured in the United States of America

10 9 8 7 6 5 4 3 2 1

For
ANICA
Brave girl, who convinced me to go,
and shared the joys and trials

and
THETA
For whom and through whom,
the struggle continues

The world is yours, as well as ours,
but in the last analysis it is yours.
You young people, full of vigor and vitality,
are in the bloom of life, like the sun
at eight or nine in the morning.
Our hope is placed on you.

—Mao Zedong

CONTENTS

ACKNOWLEDGEMENTS

All books are collective projects. I would like to thank first the editors of Monthly Review Press, and especially Ethan Young for his thorough and careful work on revising the manuscript for this book, which has helped to make readable my sometimes endless sentences and paragraphs. His patience, which was no doubt sorely tried on more than one occasion, was particularly valued, allowing me the time and space needed to complete this study. I also want to express appreciation to the journals *Monthly Review* and *Socialism and Democracy* for publishing articles on which portions of this work are based.

I would like to thank William Hinton for reading earlier drafts of parts of the material in this book, and offering both encouragement and critical comments. But his contribution goes far beyond this. The analysis presented in this work would not have been possible without the understanding of the Chinese revolution which his studies have provided over the past several decades. Almost uniquely, Hinton has kept faith with the revolutionary goals of that struggle, never uncritically, but always refusing to yield to the fashions of the moment. His devotion to those at the base of Chinese society and to their lives and struggles is the bedrock on which this work too rests. Remaining problems with this study are, of course, my responsibility alone.

But this book required a collective effort in more than the usual ways. Though I initiated the journey to China on which it is based, when it came to actually deciding to go, I found it extremely difficult to overcome the fears and doubts that came with lengthening middle age, and which threatened to turn into a more general paralysis of later life. It was only through the support and urging of many relatives, friends, and associates that I overcame these hesitancies, just as it was their practical assistance that enabled us to make this trip. I will not list them all here: most would probably be surprised to see their names included, and I would be embarrassed if I left someone out. But they know who they are, and I thank them for their love and faith, which allowed me to undertake one of the most transforming experiences of my life.

I had become jaded with what seemed like the *de rigueur* thanking of spouses and other relatives by the authors of books—until I actually wrote one. A book really is a family affair. This goes far beyond the lost time together and unfairly shifted household burdens. My daughter Theta, brother Jon, and several other relatives, offered various forms of encouragement and aid, as well as their own observations, that have helped bring this work to completion. Our daughter, Anica, who was just eight at the time, opened doors for us in China that would never have been passable otherwise—and, after only five very trying months in a Chinese school, served as our translator when we later travelled alone. My wife, Barbara Leon, shared the entire project, and many of the experiences and insights in this work come from her. She also served as the first editor and advisor on this book—a mutual role in our writing that is among the most valued aspects of years of work together.

But it is, finally, the Chinese people themselves, who must be thanked for whatever this study has to offer. Nothing could have prepared us for the love and warmth with which we were greeted when we arrived in their country, by administrators and faculty at the university where we worked, but above all by the students and other young persons we had the opportunity to teach and live among. They not only freely shared with us their views on China and the world, but on occasions too numerous to recall, took us around the campus and city, invited us to their rooms and the homes of their families, helped us with bureaucratic tangles and brought us medicines when we were sick, taught us to cook and suffered through our miserable efforts at playing ping-pong—in every way making our stay among them as rich and enjoyable as was possible.

In the last analysis, however, it is the Chinese workers and peasants who are due the ultimate expression of appreciation for this book. Though our own personal contact with them was minimal, it was the revolutionary socialist society which they had created, the remnants of which we were privileged to experience at first hand, that enveloped us while we were in China and which forms the basis for this study. Just as the Chinese revolution, more than any other, inspired my youth, so the ongoing struggles of workers, peasants, and students today were what made the time among them in China so transforming. It is their living example that renewed my determination to keep fighting on, for a just, democratic, and egalitarian socialist world, for them and for us.

White cat, black cat, if it catches mice it is a good cat.

Deng Xiaoping

We must acknowledge the existence of a struggle of class against class, and admit the possibility of a restoration of reactionary classes. We must raise our vigilance and properly educate our youth as well as the cadres, the masses and the middle- and basic-level cadres. Old cadres must also study these problems and be educated. Otherwise a country like ours can still move toward its opposite. Even to move towards its opposite would not matter too much because there would still be the negation of the negation, and afterwards we might move towards our opposite yet again. If our children's generation go in for revisionism and move towards their opposite, so that although they still nominally have socialism it is in fact capitalism, then our grandsons will certainly rise up in revolt and overthrow their fathers, because the masses will not be satisfied. Therefore, from now on we must talk about this every year, every month, every day.

Mao Zedong

INTRODUCTION:
THE "THIRD WAY"

China today stands at the brink, facing fundamental choices as to the direction it will take going into the twenty-first century. The balancing act of the Chinese leadership between the revolutionary socialism implemented under Mao Zedong, emphasizing public ownership and welfare, mass-based collectivism, and egalitarianism, and the "market reforms" of Deng Xiaoping, with their increasingly capitalistic characteristics, privatized forms of property, and class polarization, have now reached a level of contradiction that must soon be resolved. When first introduced almost twenty years ago, "marketization" had the stated intent of tempering the rigidity of a centralized state economy through a limited degree of small-scale private enterprise and unregulated sales. Though from the first there were basic transformations, especially in the rural areas, the role of the market itself was to be constrained within an economy that was still socialist overall. These initial limits, however, have been constantly exceeded, through a series of expansions into ever wider regions of the country and broader economic sectors, and incremental steps in the exploitation of hired labor, as well as by increasingly close ties with the global capitalist system.

The resulting state of suspension called "market socialism," which claims to combine the best of both worlds, has instead increasingly shown the worst distortions that could come of attempting to unite these two forms of social organization in a single system. Thus the socialist side of Chinese society has left in place an overarching party and state authority which still dominates most aspects of life, yet every day provides fewer of the former rewards of collective economic security and guaranteed forms of social welfare, while its capitalist aspects more closely resemble the most rapacious and uncontrolled stages of early Western development than a modern and regulated market system. As what is left of socialism crumbles beneath the blows of this sort of marketization, moreover, not only capitalistic but even feudalistic forms are reappearing, a throwback to the worst aspects of the premodern era. At the same time, new class forces, which can no longer be contained within the limits of market reforms as originally conceived, are being generated, making the present "mix" of contradictory tendencies daily less viable.

The "third way" between socialism and capitalism is thus increasingly unstable and socially insupportable. As a result, the Chinese people must soon decide whether they will go "all the way," as it were, toward full recapitalization and privatization of the economy, or turn "backward"—which would of necessity entail a new and even more radical move forward—to a revolutionary socialist society. This decisive choice makes virtually unavoidable a showdown between those who favor further consolidation of private capitalism, and those who still cling to the goal of socialism. The present leaders may find ways to postpone this conflict or, if it comes, to prevent it from turning into an open clash between the opposing social tendencies. But with contradictions in society deepening, the likelihood of a sharp outbreak of tensions rises with every step toward fuller implementation of "market socialism," and a renewal of cataclysmic social struggle cannot be ruled out.

In a common exercise of wishful thinking, many analysts in the West, especially those who support the current policy of marketization and its parallel of "opening to the outside world," picture China as primarily torn between economic liberalization and decentralization, and a political system that is still tightly controlled by a rigid centralized authority. In this view, the major choice facing Chinese society is between the "market," which is seen to require greater "freedom," and the continued domination of a repressive state power, which is pictured as not only stifling personal liberties, but still unnecessarily intervening in the economy as well. The widely held assumption in the West, whether explicit or implicit, that "free markets" and "democracy" are all but equivalent, reinforces this outlook. While such attitudes have a certain base in Chinese reality, since the new class forces being generated by marketization are in some instances also at the forefront of demanding political liberalization—notably among certain of the exiles from the 1989 Tiananmen movement and their Western supporters—this way of viewing the current situation tends to obscure the unity of economic and political power in the present leadership, and the fundamental choices which must be made within both of these spheres together as to their future direction.

This unification in China between the realms of economy and politics is nowhere better illustrated than in the powerful role in "business" played by top government and party leaders, and especially by their family members, who use their official positions for personal benefit. These are the very elements who have led the market reform drive, based on the combination—not the opposition—of state power and private investment, and it is they, more than any others, who have enriched themselves as a result of their own policies. Even those activities which are ostensibly most representative of the "free market" have therefore been carried out under the political protection and sponsorship of the top party and governmental leadership.

This relationship is made more apparent by reference to the history of how "marketization" was first introduced. The current "market reforms" did not emerge from some spontaneous and liberal economic process, nor even by simply removing earlier statist restraints on entrepreneurial initiative. Quite the contrary, "markets" were imposed on the Chinese people by government fiat, notably in the forcible breaking up of the agricultural commune system which had been developed under the leadership of Mao Zedong, to be replaced with a system of individual family contracts, and in the equally rapid and forcible demolition of socialist forms of collective public welfare now being imposed on state-owned enterprises and all the other major institutional centers of the society, including universities. Thus it is not primarily through the working of "free markets" per se that the economy has, in the first instance, been radically transformed, but rather by the very use of that state power and Communist Party control which Western observers so often deplore.

Had the Chinese people been allowed to freely choose their own course in the years when the reforms were being implemented, marketization might never have been introduced, or at least not so universally or in its present extreme form. If they are able to win a freer choice in the future, the people of China might opt to move away once again from "free markets" and the current rush toward capitalism, and turn back toward the revolutionary socialism and collectivism of the past. Thus political openness and economic "freedom" may very well work in opposite directions, not in parallel. Such a prospect would no doubt temper much of the present support in the West for Chinese democratization, should it take a socialist not capitalist direction. By the same token, far from leading to greater democracy, further development of marketization is likely to entrench even more completely the current political structure. At present, the basic choice facing China is thus not between "free market" forces and rigid control over politics, but rather over what direction the state-dominated economic system itself will take. But whatever the outcome, for the foreseeable future, it will most likely be the Communist Party itself and its government which makes the decision, and imposes it on the rest of the society.

Those basic differences and conflicts which do still exist over the direction of the economy, and thus in politics as well, are about the relations of production, that is, whether and in what degree exploitation and the appropriation of wealth from others will be allowed. They are in essence class struggles. The contradictions arising in the Chinese economy and state cannot be adequately grasped and analyzed without identifying the classes which are contending for control, either moving to take advantage of the opportunities opened up by marketization, or struggling to hold on to former revolutionary gains and socialist goals—in each case requiring both economic and political power.

The nature of the struggle of classes in China has, however, tended to be obscured. In the first instance, as Mao explained during the Cultural Revolution, the idea had been promoted and spread that under "socialism," even in its early transitional stages, class divisions no longer exist. Though such a concept has been largely discredited, especially in the aftermath of the collapse of the Soviet Bloc, its effects linger. Class analysis has been the weak link even in many left studies of "actually existing socialist" countries, including China. In the West, moreover, the conflict of classes has been further obscured by the crushing of the Tiananmen Square movement in June 1989, which focused attention on the apparent clash between the Communist party and state on the one side and Chinese "civil society" on the other. In the aftermath of these events, many analysts turned toward the conflict of popular forces versus a repressive governmental apparatus, without regard to class forces on either side. In such a view, as commonly put forth in the West, the broad populace can create a counter hegemony to the state through organization of a wide range of social movements, bypassing, as it were, the need for a struggle of classes per se. But as the recent transformations of Soviet Bloc nations reveal, the freeing of civil society from "actually existing socialism" tends to heighten the class struggle, not to submerge it further. So too, the social polarization of China today is increasing, raising the probability of sharper future conflicts between the classes, that will occur both inside and outside the governmental structures.

Anti-statist and democratic forces were of course prominent in the Tiananmen movement and especially in the aftermath of the events of the summer of 1989. But those Chinese supporting greater popular control of the political realm are themselves deeply divided, with some favoring even more rapid movement toward the "market," and others supporting a return to a more egalitarian and participatory socialism. Many, almost certainly the vast majority, lie somewhere in between. Moreover, these same conflicting tendencies are reflected among the party and state officials themselves. There are persistent reports that sharp differences continue to be expressed even at the most exalted levels of the political and economic system over the policies the government should pursue. Discussions based on concepts of civil society versus the state therefore tend to obscure the full range of the debate both among those who hold official power and within the masses of the people at large over the direction China should take. Thus the picture of Communist "statism" versus popular forces, however valid it may be up to a point, is inadequate as a basis for the analysis of the current contradictions in Chinese society, and it will almost certainly be an insufficient tool for comprehending future events.

Therefore, while a new broad-based popular struggle against the state and party is possible, there are still, at each level and in every sector of Chinese society, those who advocate a more rapid move to private capitalism and those who struggle to maintain the ideals and practices of the socialist system. Even within the same individual, there is quite often ambivalence and conflicting feelings over how far to go in "market reform," the dismantling of governmental social programs, and the proper role of the state and the party. This leads to complex and constantly shifting alliances at the top, and contradictory sentiments among the masses, that cannot easily be summarized, much less analyzed, by simplistic "we" and "they" formulations.

As has happened so many times in Chinese history, these contending social forces are reaching flashpoint at the very time that the dominant figure in China reaches the end of life. The passing of Deng Xiaoping from the scene, removing the one person still able to impose overall policy, will almost inevitably trigger a new level of struggle even within the various factions which support the dominant marketization program. But it is also likely to present the last foreseeable opportunity, for those who have never accepted the direction of current policies and those who are only now beginning to realize and fear the full extent of social transformation which will flow from continued reforms, to attempt to reverse the direction currently being taken by the party and state.

If earlier such periods, notably following the death of Mao Zedong, are any precedent, there is likely to be a short stretch of pledges of fealty to the policies of the departed leader and agreement to rally around an heir apparent, in this instance President Jiang Zemin, who has had the advantage of several years in power already. But it is the nature of these appointees, raised in the shadow of their sponsors, to be weak and uncharismatic, and to lack the personal power to deal with the complexity of choices and factions which surround them once the dominant leader has departed. Thus the emergence of new leaders, with their own visions of society and their own ranks of dedicated followers, may mark the near future. There is already a growing debate, both within China and abroad, over where the country will go next and who will come out on top—analyses rife with palace intrigues and factional maneuvering.

What is generally missing from such calculations, however, is the role of the mass of the Chinese people, the peasants and rural laborers, urban working class, small entrepreneurs, and highly educated intellectuals. In the long history of China these classes have never had adequate means for the expression of their own political and economic will. Even during the most radical periods since the Communist triumph, notably in the Cultural Revolution, the rallying of the masses never led to the national development of institutionalized forms of popular representation adequate to allow the population as a whole to help direct the overall governing of society. This lack of regularized processes has been a major weakness in the building of Chinese socialism, and helped to open the door to the current capitalistic marketization. Any renewal of the movement toward a socialist society will have to address this historic limitation.

Yet nowhere more than in China has the dictum of Mao that "the people, and the people alone, are the motive force in the making of world history" been more profoundly felt, both for centuries past and in the present.[1] It is not only in the modern revolutionary period, but for thousands of years before, that the role of the mass of the Chinese population has been crucial in the ultimate determination of the course of events. The armies of China, drawn for millennia from the vast rural population, have always had the final say, from the earliest dynasties to the crushing of demonstrators in and around Tiananmen Square in 1989. While historically the peasant army has been the tool of the powerful, these same peasants have also shown over and over again the ability to mobilize on their own behalf behind leaders drawn in part from their own ranks, and have more than once changed the course of Chinese history, most recently and profoundly in the Communist Revolution itself. In China too, as much as in any country, the industrial workers, and the students and intellectuals, have been at the forefront in the modern struggles for social justice, national liberation, and socialism, and their actions have decisively shaped the form of Chinese society. That a people with such a legacy of millennial rebelliousness and revolutionary acts will be quiescent in the face of the profound transformations now taking place in China defies both the historical record and the logic of the present.

Lack of the more formal institutions of representation should never be taken, therefore, as a sign of powerlessness on the part of the Chinese masses. Rather, their very inability to exert power through direct control over the political and economic system has led throughout the history of China to explosions whose suddenness and ferocity can only surprise those unfamiliar with its past. Chinese leaders, well-versed in the historical lessons of their society, have always had to keep one eye over their shoulders, with a view to the unleashed might of the masses, constantly threatening to erupt. Those who replace Deng Xiaoping at the pinnacle of the party and state will surely be no exception to this rule. It was the greatest achievement of Mao Zedong that, reversing centuries of practice, he embraced, rather than feared, the power of the people, and led this massive popular force in the revolutionary transformation of the entire social order, on a scale never previously attempted. It is this which is the abiding legacy of the Chinese Communists as a whole. Only those who, in turn, help release the power of the masses once again toward the realization of their own interests, will have any chance for ultimate success in leading the future China.

It is this "bottom-up" dimension to the issue of where Chinese society will go next that is lacking in so many of the current analyses of the situation in that country. With 1.2 billion people, in a vast and varied land, and without easy forms of measuring popular attitudes, only a fool—especially one from the West—would dare to state what "the masses" think. But numerous discussions in China, and observation of those straws in the wind which make it into the highly regulated mass communication media, suggest that far from being at ease with the current direction of events, the Chinese are increasingly troubled by what is happening to their society. Despite quite widespread support for the general direction of "marketization," at least among the more privileged rural and urbanized strata, there is building concern, not only with the direct effects of market reform, but at the loss of closeness of relationships with relatives and friends that in earlier times eased the weight of a massive society. Many, especially among the middle aged and older generation, feel increasingly out of place in the new China. But even young people often feel disoriented by the rapidly altering conditions of life and of the ideological justifications for them. These changes are being felt in every area of the social order. Far beyond all previous shifts of "line," the transformations being wrought by the current marketization are sweeping away the older cultural forms, and striking at the basic underpinning of Chinese society. The resulting tensions, having already exploded once in the days of Tiananmen, are unlikely to be permanently suppressed or coopted, especially as power changes hands once again at the top, with all the implications of a new turning point. Thus the uneasy domestic calm of the present is likely soon to be broken.

In their relations with the rest of the world as well, the Chinese must soon decide how far they want to go in transforming their society. The flow of capital and of cultural importations now sweeping into China has already begun to overwhelm national economic control and traditional social patterns. The threat of outside domination, as ancient as Chinese society itself, has always had the capacity to set off repercussions in the domestic economy and political structure. At the same time, as China seeks to reassert its historic position as the "Middle Kingdom," not only as the dominant society within East Asia, but as the most advanced and powerful in the entire world, the potential escalates for the situation to lead in the not very distant future to clashes with the current global powers, resulting in unforeseeable consequences. Thus just as in its domestic life, so too in its world position, China faces the most fundamental decisions, between pursuing its nationalistic interests and renewed claims to international power, and taking actions more acceptable to the U.S.-dominated system.

To examine these contradictory forces in Chinese society is the goal of this work. In the fall and winter of 1993-1994, my wife and I taught some 150 graduate students attending Jilin University of Technology in Changchun, in the Chinese Northeast. Being located in this rather isolated city proved to have its advantages, despite the bitter winter cold and rather drab (by Chinese standards) historical and cultural setting. For unlike the Southern and coastal provinces, this region of China was still relatively untouched by the forces of "marketization." True, Changchun, like virtually every other city in the country, is now undergoing a rapid and massive physical and economic transformation. But the underlying social relations while we were there were still largely based on the "old" socialism. In conversations with faculty and university staff and visits to local factories, but above all from the marvelous young people, with whom we had the most daily contact, we learned about the complexities of the system and the profound contradictions and ambivalences rending Chinese society as it strives to reconcile its socialist past with the "market."

The students that we taught came in the vast majority from Jilin and the other Northeastern and North Central provinces, and only a relative handful of them had direct knowledge of the new marketization conditions of the South, either through family ties or job experience. Thus both the overall social setting of Changchun and the attitudes of our students still reflected much of the socialism now rapidly vanishing elsewhere in China. The view which this experience accorded us of the "old" socialist relations of the Chinese Revolution threw into especially sharp relief the rapid transformation which was occurring right before our eyes, even in the Northeast. It also provided a base against which to measure the even more dramatic changes and evidence of social breakdown in other parts of the country, which we observed during more than a month of travel that followed our stay in Changchun. From this collision of past and present came a heightened understanding of the kinds of doubts and ambivalences that had been expressed by our students, and a clearer sense of the troubling naivete with which they had confronted "the market" and the possibility of combining it permanently with socialism.

In the two years which have passed since our time in Changchun, there has been an ever more rapid escalation of the changes which were becoming more obvious even while we were there. Continuing contacts with China make clear that some young people are deeply troubled by these policies, further heightening the tensions we had already felt. Yet the concerns expressed by these most privileged of Chinese students can be but a faint reflection of the views of those workers and peasants, and especially the youth—for whom, in growing numbers, the policies of reform are themselves a threat to survival. For educated young people, marketization represents an exciting if also dangerous challenge—but their education will tend to carry them through, as it has for the privileged elite of Chinese for centuries, even if they fail to realize their full potential. But for vast numbers of workers and peasants, losing out in the market can be a short step to impoverishment and even total destitution.

While many in the working classes too have welcomed the opportunities opened up by the market, for those who fail to "make it" in the ever more desperate struggle to "get rich," the future can only be grim. It is in their lives that the costs of juxtaposing old socialist forms and new market relations are felt most sharply, and it is by their actions that the contradictory class forces will be most profoundly fought out. Though our own direct knowledge came above all from the students, therefore, it is the broader masses of peasants and workers, and their role in the conflicts now looming, who will provide the main impetus for the direction China takes in the near future, with enormous implications for the world as a whole. It is, as Mao said, "the people, and the people alone" who will render the ultimate verdict on the contradictions of "market socialism," and it is they who form the basis for this analysis of Chinese society.

CHINA AT THE BRINK

I. The Capitalist Superhighway

In the Chinese board game *wei qi*, better known to many in the United States by its Japanese name *go*, two players alternate in placing white and black stones on a grid of lines, trying to surround and capture the opposing pieces. A more experienced player will open the game by racing around the board, leaving a piece here and there in what, to the novice, seems to be an arbitrary pattern, before settling down to more concentrated play in one or two areas. Sometimes it is only hours later that these apparently random moves are shown to be decisive, as a lone stone, off in one corner, suddenly holds the strategic position that provides the key to victory in a closely contested match.

China today is like a vast *wei qi* board, on which giant players—primarily the government and foreign investors, but also increasingly the new private Chinese entrepreneurs—are making their opening moves, scattering pieces across the country. Many of these investments have little immediate economic basis, as the surrounding region is not sufficiently developed to support them. Rather, they are speculative gambles that the concentrated play, which actually began some years ago in the South and on the Eastern Seaboard, will move northward and inland to where the new money is being invested, and that the players will prove to be strategically located in the endgame. With every region and city hoping that it will be the next "hot spot" in the economic boom, great amounts of risk capital are being thrown around in anticipation of quick gains. In some cases houses are even being torn down and land cleared, just in case it is needed for rapid development later. At the same time, since no one knows how long this particular game will last, where it will go next, or even if it will be "completed," there is a mad scramble for each to get what they can now, and never mind who wins or loses in the end.

The individual moves of single investors are not occurring in isolation, however. In theory, at least, they are part of a social plan, the attempt, now fifteen years old, to reorient toward markets and profitmaking, and to "open up to the world" and especially to foreign capital. All of China is now engaged in a massive gamble, to see if it can reach a permanent level of higher development through what the government calls "reforms" to achieve "market socialism" or "a socialist system with special Chinese characteristics," while retaining national control of the economy, preserving some degree of social ownership and planning, and avoiding the worst dislocations normally associated with third world capitalization.

In this new and still largely untested mix, the older public enterprises and those in the newer private sector are expected to compete, stimulating each other to higher levels of production, efficiency and profitability. But in practice, the government or "socialist" units have been told to get money where and how they can, which means looking for their own profitmaking projects, typically by joining with foreign capitalists for investments in China itself or even abroad. In these enterprises, the Chinese side retains majority control, and the entire investment normally reverts to China after a period of no more than fifty years. These "joint ventures" are thus the archetypical expression of the new system, a hybrid form which is supposed to represent the "special characteristics" of Chinese socialism. In this way, the two parts of the system are closely combined, creating a melange of public and private funds, in which the line that in theory separates socialist and capitalist forms becomes increasingly blurred.

Despite the nominal retention of majority control through public or "socialistic" ownership, however, for the moment it is the "market" side of this equation which is clearly dominant, fueled by a massive influx of foreign capital. The whole nation is in a frenzy of development, as cities across the country compete with each other to see how rapidly they can open enterprise zones and attract joint ventures that will bring in money from abroad. The scale of this activity is staggering, and it is still accelerating. In the first eight months of 1993, 44,000 overseas-funded enterprises were approved to be set up in China, already equalling the total for all of 1992. Of these, over 28,000 were Sino-foreign joint ventures, up 250 percent over the same period the previous year; almost 6,000 others were cooperative firms, usually smaller businesses run by their own owner-employees, up 210 percent. The remaining 10,000-plus enterprises, however, were wholly owned by foreign investors, and it is this sector which is expanding most rapidly, increasing 312 percent over 1992. By April 1994, more than 186,000 foreign-funded enterprises had been approved, with a pledged capitalization from abroad of some $150 billion, and actual investment of just under half that amount, with $30 billion invested in 1993 alone. Making up this total were 108,000 joint ventures, 25,500 cooperatives, and more than 34,000 solely foreign-financed firms. The average size of each investment has also been growing rapidly, especially since 1991.

Hong Kong accounts for by far the largest proportion of the new enterprises, with almost 28,000, followed by Taiwan with close to 6,000. Much of the foreign investment, therefore, is really a merging of the "socialist" economy of the mainland with the "market" of the two islands, in what the dominant architect of the present policies, Deng Xiaoping, calls "one country with two systems." This anticipates the absorption of Hong Kong scheduled for 1997, and the intention to recover Taiwan also within the near future. Hong Kong and Macao investors alone employ more than 3 million workers in Guangdong Province, the center of the new policies, and the output value of foreign-funded firms there is now equal to one-third the industrial production of those two colonies. Among the other top ten investors from abroad, the United States is third with some 3,200 firms, with Canada, Japan, and other Pacific Rim nations completing the list. Manufacturing holds first place among these foreign-funded investments, but the money is going everywhere, into retail and services, finance and insurance, infrastructure projects, and even education and culture.

The true boom areas, however, have been real estate and construction, which soared by multiples of ten and thirteen, respectively, as part of an explosion in the market for property in the first half of 1993. Here the full impact of the massive economic infusion is most apparent. The face of China, especially its urban centers, is continuing to be transformed, sometimes virtually overnight. Large office buildings, hotels, and housing complexes are rising everywhere. Even if they are only twenty stories high, many of them are virtual skyscrapers in contrast to the traditionally low profile of the Chinese cities that surround them. It is no longer just in the older areas of "marketization" in the South and East, nor in the biggest urban centers like Shanghai and Beijing that this is happening, but in medium-sized and even smaller cities in northern and inland areas as well.

Changchun is the capital of the Northeastern province of Jilin, a center of the auto industry with many universities, and relatively small by Chinese standards with only 2 million people. The heart of the city is being remade with an enormous new railroad station as its centerpiece, and several office towers nearby. Parts of the downtown look almost as if they had been bombed out, so many buildings stand in a state of partial completion with gaping windows and doors, and surrounding streets full of rubble. But unlike the United States, where such sights are usually the sign of urban decay and economic collapse, in China today they are a mark of metropolitan growth and rapid expansion of the economy. Phrases like "that building wasn't here last year" are constantly heard, and some longtime residents seem almost in a state of shock as they observe the transformation of their environment that has occurred in just three or four years.

Viewing all this enormous activity, it is necessary to keep reminding oneself that, increasingly, the engine which is driving it is the massive infusion of capital from abroad, albeit with a large, and even majority, Chinese admixture. Ask what a new building is for, and the answer may be an office complex, bank, department store, housing project, or hospital. But inquire about who owns it, and the almost invariable reply is "joint venture." Everything, it seems, is being financed at least in part by foreign investors. Both rapid economic growth and higher incomes increasingly depend on the input of ever larger amounts of capital from abroad.

In Jiangsu Province, which stretches north from Shanghai, Vice-Governor Wang Rongbing speaks of raising the per capita GDP from under 1,100 yuan or $133 at present to 7,600 yuan or $916 by the end of the century, tripling again to 23,000 yuan or $2,770 by 2010.[1] But, as he points out, this can only be achieved by "internationalizing the economy." In the southern part of the province, such internationalization is already highly advanced: one-third of all industrial production is for the export market, joint ventures in early 1995 accounted for an equivalent proportion of manufacturing firms, and overseas capital owned an equal share of fixed assets. Some 26,000 foreign-funded firms have absorbed $10.7 billion in financing from abroad, a figure expected to rise to $60 billion by the end of the century. The province already ranks second in the country in both exports and utilization of foreign capital. But even this is not sufficient. "'We'll open our economy in an all-round way to the rest of the world,' Wang said."[2] In this manner, the new Chinese prosperity, especially in the booming centers of the South and Eastern Coast, is increasingly dependent on overseas financing to sustain present growth and future hopes.

In Shanghai itself, 3,752 foreign-funded enterprises were approved in 1993, close to the total for the previous fourteen years combined, and $3.7 billion—more than half the $6.8 billion invested from abroad—went into real estate. These firms already account for close to 20 percent of the output of industry in the city, the largest in China, and a majority of the industrial enterprises there will most likely be transformed with some input of capital from abroad by the end of the century. Even in a relatively small regional center like Changchun, when the authorities held a celebration of the real estate industry in 1993—complete with a military band, fashionable young women holding a symbolic ribbon to be cut, and a lavish banquet—the investors represented came not only from Hong Kong and elsewhere in the South, but from as far away as Canada, teaming up with local firms and government agencies.

By the same token, however, without the constant flow of capital from abroad, much—or in some areas, even most—of this construction would come to a screeching halt, or would never even be started. As Zhang Guangyi, an official from the State Economic and Trade Commission, noted, "[P]resent domestic capital cannot meet the demands of China's booming economy."[3] As a result, in the daily, relentless struggle to keep the foreign money coming, there is virtually nothing that is not up for sale. In Beijing, for example, the city government has even decided to experiment with selling the busiest bridges and major overpasses to multinational corporations, which are then allowed to "buy out the bridge's name and have their own put up on a big sign."[4] This policy began after Lufthansa asked to buy the bridge near its shopping center, and now entire neighborhoods are losing their traditional Chinese names and coming to be known instead by the foreign firm which dominates commercial activity there. Even the canyon walls in the Yangtze Three Gorges region, soon to be devastated by a massive dam, are being sold off to potential advertisers.

The greatest pressure which is generated by this constant effort to attract capitalists from abroad, however, is that they demand a "normal" profit on their investments. In the "Wild South" atmosphere of much that is occurring, with low wage rates and economic rules being made up as they go along, the margin of profits can be very high indeed. This is especially the case for foreign capitalists, who are usually subject to fewer economic, labor, and environmental controls than in their home countries. A survey of overseas-funded firms conducted by the Washington-based U.S.-China Business Council found that "most of the enterprises responding to the survey pegged their long-term profit target at between 11 to 25 percent."[5] No effort is made to make investors from abroad limit their profit rates or otherwise behave in a more socialist spirit. Quite the contrary, projects funded with foreign capital are commonly given special incentives, such as tax breaks, to ensure their profitability for years to come. Usually they are also granted the most precious right of all, to hire and fire employees at will and to set their own wage and salary rates. At the Changchun real estate fair, these incentives were flaunted in slick brochures as a lure to potential investors and customers.

For foreign capitalists, therefore, the opportunity for quick profits is especially alluring. "Much of the investment is aimed at producing products for the outside world, taking advantage of $2- to $4-a-day wages for literate, healthy and eager young employees," as the *New York Times* reported.[6] It is estimated that by employing 3 million workers on the mainland, Hong Kong joint-venture investors save almost $12 billion annually on wages, and real estate owners from the colony report that their holdings across the border are their most lucrative ones. Or as a municipal government official put it in explaining the attraction for investors in Behai, a coastal beach town now being developed as a major tourist center largely with Hong Kong money: "'Foreigners are confident that they will earn big bucks very soon.'"[7] Drawn by the promise of quick returns, China today is second only to the United States as a recipient of foreign investment, and by one estimate has attracted 40 percent of the money put into developing countries in the last fifteen years. It has also become the leading recipient of financing by the World Bank, which expects profits on its loans.

The consequences of the shift to profit maximization and especially the "special rights" granted to foreign investors and joint ventures are, however, increasingly disastrous for the working class. The widely reported November 19, 1993 fire in the Zhili Toy Factory in Shenzhen, Guangdong Province, killed eighty-one workers and injured another forty-two, trapped behind locked doors in a "'cage-like workshop ... to prevent workers from stealing the products.'"[8] But as was the case in the Triangle Shirtwaist inferno in New York eighty-two years earlier, of which it was so reminiscent, Zhili ripped the lid off a growing number of Chinese sweatshop factories, exposing an entire system of brutal exploitation and hazardous working conditions. Even before the fire, surveys had found that 61 percent of the employees in enterprises like Zhili work virtually continuously without a day off, and over one-third of the workers report frequently being forced to labor extra daily hours, in a majority of cases without any additional pay, never mind overtime. Some 28 percent tell of no safety measures being taken by their employers. More than half the female workers get no maternity insurance, a third of the employees have no contracts, and an equal number are unaware of their contractual provisions. Overall, infringement of the rights of employees were found at 90 percent of the firms. Since only one-fifth of the 5 million Chinese working for foreign-funded enterprises nationwide are organized in trade unions, such disregard of existing laws has been particularly easy.

Typically, even though Zhili had previously been cited for violation of factory laws, nothing had been done to enforce the regulations, the result of collusion between its owner and local officials. But the situation found in Shenzhen is just the tip of the iceberg. In Guangdong alone, the number of fatalities in industrial accidents climbed to 836 in 1992, jumping 63 percent in just one year, while throughout China 15,000 workers died, up 3.3 percent from 1991. This was followed by a series of disasters in the first months of 1993, resulting in a "horrific increase," with more than 60,000 dying between January and October alone. While "the number of accidents was particularly marked in foreign-funded firms and collectively-run mines,"[9] nevertheless, these conditions have spread to state-run enterprises as well. Typical were the deaths of 175 coal miners during a single week in January, 1994, in six separate major accidents. "The root cause," stated the Minister of Coal Industry, "is that some officials put profits before security."[10]

Clearly, today, whatever the name of the system, increasing numbers of Chinese are working and dying to produce "big bucks" for those who have capital to invest, especially from abroad. In spite of the official rhetoric, therefore, much of China seems to be taking not just what Mao called "the capitalist road," it, but a capitalistic super-highway—symbolized by the actual superhighways being built around major Southern cities, mostly financed by capital from abroad in joint ventures or as wholly overseas-funded enterprises, with their profits generated by toll charges. Not just in the factories, but in society as a whole, the Chinese, increasingly, are being employed by, taxed for, and mortgaged to outside economic forces. Such a massive dependence on and preferential treatment of private foreign capital, however, is more and more at odds with the still officially proclaimed socialistic basis of the system.

II. The Class Basis of "Market Socialism"

It might be stated as a general principle, that it does not matter if a regime calls itself red or white, as long as it exploits the working classes for profit. Thus despite the continued claim by the government that its system is socialist, it is possible to argue that China is already under a system of state capitalism in which, even with a high degree of public ownership, the workers and peasants are exploited for the benefit of officials and managers. That a statist Chinese bourgeoisie has come into being, often closely associated with openly capitalistic domestic entrepreneurs and foreign investors, seems beyond dispute. Elements of these class forces are present in the highest echelons of the government and party, including the military. It is among the families of the leading authorities in particular that the melding of official power and the appropriation of wealth has often gone furthest. But the use of the state as a base for personal profiteering, both legal and illegal, has spread to all levels of the society.

A case therefore can be made that all the talk of market socialism is nothing but a cynical euphemism, the last defense of a ruling Communist party which cannot move openly to capitalism without losing any remnant of its ideological legitimacy. The character of this mix of marketized and socialist aspects, not only in the economy, but in the ideology of the current leadership, is exemplified by the deeds and words of Mu Qizhong, one of the largest private entrepreneurs in China today, head of an economic group worth 1.5 billion yuan or some $260 million. Having bought up many unprofitable state enterprises in China, Mu began turning his sights on the former Soviet Union. "The key to success," he declared, "is to take advantage of the low production costs of enterprises in socialist countries, or in countries transforming to a market economy." By providing the "'missing link'" of marketization to such firms, "we can realize much higher profits than our capitalist counterparts [sic]." With an ideological cynicism that perfectly exemplifies the reforms, Mu concludes that his survival where so many others like him have failed is due to his personal philosophy: "I'm economically radical but politically I don't rock the boat.... I hold that China can only choose socialism."[11]

Yet tempting as it may be to adopt a "state capitalist" analysis of the current Chinese leadership, and accurate as it undoubtedly is up to a point, this formula is perhaps too simplistic to capture the complexity of the contradictory forces presently contending in China. Though a full-blown system of capitalism may now be emerging, the path by which it has developed continues to shape the conflicting forces and ideologies which are still so much in evidence, and which may radically affect the future. When Mao Zedong attacked his opponents as "taking the capitalist road," he caught perfectly the contradictory mix of characteristics which marked their policies, maintaining basic elements of public ownership and state control, but freeing the market in such ways as to lead toward full recapitalization. However, unlike his early analyses of the classes of rural China, so precise in their measurement of each stratum and its economic and political tendencies, Mao used sweeping terms in dealing with the "capitalist roaders" that failed to single out the particular class interests which marked the character of their system and the contradictions in their own ranks. In the absence of such a study, both opponents and analysts of the reformers have been left in basic respects ideologically and theoretically disarmed.

"Market socialism" in its origins can best be understood as the expression of the "middle class" or petty bourgeois side of the Chinese revolution, an element which was certain to have a strong base in a country overwhelmingly rural and economically underdeveloped. Thus the "capitalist roaders" typically represented the upper strata of the peasantry, the more skilled workers, and the professional elite, against the poor peasants, common laborers, and less privileged students and intellectuals favored by Mao and his supporters. The policy of market socialism therefore reflected the dual nature of the petty bourgeoisie, a class of laborers who are at the same time owners of property, committed to the development of "business," but fearful of the power of their bigger competitors as well as the independent strength of the proletariat. This class is typically capable of combining an interest in private appropriation with a degree of socialistic restraint on both capital and labor.

It is no accident, therefore, that the early efforts at reform focused on breaking up the agricultural communes and promoting separate family production contracts among the peasantry, the potential petty bourgeoisie par excellence. The new policies tapped the class enthusiasm of many peasants for individual ownership and production, and for sales in the private market, an historical tendency especially strong among the better-off elements in rural China. Thus the reformers turned first to a segment of the Chinese population most susceptible to their appeals, but they enforced the changes across the board by forcibly breaking up even those communes which were succeeding and had wide mass support. In the process they destroyed the most viable collective farms and threw all peasants on the mercy of the market, though many were opposed ideologically or unprepared in practice for the struggle for survival there.

These policies can be seen as the freeing of the class interests of the upwardly-mobile peasants, with their desire to "get rich quick." The new reforms did produce a surge of production and income, based on freer exchange and credit, increased prices for farm goods, a growth in non-agricultural sideline occupations, and the release of surplus peasant labor, much of which was employed to fill the pent-up demand for consumer goods through light industrial development in the townships and cities. No longer constrained by the need to worry about what would happen to their poorer or weaker neighbors, many of the peasant entrepreneurs managed to turn themselves in a few short years into petty bourgeois small farmers and traders, raising their productive efficiency through capital investments. In increasing numbers, they have freed themselves from the ancient poverty of the

Chinese peasantry, building new "modern" houses and acquiring the same kinds of consumer goods available to those in urban centers.

Yet at the same time, in its early years, market socialism was supposed to be carried out within strict limits, especially as to the hiring of labor, so as to prevent a rural "big bourgeoisie" from developing and in turn crushing the emergent agricultural middle class. Until recently, many township enterprises were also restricted by legal restraints, which have served both to limit their degree of privatization and their scale. In this way, the reformers attempted to have their cake and eat it too, combining the drive of private market initiatives with socialistic limits, to provide a uniquely balanced system.

When the reforms were in turn introduced to the urban areas, they again began with the promotion of small-scale entrepreneurship, especially among retailers, the sector which even today has gone furthest in privatizing. Here too, however, limitations were set on private exploitation, notably through the requirement that employment be limited to family members and a few hired workers, generally restricted to no more than seven. This goal of promoting productivity through individual entrepreneurial initiative, but without releasing the full consequences of private capitalization, continues to be evident in the form of cooperative firms, which are in general relatively small-scale, and have been limited in their ownership to those active in the business. The major role of the cooperatives, attests to their centrality in the reform program. By 1991, the 2.4 million such collective firms had over 36 million employees, equal to one-third of those in state-owned enterprises, and their output was growing at almost double the rate of the latter.

Thus while the largest rewards of "marketization" have been concentrated at the top, support for these policies among the population has been based on the spreading out of economic wealth through a variety of economic forms and among many strata. In the suburban agricultural belt surrounding Shanghai, for example, in what are sometimes referred to as "urban villages," per capita income among farmers has risen to 2,650 yuan or $305, almost three times the national average for all farming communities. Most of these former peasants have used their new-found wealth to build new houses, often multi-storied, with living space climbing to forty square meters per person. In the cities too, a visit to both "old" and "new" homes makes clear why those professionals who today can enjoy modern apartments with ample rooms and can buy their children electric pianos and relax in front of a VCR may well support reforms. The growth of a broadly based middle class among both peasants and urban entrepreneurs and employees, however limited their proportion of the population may be, has provided a popular underpinning for market socialism.

But many among the broader masses as well have benefitted to a significant degree from rapid economic growth and the consumerism which it promotes. The number of peasants in deepest impoverishment is said to have dropped from 250 million in 1978 to 70 million today. Changchun university students from poorer peasant backgrounds speak of the transformation of their villages, with investments in modern farm implements and new consumer goods. For the working people in that city, who previously had to live through the winter largely on cabbage and root crops and buy what few other vegetables and fruits were available off the frozen sidewalks, the plethora of bananas, oranges, strawberries, greens, and meats of all kinds that can now be purchased in indoor markets year-round have changed their lives and their diet. Across the nation, meat consumption per capita has increased some two and a half times since 1980. Millions of workers have gained new housing during reforms, built by their enterprises, so that the two or three families that used to share a single apartment now each have their own separate homes. Between 1979 and 1994, per capita living space in the cities rose from 6.4 to 10.6 square meters. Urban households now routinely have washing machines, refrigerators, and even color television sets. Within the last few months, the work week in state-owned firms has been lowered from forty-eight hours to forty-four, a major and widely welcomed improvement. Thus the reforms have not simply boosted the GNP of China as a whole, nor benefitted a wealthy elite alone, but have improved living and working conditions for a large proportion of the population, and have included broadly based elements of income distribution.

As long as the old socialist system still held the strongholds of the large state-owned industries and institutions, however, the entrepreneurial path to development could not be fully implemented, and the interests of the emerging middle class would not be secure. Small commodity production serves as an inadequate basis for a modern economy. That base can only be built on the massive industrial enterprises which until recently has been largely state-owned in China. Once the issue of "modernization" of the entire economy is fully addressed, therefore, the idea that "the market" and individual entrepreneurial initiative based on material rewards can best stimulate production cannot be kept within petty bourgeois limits. The reformers bypassed this problem temporarily by turning to foreign capital and stimulating the isolated development of Special Economic Zones. But the question of how to deal with the large public firms which formed the heart of the Chinese socialist system in industry could not be put off forever. Here, however, market socialism confronted a different set of difficulties than those present in small-scale production.

The scale of modern industrial enterprises or large professional institutions does not lend itself easily to the combination of "free market" economics with the kinds of socialistic restraints which had earlier been imposed on small-scale entrepreneurs. The contracting out of a major factory to semiprivate ownership immediately creates an exploitable working class capable of supporting a full-scale system of capitalism, while these same large industrial enterprises offer enormous opportunities to "get rich quick," at levels which are inconceivable to the petty bourgeoisie, for those in control of apportioning financing and trade. When these industries are tied into the functions of the state itself, the greatest openings are generated for instant wealth on an enormous scale. Nor can the problems facing state-owned enterprises be corrected by internal entrepreneurial initiative alone, since they require massive outside investments and technical aid. These could only be obtained, given the rate at which the reformers were compelled by "the market" to drive expansion, by turning in large part to foreign, that is capitalist, investors.

From the beginning, therefore, the very character of modern mass production threatened to break the class limitations of the petty bourgeois market socialist program. But it is just these changes in the structure of classes that were resisted in the state enterprises. First, the reformers faced the mass of workers, whose class interests were threatened by the loss of socialist securities and of a relative egalitarianism, without the compensating opportunity to "get rich" through private participation in the market available to the petty bourgeoisie. The old managerial stratum of these enterprises often shared similar fears about their potential losses under a more privatized system.

Thus special caution was required here by the reformers to overcome the remnants of their opponents and the resistance of those with different class interests. To remove these barriers, the state-owned enterprises which lay at the center of the socialist system had to be gradually "surrounded," first from the countryside, then by urban entrepreneurs, and finally through development of the South and a massive influx of foreign capital. The hesitancy of this approach, however, has left market socialism in a kind of limbo, half-way between its two inherent poles, but without a clear "middle" strategy.

Nowhere is the resulting policy confusion more evident than in the current debate over property rights in state-owned enterprises. In most firms the move has already been made toward a semiprivate form of ownership, in which each enterprise essentially controls its own finances and retains a large portion of its profits, though it continues to be subject to governmental regulation and must share at least a portion of its income with the state. In government newspaper articles and editorials, however, it is openly admitted that the question of who actually owns these institutions is no longer certain. Having increasingly turned over managerial authority to each enterprise, the state finds that its own continued ownership and control hinders their independent progress. Yet to relinquish the last vestiges of government possession is to abandon all pretence of a socialist system.

Both in theory and in practice, therefore, a wide range of solutions are being proposed and tried, centering around the concepts that 51 percent state control still constitutes "socialism," even if it is combined with minority private interests, or that "public" can mean any form of owning that continues to have at least some collective dimension. The Chinese government is now experimenting with many new corporate forms, in an effort to combine a degree of privatized ownership with the development of socialist enterprises, including shareholding systems which are more limited than those typical in capitalist countries. A major debate is raging, both at official levels and in the press, universities, and enterprises themselves, over how far to go in the privatization of these firms. Yet in the answer to that question lies much of the future direction of the entire system.

That the issue of who owns the state enterprises should only now be facing "final" resolution, fifteen years after the beginning of reform, indicates the deepening of the contradictions reached by market socialism. The length of time that it has taken to bring the public sector of the Chinese economy to the point of complete "marketization" can thus be read in various ways. On the one hand, it attests to the ideological skill and patience of Deng Xiaoping and his supporters, who have striven to devise a theoretically worked out program, and to introduce it gradually, not getting ahead of themselves. This in turn reflects the contradictory nature of market socialism, which necessitates a constant effort to balance the needs of privatized initiative with a degree of public control. At the same time, having suffered so much for their "reformist" ideas during the Cultural Revolution, Deng and those around him are still very defensive after fifteen years in power to the charge that they are leading China to capitalism. Thus the gradualism of reforms also indicates the degree to which its advocates must be careful not to reawaken the opposition to their policies among those class elements who are most likely to lose out in the radical economic transformation.

Despite attempts to control the process, however, as state-owned firms are reformed, the contradictions of marketization are coming to a head in ways which threaten to release again the open struggle among classes. On the one hand, as the large industries shift to reform policies, and as goods from abroad are increasingly allowed to flood the market, their competition undermines the earlier base created among the emerging middle class. At the same time, limits on the hiring of labor have fallen to allow small producers to compete with larger ones. Thus from the petty bourgeoisie itself, new big capitalists emerge, to join those already present among the foreign investors and large-scale domestic entrepreneurs, and the officials and managers who are their partners. The mix of private entrepreneurial and social-istic elements which served the reformers so well at the start, therefore, has begun to break down under the class dynamics and productive requirements of large industry and global markets. These contradic-tions make it increasingly impossible to defend the market socialist system ideologically. They also render more and more irrelevant whether the subjective goals of the present leadership are to reestablish a capitalist system or not, for the very nature of their program leads inevitably in that direction unless it is altered by a reversal of policy and a renewal of revolutionary socialism.

III. From "Iron Rice Bowls" to "Socialist Pawnshops"

If it is difficult to measure precisely what there is that is still socialist about the Chinese political and economic system, or even what the word means now in the language of the government, it is striking, after fifteen years of marketization reforms, how much of socialism still remains. The term "iron rice bowl," so eagerly seized upon and so widely disparaged in many Western analyses, does not do justice to the complex of rights and guarantees which were won through social-ist revolution in China. Under this system, the government effectively guaranteed that all adults were able to work, and until recently virtu-ally every person working for public enterprises had jobs from which it was essentially impossible to fire them, at least without providing equivalent employment.

But this "iron" security against joblessness only begins to capture the complex of social relations which being employed by the state represents in China. For a job with a government institution almost always comes with employer-provided housing in nearby apartment complexes at minimal maintenance cost, free health care and maternity payments, worker compensation and other forms of insurance, a pension, and frequently other resources, such as schools or recreational facilities. Thus employment in a work unit provides a full set of social benefits in an enveloping community setting. This all-encompassing system, even at the very low overall level of the Chinese economy, allowed conditions of society completely unfamiliar in the vastly more wealthy United States: essentially no unemployment, begging, or homelessness, virtually no crime, no shantytown slums, and even among the very poor, no "underclass" of social outcasts in desperate and degraded poverty.

Nor were these relations only of quantitative security. In the automobile factories of Changchun, workers on the floor in early 1994 were still commonly paid at least two times the income earned by faculty at nearby universities, though there were certainly more poorly paid laborers in the city, and some professors were able to make much more. Relative egalitarianism in class relations is further exemplified by the president of the largest auto factory in Changchun living in an apartment building only marginally more attractive than those provided for the 100,000 other employees in the plant. These egalitarian practices were national in scope, not a local aberration.

> According to a 1988 survey by the Beijing Statistics Bureau, urban intellectuals earned on average 11.3 percent less than urban workers. Moreover, average salaries of college-educated workers were less than for those who were illiterate or had primary educations or less.[12]

Adding to this economic and social egalitarianism, in work units, including universities, there is also a political hierarchy that may differ greatly from the administrative channels, with important effects on the relationship of classes. A driver and one of the gatekeepers at the university where we taught in Changchun, for example, were said to have considerable power in the party structure, despite their lowly occupations.

Thus while Chinese workers have lacked certain formal or legal rights, such as the freedom to form independent unions and to strike, which, as often in the breach as in practice, they are supposed to have in the West, this should not suggest by any means that they are powerless. When the question is asked why, fifteen years after the end of the Cultural Revolution, someone working on an auto factory shop floor could still earn more than a professor, the answer given is that the workers simply would not put up with any change. If salaries for professionals were to be raised, those in the factories would demand a similar wage increase, finding ways to limit their output until they got it. Thus the "iron rice bowl" rested on a healthy respect for the working class and its power, as well as more quantitative forms of social security.

Similarly, until 1995 university students received an almost free education, having to pay only limited fees and meet some of their living costs, and while they recently were given the right to seek employment not provided by the government, most could still apply to the state for guaranteed jobs, with housing and health care. These students are chosen through a national system of examinations which, though hardly foolproof in terms of egalitarianism, given the different advantages provided by family background, nevertheless offer the chance for higher education to all levels of the society. At the university where we taught, one-half of the student body came directly from work units, including the auto plants. Half the university students there, as across the nation, also come from rural families, a percentage below their proportion in the population, but still quite substantial overall.

The "iron rice bowl" is therefore not just a kind of job security, or even an economic system alone, but a form of socialism which organizes society in its entirety, including its class relations and degree of egalitarianism. These socialistic elements have remained surprisingly resistant to direct attack over the past fifteen years. Thus the reformers who dominate the government are just now beginning to succeed in the total dismantling of the previous system, and even at this late date they can do so only through a kind of outflanking maneuver. It is in this effort that the foreign enterprises and joint ventures have been given a central role as the entering wedge to split apart the existing social relations. It is their heavily exploited workers, in turn, who have been used as shock troops of a kind, as cannon fodder in the economic war to break the back of the old system and to force the Chinese working class to accept the new marketization forces.

As a result, though private and foreign-funded enterprises still account for a small part of the total economy, their impact is out of all proportion to their share of economic activity. After extremely rapid growth, by the end of 1993, the portion of Chinese investment in fixed assets utilizing funds from abroad was still only 13 percent, and the labor force in this sector was between 5 and 6 million, a tiny part of the overall figure of 145 million engaged in work outside of agriculture. But the role of the private and foreign-funded sectors is far greater than their size alone would indicate, for they are the most dynamic element in the economy, and are already the main producers in some leading industries, especially high-tech ones. Even more fundamentally, they are viewed by the government and public alike as the vanguard of the new social relations.

The firms owned or funded from abroad have become the model around which "market socialism" is being created, and which the state-owned enterprises are in turn expected to follow. It is here that experimentation is being carried out into how far China can go in dismantling the old socialist forms of planning, management, and social services, without totally losing control of the regulation of society by the party and the state. So too, the higher salaries and less controlled working conditions of these sectors have made "the South" a kind of magnet for the entire country, resulting not only in the massive physical movement of people to that region, but also in a form of mental reorientation even among those who resist the temptation to seek their fortunes there, not unlike the role of the West in U.S. development. Finally, it is in the private and semi-private sectors that new class elements are being created which are incompatible with socialism in any recognizable form.

Thus the model for government units today is the privately owned company which can make its own way in the world economy without public support. This is reinforced by the "pecking order" of preferential policies, such as tax breaks, which favor first and foremost foreign investors and joint ventures, and then those state-owned enterprises which invest in newly created economic zones. These same benefits, however, are largely unavailable to older government units and the small cooperative firms. This puts the latter at a decided disadvantage in the competition with foreign enterprises and joint ventures, leading to many bitter complaints, though investors from abroad in turn accuse state ministries of showing preference to their own firms.

Despite these conflicting claims, it is those public enterprises which lag behind in the process of semiprivatization which are officially blamed for the remaining "backwardness" and lack of development in China, and they are constantly being exhorted to accept the market reforms, open up to the outside world, and adopt "modern" management methods, i.e., those which have been developed by and for the capitalist system. Both economically and ideologically, therefore, the "competition" between public firms and private and semi-private ventures, between domestic socialism and foreign-funded capitalism and semi-capitalism, is very unequal. While foreign enterprises and joint ventures have been left free to practice capitalistic methods with little or no effort to make them abide by socialist principles, the drive to change the state-owned firms in the direction of marketization has been constant and relentless.

In defending these policies, the same Chinese ideologists—beginning with Deng Xiaoping himself—who insist that the market is not incompatible with socialism, at the same time undialectically point to state ownership as a sign that the system is still socialist. Thus as long as "the public" owns a major portion of the economy, the latter is said to represent "socialism." Governmental ownership in and of itself, however, cannot be accepted as an adequate definition of a socialist system, for a degree of public control of the means of production is by no means incompatible with their capitalistic exploitation. Nowhere is this more evident than in the case of land, which remains totally owned by the Chinese state, but which nevertheless supports a flourishing private real estate market based on the long-term leasing of individual plots, with the right to sell such leases and any buildings erected on the property. As noted above, these are among the most profitable investments.

Just how socialist property is to be used to support a capitalistic class is exemplified by Bei Zhaohan, chairman of a state-owned conglomerate based in Guangzhou, who "seems not so different from Western business tycoons."

> "We want to get into property development," said Mr. Bei, a dynamic 52-year-old man with a well-tailored suit and boardroom manners, "because I see that the richest people everywhere—in the U.S., in Japan, in Hong Kong—are all property magnates."[13]

Thus though the largest single sector of the economy is indeed still located in public enterprises under the authority of governmental ministries, as a result of marketization, these state-owned enterprises can, and often do, generate profits by methods not easily distinguishable from those of capitalism, especially in their joint ventures with foreign investors. Returns can be very high indeed. Auto industry profit rates are said to be two to six times above the international average. But even where the goal of the investment may have a social purpose, for instance to improve worker housing, the method of operation must be such as to put profits first, for otherwise the needed foreign funding will simply not be available and the sponsoring enterprise will not survive.

No sector of Chinese society has remained untouched by such developments. The People's Liberation Army, in particular, once the last bastion of socialist ideals and rigor, has become a massive investor in all kinds of profit-making enterprises, including in sectors as totally unrelated to defense as modern tourist hotels, in a move disturbingly similar to the process which has occurred in many countries of Latin America, Africa, and other parts of Asia. The armed forces are now said to own anywhere from $5 to $10 billion in nonmilitary investments, and profit-making has become so much their focus that their ability to fight effectively is subject to doubt. Many public agencies, including the army, have also invested heavily abroad under conditions which lack even the pretense of socialistic methods. Thus by 1993, China owned or participated in some 4,400 enterprises in 120 or so countries, with an investment of over $5 billion.

The profits generated by these government-owned units, while remaining ostensibly the property of their enterprises, can be, and today in China increasingly are, diverted into a wide range of essentially private perks. Especially singled out for official condemnation has been the practice of buying luxury automobiles, which are then used for nonofficial purposes, such as driving the children of leading functionaries to schools. Primary school students in Changchun received national media coverage when they wrote a letter to local officials complaining of this practice among their classmates, and in early 1994 the Jilin Province authorities went so far as to seize 188 automobiles "clamping down on corrupt officials and company bosses who have used public funds to buy luxury cars."[14]

Such abuses have become so widespread that a national ban on the purchase of such vehicles by state-owned enterprises was enacted, considerably deflating the car industry after its rapid recent climb. As a result, at the First Auto Works in Changchun, the largest in China, the assembly line was being shut down early each day during the winter of 1993-1994 for lack of work, and trucks were being stockpiled at the airport and on empty lots around the city. But even such disruptive control measures only scratch the surface of the deeper change in relations, which allows each company to profit from its own economic activities, with the benefits flowing largely to the employees of the specific firm, and especially leading managers. Public ownership per se, therefore, is no guarantee against an essentially capitalist relationship, whether between employer and worker, or through the exchange of goods and services in the marketplace.

The full assault on the iron rice bowl form of socialism, however, cannot be carried out without dismantling all the social securities and class relations of which it is composed. It is these transformations which are now being pushed at full speed by the government. Most notably, job security is rapidly crumbling. In the past few years, managers have increasingly been given the right to reduce the work force. In Jilin Province alone, 120,000 workers had been let go as of mid-1995. By 1996 the coal industry had already fired 100,000 workers, with plans to get rid of many times that number in coming years. The China National Coal Corporation, only one of the large state-run firms, announced plans to "excess" 400,000 of its 3 million employees by the end of 1995. As a transitional measure, companies were required to find or create alternate employment for their dismissed workers, and the coal industry claims to have done so for those already fired, while promising $1,720 "to help start a business or find work elsewhere" for those let go in the future.[15]

But such programs often involve a downgrading into lighter industrial or service work at a lower wage rate, with subsidies that are gradually reduced over a few years. Thus even if workers retain jobs, they are unlikely over the long run to claim the same social rewards as previously. At the Changchun Number One Auto Plant, for example, with around 15,000 scheduled for dismissal, only a kind of make-work system of odd jobs has been proposed as compensation, a complete come-down from the dignity and security which those on the production line had enjoyed. At Wuhan Steel, 70,000 of the former 120,000 employees lost their jobs and were placed in subsidiary companies, with a subsidy for their lower pay that dropped annually and was scheduled to be finally ended in 1995.

> "'This is not unemployment!' Zhao Wenyuan, vice president of Wuhan Steel, said in horror. 'Absolutely not. Unemployment is when you push people out on their own into society. We're not doing that at all.'"[16]

But though some of the spinoff enterprises prove to be successful in their own right, for many workers, the jobs created are little more than a "half-way house" to future unemployment. Others are helped to set up small businesses, joining the legions of "self-employed," or the already overcrowded informal economy. For the ever-expanding numbers of such workers, semantic arguments over what "unemployment" is mean little.

> On the market street of Wuhan, laid-off women sit by displays of bowls, clothes and whatever products that [sic] can find to sell on consignment. "Most of these people here have been let go," a young woman said, sweeping her hand toward the crowds of people on the street. "We're all trying to make a living....
> "It's terrible," she added.

But despite the growing mass of such "informal economy" workers, officials persist in calling the system in China "socialism."

> "We are still a socialist country," said Li Pan, deputy secretary general of the Wuhan municipal government. "We can't just throw people into the streets. We must give them a way out. If they can't move from one iron rice bowl to another, we have to at least give them a rice bowl made of mud."[17]

It would be difficult to find a more perfect expression of how the concept of "socialism" in China today has become "muddied," with what were once its guarantees of a stable and secure life replaced by the porous and easily shattered promises of "market" reforms.

But even this limited degree of job protection is being lost, as the requirement for enterprises to provide new employment for their dismissed workers is dropped. Most ominously, the reemployment rate, which had been running at about 70 percent for several years, dropped to 20 percent in 1993. Key to this development is the new contract system, introduced since 1986 on an increasingly wide scale, in which workers either individually or through labor unions bargain directly with their employers. Under this contractual arrangement employees are paid according to their production, and they are allowed greater freedom in changing jobs. At the same time, enterprises gain expanded rights to hire and fire workers and to set their own wage and salary rates. Some 23.3 million employees, or about 25 percent of the workforce in state-owned firms, have signed such contracts, and in Shanghai the proportion has already reached 98 percent. Most new workers nationwide are hired under such terms. The contract system has been used in particular to "rationalize" unprofitable state enterprises, through a combination of firings and production-related raises for at least some of those who remain. At the same time, laid-off management personnel are generally given new assignments, feeding worker resentment.

Such power to slash the work force with no alternative employment cannot be safely granted to managers, therefore, without creating the danger of a social explosion, unless some form of unemployment insurance and job placement service is also in place. The government is now racing to complete such a program, and makes clear that it is itching to get rid of millions more workers from state-owned firms once this system is sufficiently developed. The state itself is planning to "excess" at least 2 million employees. At the same time, the "model" of private firms and joint ventures, which generally provide few or no benefits such as housing, insurance, health care, and pensions, is being universalized, by creating either government-run programs or, increasingly, private companies to offer these services. Workers are now being forced to buy their houses from their employers, in a kind of condominium arrangement, compelling them into the real estate market. Though the opportunity to own a home is often welcomed, such plans are increasingly forced on all employees, whether they wish it or not. Public housing in the cities is also being sold off. To replace the former employment benefits, foreign firms, such as Pensions 2000, the largest pension fund in the United States, are now exploring this new market.

These developments are leaving millions of workers without the social securities which they have enjoyed up until now, despite marketization, and this is resulting in the revival of conditions not seen for several decades.

The contradictory results that have been created by the ambiguous mix that is the Chinese market socialist system today is well captured by a small article from Shenzhen. Without apparent irony, the story reported:

> Pawnshops, once thought of as a means for the rich to exploit the poor, have revived in this boom town.
> There are now six local-government approved pawn companies.

And they have become a valuable short-term source of limited amounts of cash for individuals and private and collectively-owned enterprises.[18]

No doubt "socialist" pawnshops, under government regulation, may be less exploitative than the old-style ones in the days of mandarin landlords and uncontrolled capitalism. But even in this age of capitalist triumphalism, there may be some left, in China and elsewhere, who believe that socialism should be made of sterner stuff.

IV. Many Must Get Poor Second

Of all the ideological pronouncements by Deng Xiaoping in advocating "market socialism," the idea that "some must get rich before others" has met with the most unqualified success. The "new wealth" enjoyed by many leading party and state functionaries, military officers, public enterprise managers, and especially businesspeople, both private entrepreneurs and those in semi-privatized ventures, is increasingly apparent. Many of these people can be found in the top hotels and the Pierre Cardin stores, flaunting their cellular phones and beepers, fancy Western-style clothes, and air of self-important indulgence so reminiscent of the Chinese elite of the Guomindang period. It is they who can afford to join the new Jingnan Yongle golf facility in Beijing with dues of $12,000, and the Country Horse Racing Club, where memberships in 1993 cost 80,000 yuan, or almost $14,000. The club advertised that 200 had already been sold to foreigners, and another 300 to "Chinese managers and senior officials in joint ventures."[19]

These same people, together with overseas Chinese and multinational corporations, are the ones who have been buying into luxury apartment buildings like the French-designed Sunshine Plaza in the capital, advertised as "The Most Splendid Contribution of China for Centuries," and the suburban Beijing Dragon Villas, in "pure American-Canadian style" with broad lawns, starting from "only" $360,000. Some have even begun buying plots in Florida. The measures of this new wealth are found in smaller things also, like private phones, installation of which "will cost roughly a year's salary for an ordinary Chinese worker," yet with the demand already in the hundreds of thousands.[20] Others can spend the equivalent of thousands of dollars on imported liquors. In Beijing, a city where the average resident earned just 197 yuan or $34 a month in 1992, single little abalone-stuffed mooncakes sold for 1,000 yuan each at the Lufthansa Shopping Center's 1993 Lunar Festival.

It is these class elements as well, no doubt, who were the purchasers of the limited-edition jewel-encrusted gold watches issued for the hundredth anniversary of the birth of Mao Zedong on December 26,

1993. The most valuable were those with seals offered by the daughter and son-in-law of Mao, costing as much as $19,388 each, and coming with $17,000 life and $20,000 property insurance policies. Mao would no doubt be flattered that even the nouveau riche of China find his memory so valuable. But such timepieces are indeed the perfect hedge in more ways than one, in these days of growing uncertainty in China: sure to rise in value if marketization continues, but "politically correct" if things once again take a leftist turn.

There are now said to be over a million people in China with more than 1 million yuan or $119,000 in new worth. Those able to take advantage of the opportunities to "get rich" under the reforms are by no means limited to top officials and businesspeople, however. A sizeable number of persons in all strata of the society are in a position to obtain new levels of wealth which set them dramatically apart from their Chinese counterparts. On Hainan Island, for example, a young farmer developed the tourist trade, earning in the first year 100,000 yuan, equal to $17,241, "an astronomical figure for the local people, whose annual income often fails to exceed 200 yuan [$34]."[21] Scientists, university professors, and even students sometimes "strike it rich." One doctoral postgraduate sold an invention in the chemical field for 2 million yuan, or $340,000, while a 1993 auction of research ideas brought eighteen scientists an average of 100,000 yuan each. It is this kind of "sudden" wealth which stands out in such stark contrast to the older socialist system with its relative egalitarianism.

But those who announced the "some must get rich first" policy, failed to add the inevitable corollary: "many must get poor second." A 1994 trip through China, beginning in the Northeast and ending in the South, provided a visual "misery index" of the impoverishment which is inseparable from marketization. In Changchun, Beijing, and west to Xian, one still saw little visual sign that the conditions of social security which have marked the socialist system up until this time have broken down. Even in the western central province of Sichuan, there was no obvious evidence of the dislocations that might be expected, given the large numbers of poor peasants who are migrating from this region to the South and East. But when one gets to booming Shanghai on the eastern seaboard, the change begins, appropriately enough on the Bund, the old imperialist center on the riverfront with its Europe-an-style buildings, where panhandling children appear, though they are not very aggressive. South to Guilin, a major tourist area, and the begging becomes more insistent, but still limited and without the sense of complete desperation. In Guangzhou, however, there can be no mistaking that the homeless peasant-worker families camped out around the railroad station and the children grabbing leftovers off tables in restaurants nearby are in a state of desperate poverty, malnutrition, illness, and total degradation. Their ranks, made up mostly of migrants from Sichuan and elsewhere, are swelling in rough proportion to the degree of "new wealth" being generated in this center of foreign investment and reform.

There are now some 200,000 children estimated to be on the streets of Chinese cities, and as one newspaper article put it, "child homelessness, which is on the up and up, is stretching government welfare resources."[22] In Shanghai, more than 3,000 child vagrants were picked up in 1992. Even in the North such conditions are spreading. In Jiamusi City, in Heilongjiang Province, there are an estimated 3,000 vagrants. Some 600 children among them were rounded up and sent back home between 1989 and 1991, but an equivalent number quickly reappeared on the streets, and by the end of 1992, there were 40 percent more homeless youths under fourteen than the year before. There have been partially successful efforts during the last year to control the flow of peasants into Guangdong as well. But the entire system of "marketization" production in that province is built largely on migrants. There are now an estimated 8 to 10 million transient workers there, the majority of them women. It is increasingly common to find situations such as that in the village of Houjie, whose 75,000 permanent residents are today outnumbered by 80,000 migrants, working on the assembly lines of the 900 local factories.

> Wages are low by American standards, but extravagant by Chinese terms: $50 to $60 a month, more than some university professors earn. Almost all of the workers are women, who are regarded by factory managers as more responsible and adroit with their hands than men, and they typically work six days a week for up to about 10 hours a day.[23]

There are also some 500,000 child laborers in the province, many of them helping to work the new sweatshops.[24] Thus the problem in Guangdong cannot be so easily solved by limiting internal immigration, nor by the municipal roundups used elsewhere. This is a major reason why homelessness and begging are more in evidence in the South than in other parts of the country.

The development of such third world phenomena is a dire change for China. Central to the policies developed by Mao in the earlier revolutionary period had been a determination to avoid just this kind of mass movement of peasants into the cities and the growth of an urban underclass of impoverished semi-migratory workers, unemployed, slum dwellers, and homeless. The scale of Chinese society makes the rise of such dislocations especially drastic. The government of China itself estimates that there are at least 100 million "excess" peasants in the countryside—equivalent to some one fifth of those still engaged in farming—and 30 to 50 million or so more already on the move looking for work, 80 percent of them young people. This is a mass of peasant labor at economic loose ends approximately equal to the number of all non-agricultural workers in the Chinese economy today. It is also equivalent to the entire work force of the United States, or the total populations of France and England combined. And this figure for "floating" labor in China is expected to climb as high as 250 million by the end of the century. Already Sichuan province alone, where one-third of the peasants are "surplus" laborers, has generated 10 million such migrants, who sent 10.7 billion yuan or $1.3 billion home in 1994. They and millions more from other impoverished regions flood the cities, providing the work force for the construction boom and performing other hard labor, while often supporting families on as little as sixty-four cents per day. Commonly housed in temporary shacks right at the work site, they could be seen everywhere in Changchun, easily distinguishable from the more permanent and stable working population in the city.

The scale of the "floating" work force is increasingly creating problems, especially for the transportation system. In an effort to control the massive flow of workers to and from their villages during the 1995 Chinese Lunar New Year, 60 percent of the migrants working on farms in Guangdong province, or over 2 million laborers, did not return home for the holidays. But such a failure to rejoin their families for the Spring Festival—a tradition that is pursued with great intensity across China—further shatters the social structure, and breaks the ties of workers with their local regions. This in turn helps to generate an increasingly permanent but unstable "underclass" in the large metropolitan centers, without familial or other societal roots.

> Wang Ju, an official in charge of residence registration in the Public Security Bureau of Beijing estimated the floating population of the city at around 1.65 million, more than one-tenth of Beijing's total population....
>
> The non-Beijing residents pose a major problem for police, family planning and other authorities.
>
> Local reports said provincials accounted for about 70 per cent of the criminal offenders caught in Beijing last year.[25]

About four fifths of the migrants in the capital find laboring jobs, and they now predominate among the 800,000 construction workers. But their numbers are overwhelming city resources.

> A new rule, designed by the Beijing authorities to limit the influx of migrants. was passed by local people's congress.
>
> On November 1, the capital began to charge new residents between 10,000 yuan ($1,170) and 100,000 yuan ($11,700) for a permanent residence

card depending on which area of the city they want to settle in—the centre or the suburbs.[26]

Even the lower of these charges would exclude many from the countryside, reversing the "open door" policy of entry into the urban areas that has been increasingly implemented under reforms.

Added to these worker-peasants drawn from the rural areas, are the growing numbers of urban unemployed, whose ranks, while still relatively small at 4 to 5 million or so, are also increasing rapidly as enterprises "rationalize" their workforce.

> 17 million overstaffed workers ... have been discharged by China's State-owned enterprises. They are the victims of businesses which have closed, merged or shifted to manufacturing of other products in recent years as a result of previous unprofitable operations. The figure is equivalent to the industrial population of France.[27]

For many of those let go from state-owned factories, there is no work available except in foreign-funded enterprises. In Tianjin, of 80,000 excessed workers, 80 percent ended up in such firms.

> Surplus workers discharged from State-owned enterprises, in turn, have formed a rich employment source for newly-built, Sino-foreign joint ventures here.

However, investment from abroad cannot sop up all such "riches."

In 1993, the unemployment rate was 2.6 percent, and 900,000 persons registered for jobless relief, compared to just 350,000 in 1992, and 100,000 more than over the previous six years combined. But many others have jobs in name only, still kept nominally on the books, while being sent home with a greatly reduced wage. Though there are claims that two thirds of all workers are now covered by an unemployment insurance plan, of the 5 million unemployed expected by the end of 1994, only 1.8 million were anticipated to be receiving benefits. With the number of unemployed increasing nationwide, the ability of the state to pay for such social services is already strained.

> "Government statistics showed, about 200 billion yuan ($23 billion) are required for compensating these surplus workers. But the country's relief funds have totalled only 2 billion yuan ($235,000).[28]

Despite efforts to create labor exchanges and to restrict hiring of low-wage rural migrants instead of those fired from urban jobs, the ranks of the latter are certain to grow rapidly, and were said to have reached 8 million by early 1995.

Thus the birth of the "new rich" is being accompanied on a vastly greater scale by the generation of a newer type of poor, who have no place to fit in except as a reserve army of labor. The way in which they are viewed as necessary to the emerging social structure was expressed by Luo Gan, a state councilor.

> Transient rural labourers are vital to maintaining the luster of big economic and financial hubs, he said.
> Studies conducted in Beijing and Hangzhou show that about 10 per cent of migrant labourers are engaged in catering, helping develop the service industry.[29]

Thus "Provincial girls account for 80 per cent of the housekeepers in Beijing."[30] Many of those dismissed from industrial jobs face a similar future. Even the reemployment program in Beijing, "mainly involves developing service industries, particularly labour-intensive ones, with the idea of absorbing surplus workers."[31] Thus the urban new rich increasingly depend on a rapidly growing servant class of poverty-stricken peasantry and discarded proletarians to "cater" to their "lustrous" needs.

The more visual manifestations of such contradictions, however, only begin to convey the depths of division beginning to open up in Chinese society. Marketization has begun to devour the very groups in whose name it was initiated and among whom it was first implemented. In the rural areas, in the early years of reform, incomes on average rose, and the historic gap between country and city began to be reduced somewhat. By the mid-1980s, however, marketization began to spread to the urban centers as well. As reforms were introduced in the major industries, including in particular more freedom in pricing, inflationary pressures grew, opening a "price scissors" between rural and urban areas.

In the last five years, costs of agricultural production materials have risen twice as rapidly as grain prices. Typical of this development, the governor of Henan Province estimates that whereas fifty kilograms of corn could be exchanged for thirty-seven kilograms of urea in 1984, by 1992 the equivalent in fertilizer was only nineteen kilograms, a loss of one-half in farm market value. Thus despite greater productivity, peasant incomes are actually falling in many places. The effects of these contradictions are uneven, however, increasing the polarization among the peasantry itself. In 1985, the gap between the annual rural per capita output value of Central and East China was just 452 yuan or fifty-two dollars compared with a 1,858 yuan or $214 difference by 1993. The two thirds of Chinese farmers in the western part of the country generate only one third of agricultural value, and "per capita income in the vast hinterland region is one quarter that in the coastal areas.... 'Do not let the disparity becomes so serious,'" a newspaper warned. "'If the gap widens further, it will stir social tension and stall the overall development of the nation.'"[32]

The very turn to small-scale household agriculture that at first promoted a spurt of entrepreneurial investment has begun to turn back on itself, leading to a rapid decline in income growth.

> From 1978 to 1984, greatly initiated by the State's household responsibility system, which granted more independent rights of production and management, the average growth rate of the farmers' incomes was around 15 per cent.

In the following four years, however, the rise in peasant income dropped radically to only 5 percent annually, and from 1989 to 1991, it declined further to just 2 percent after inflation. Though up to 40 percent of the rural population gave up regular agricultural work and went into township enterprises, and tens of millions more left for the cities, rural underemployment continued to rise given the inadequate base for farm production.

> First, farmers' small production scale—6.3 mu (0.42 hectare) farmland per household—had directly affected their incomes and investment level.
> Most of the funds farmers invested in simple production come from self-accumulation.
> Statistics show in 1992 that bank loans for agricultural purpose was 2.18 yuan (26 cents) per capita.
> The farmers' low income level and weak inability to invest has greatly limited their investment scale and causes the production to remain at a standstill.[33]

Once the "capital" inherited from the breakup of the communes was exhausted, the capacity of farmers for "self-accumulation" proved very small. Thrown on their own limited resources on tiny farms, while the attention of the government and financial institutions turned to non-agricultural sectors, the gains of the early years of reform have turned into their opposite for many peasants, and they have seen their early income growth rapidly disappear.

At the same time, illegal fees, charges, fines, demands for "contributions," and even outright extortion and labor duties reminiscent of feudal landlord times, have been levied on farmers, often amounting to 10 percent or more of their income, at least double the funds they are supposed to owe public bodies. When the government in 1993 belatedly moved to reduce such extra levies, it was estimated that the saving to peasants was more than 10 billion yuan, or $1.7 billion, but this only indicates how much they had already lost. Despite such efforts at control, in the first half of 1994, governmental levies on farmers increased 41 percent, while income grew by only 9.4 percent. Even more drastic has been the widespread practice of paying peasants in I.O.U.'s, which were not always redeemed promptly or at their equivalent value, due to inflation. As a result of such policies and of the price spread, the nationwide average income in the countryside went up 3.4 percent in 1993, to 921 yuan or $106, while urban residents saw a gain of 10.2 percent, to 2,337 yuan or $269. The ratio of per capita income between the rural and urban population, which fell from 1:2.4 to 1:1.7 between 1979 and 1984, has risen to 1:2.7 today, or slightly higher than pre-reform levels.

The reforms have more than economic effects, however. The rural medical cooperative system, begun in the 1950s—and greatly expanded by the "barefoot doctors" program launched in 1966 at the start of the Cultural Revolution—has been largely shattered. Today, inexpensive preventive services for the masses are giving way to high-tech and costly equipment for the relative few.

> Among the most fundamental problems facing the Chinese system is the shortage of doctors in some rural areas, particularly since the dismantling in the early 1980's of the communes that used to provide health care services. In some poor areas, villages have neglected health care since the communes fell apart, and schistosomiasis—a disease caused by parasites that live in the blood vessels of humans and animals— spread as communities stopped mass mobilization efforts to combat the parasite.
>
> These problems seem to have been partly resolved, and now there is again a determined effort to stamp out schistosomiasis. But problems have surfaced, including surging costs as hospitals compete with each other to buy fancy equipment like brain scanners.[34]

Funding for village medical cooperatives has evaporated, first through the shift to the individual household responsibility system and destruction of the communal structure, resulting in a breakdown of the local revenue base, second as a consequence of the favoring of urban residents over peasants, leading to a drop in the proportion of the national health care budget received by the rural medical service from 21 percent in 1978 to 10 percent in 1991. The growing polarization in access to services is indicated in a 1994 report from Minister of Public Health Chen Minzang.

> A survey of 65 counties conducted by the Ministry of Public Health in 1993 found that spending on public health was just 4 per cent of the counties' budgets.
>
> Further, 20 per cent of Chinese farmers cannot afford medical care.
>
> "There is a widening gap between urban and rural residents in terms of access and the ability to pay for medical care," according to Chen.[35]

By 1994 only 5 percent of villages nationwide were able to afford funding of cooperative health services, leading to a drastic exodus of doctors either to private practice or to more urbanized centers.

Now, as in so many other sectors of the economy, a scramble is underway to find alternative sources of funds from the state or private institutions, or to tap individuals and villages to support a separate system of "medical foundations." Despite apparent success—the government claimed that 89 percent of villages had set up health centers by 1993—these new solutions are certain to be far from universal, and will undoubtedly leave millions of poorer peasantry without health care. Thus,

> Another challenge is the growing number of migrant families, who move to the cities with or without permission to find whatever jobs they can. They pay for their own health care, and often break the rules and give birth to more children than they are allowed to.
> "Our biggest headache is the migrants, because they don't get checkups and they're afraid we'll report them if they have an extra child," said Zhang Huizhong, director of pediatrics at Shanghai's Ninth People's Hospital. "Even if they're sick they don't come to see a doctor."[36]

But those who remain in stable rural occupations and are relatively well off are also finding medical care an often ruinous burden. Thus, "as a result of the disintegration of the co-operative system, the peasants are suffering," and even "once-rich farmers have become impoverished when they have to pay by themselves for an operation or medical treatment."[37]

What is especially significant about these developments is that the peasantry as a whole have begun to suffer as a class, regardless of their individual wealth, and that the farming regions are being increasingly stripped of income to pay for the high-flying profiteering and rising consumption levels in the cities, and to make up for the township revenues lost when communal structures were dissolved. Especially ominous is the disintegration of much of the agricultural technology support system, which like everything else has been semi-privatized and cannot compete with more lucrative ventures. In an economy which must feed more than one fifth of the population of the globe, however, and where three quarters of the people are still wholly or partially dependent on farming for their livelihood and basic survival, such developments can have extremely dire consequences.

Cutbacks in the purchase of costly fertilizers and pesticides, production by peasants only of what is needed for their own survival, or the intentional withholding of grain from markets in an effort to drive up prices, have all increased. Peasant per capita investment in agriculture actually fell in real terms over the last four years, and as a result acreage under cultivation suffers further deterioration, as declining infrastructure maintenance means more environmental damage. In 1978, of the one third of arable land affected by unfavorable weather,

42 percent reported severe losses, while by 1992 the proportion of heavily damaged acreage had risen to 50 percent.

Already living off only one quarter of the world average of agricultural acreage per capita, with its population growing at 10 million per year, China is suffering further from the effects of marketization, as peasants abandon their lands to pursue more lucrative fields.

> To make matters worse, in some places, stretches of farmland are going out of cultivation mainly because the farmers have moved to posts with higher incomes.
>
> For example, in 1992, some 6,600 hectares of farmland in Feidong County, Anhui Province has been abandoned by farmers.
>
> Though the local governments have made great efforts to resume cultivation of such farmland, 30 per cent of it still lies wasting.
>
> We cannot simply blame rural labourers for their reluctance to take up farming.
>
> After all, under a market economy, farmers apparently not only have more chances, but a right to choose their favoured occupation.[38]

The issue is not individual "chances" or "rights," however, so much as government policies which discourage growing numbers of peasants from considering farming to be economically viable, as their costs rise and incomes stagnate compared to non-farm jobs. Abandoned farms can have a serious effect on the local economy, but it is also a matter of grave national concern. With estimates that China is already 20 million hectares short of the amount needed to feed its swelling population, even relatively small additional losses of farmland are a very serious matter. Yet throughout the Chinese countryside, almost 750,000 hectares devoted to agriculture were lost during 1992 and 1993, and land planted in all the main crops was reduced by over 4.4 million hectares. Cropland losses were around 1 million hectares in 1994 alone.

The drop in lands devoted to grain, which Mao had urged be taken as the "key link" in economic development, is even more dramatic, and by 1994 had fallen "below the warning line."[39] Some even see a growing threat to the very ability of the Chinese to feed themselves.

> China's area of farmland under grain dropped to 109.2 million hectares last year, 800,000 hectares below the national security line.
>
> If this dwindling area of farmland isn't checked, another line, 1.2 billion people's bread-and-butter [sic] line, is likely to be threatened.[40]

Other estimates suggest an even more extreme decline in lands used for raising grains, when viewed over a longer period of time, falling from 112 million hectares in 1957 to 95.4 million in 1992. In the former year, "83.7 per cent of cultivated land was devoted to grain production; by 1983, the figure had dropped to 76.4 per cent, and in 1992, it was down to 74.1 per cent."[41]

Stating that "rural economic readjustment has ignored the overall agricultural balance in recent years," Deng Yiming, senior research fellow with the Rural Development Institute of the Chinese Academy of Sciences and deputy secretary-general of the Chinese Rural Economy Management Research Institute, "expressed also the worry that per capita grain output could be lower in 2000 than it is today. That could result in higher grain prices and disrupt the country's economic situation as a whole."

> In 1994, China produced 444.6 billion kilograms of grain, a decrease of 11.9 billion kilograms from 1993. The per capita output was 370 kilograms.
>
> With the yearly 1.2 per growth of population taken into account, the recommended minimum 400 kilograms per capita grain production seems almost impossible to attain by the end of the century, Deng said.[42]

The causes, according to Deng, are the conversion of croplands into forests, grazing land, and fishponds—which are often more profitable in the new market economy—and for infrastructure and rural enterprise growth, and "unrestricted building of houses and tombs." Another major loss has been for golf courses, which have multiplied to serve foreign visitors and the Chinese new rich; forty have been built in the Pearl River region of Guangdong alone.

There has therefore been a rapid fall in cultivated acreage, compounded by the generally unplanned and wasteful conversion of farmland to other uses. In Guangdong, most notably, there was a reduction in agricultural lands of 667,000 hectares during 1991 through 1993. Grain output there declined 3.4 percent and 9.9 percent, respectively, in 1992 and 1993, the latter year showing the greatest loss since 1955. The Ministry of Agriculture states that production of cereals and cotton have dropped in most southern provinces, where the seacoast rice harvest has fallen by 10 million tons, a three month supply for regional cities. Some former grain-exporting provinces now have to import grains.

In an attempt to overcome these rapidly growing losses, there have been major conversions of waste and marginal lands to agricultural production in the past few years. Through such measures, Guangdong reversed earlier declines and achieved a record grain harvest in 1994. But nationally, this has so far been a losing battle. In 1994, 713,000 hectares of existing farmland were taken for other uses, while only 316,660 new hectares were developed for crops. The resulting net drop was a 14 per cent increase over the similar losses in 1993. "In recent years, the country has consistently diverted 400,000 to 466,000, hectares of farmland annually for non-agricultural uses.... And this trend seems difficult to control."[43] The basic contradiction here is that the conversion of marginal and waste lands to agriculture clearly has finite limits and often results in lower productivity even with more costly inputs, while the diversion of farmland to other uses is relentless and largely irreversible, and tends to absorb just those flat and fertile fields which are the most productive.

Between 1978 and 1993, arable land had already dropped from 1.6 to 1.2 mu (about 15 hectares) per capita, but according to an estimate by the Chinese Academy of Agricultural Sciences,

> cultivated land is expected to decline by 2 million mu (133,400 hectares) each year. By 2030, it is expected to drop to 1.35 billion mu (90 million hectares). The per capita cultivated land will be 0.83 mu (0.06 hectare), compared with 1.19 mu (0.08 hectare) in 1994.[44]

This means that early in the next century, arable acreage will have fallen to only one half the amount per person that existed when the reforms began.

Thus the land versus population squeeze is rapidly becoming more dire, and is projected to continue unreversed for many decades. Despite this, the Academy and some other researchers remain optimistic that food needs can be met, through expanded use of former waste and marginal lands, new seed strains, and the increased dependence on chemical fertilizers and irrigation. They count on growing economic development and rising demand for a variety of foods on the part of the expanding population to stimulate technological advances in agriculture. But in the meantime, overall grain output has stalled out. Having increased about 50 billion kilograms every five to six years from 1952 on, it has "hovered around 450 billion kilograms ever since 1989," and dropped 11.9 million tons in 1994 alone, a 2.7 percent loss.[45]

In addition, optimistic long-range forecasts may fail to sufficiently take into account the nature of marketization, which constantly generates negative factors that cancel out positive gains. Thus even as "China expects to develop vast wastelands to meet the needs of the country's increasing population and rapidly developing food industry," the uncontrolled nature of the market corrupts the very process.[46]

> The State Land Administration (SLA), China's premier land authority, is drafting a new rule to curb the random auction of unused land without undisputed ownership and to regulate the blind sale of such land in rural areas....
> One proposed measure is to strengthen the government's overall planning and management of unused land by incorporating mountains, slopes, gullies and ravines which are arable but have not yet been cultivated or developed for agricultural purposes into local development programmes.[47]

The necessity for such measures resulted from the buying up of vast amounts of marginal and waste land for speculative purposes.

> The auction of unused land became very popular last year in China's 15 northern provinces, autonomous regions and municipalities.
> Since that time, 800,000 hectares of unused land have been auctioned off in rural areas, an SLA official said yesterday.
> Many urban individuals, units and overseas investors have bought unused land in the auctions for low prices and pocketed most of the profits.[48]

The very land needed for agricultural expansion, in other words, is being gobbled up for speculative purposes, largely by those with no interest in farm production per se, and at twice the rate of the disappearance of croplands resulting from their being turned to nonfarming usages. In this anarchic market situation, any rational increase in the conversion of marginal or waste lands to meet governmental goals for food production becomes hostage to the profit motives of speculators, and even local agricultural planning can only be advanced by fending off predatory investors, including those from outside China.

Another result of these growing contradictions in the countryside has been sudden rises in food prices, which in the main urban areas soared by more than 25 percent in early 1993 compared to a year earlier. Grain was up by 40 percent, and such staples as fresh vegetables had more than doubled. Typically, when urban state-supported vegetable shops lost their subsidies under the reforms, many of them turned to other businesses, and they now control only 10 to 15 percent of the market, the rest dominated by private owners. As a result, vegetables, whose retail prices used to be only 10 to 20 percent above wholesale levels, were being sold on the streets in the spring of 1994 for double their cost to retailers. Such inflation contributes, at the same time, to a rapidly growing gap between urban rich and poor. Shanghai is typical, where despite a gradually rising level of average wealth, the spread between the income of the lowest 10 percent of the population and those at the top increased 66 percent just between 1992 and 1993. The "middle class" is being especially hard hit, with 30 to 40 percent of those surveyed in large cities stating that they were finding it increasingly difficult to maintain a decent standard of living.

Here again, the main losers have been those the government had earlier favored, most notably professionals and workers in state institutions and enterprises on fixed incomes, which have been virtually frozen in a highly inflationary economy. Large numbers of academics, for example, have been forced to moonlight at all kinds of activities, often unrelated to their normal work, just to make ends meet. Many neglect their university duties to serve as advisers to enterprises, or even to go into business for themselves. Others have moved south, where in joint ventures they can rapidly increase their income, but often at the cost of leaving their earlier professional fields, or even their families, behind. Across the country, a bidding war has broken out, with rapidly developing areas offering lures such as high salaries, extra housing, and even cars, to attract needed professionals. This "brain drain" has had serious consequences in many poor or outlying regions, those which can least afford the loss of their skilled personnel. This has led to a sharp national polarization in availability of "human capital" as well.

> Provinces, municipalities and autonomous regions across the country have been trying their best to attract professionals and technical personnel since the country started its reform and opening up 16 years ago. The developed coastal regions have been winning the "talent war" because of their economic strength.
> Incomplete statistics show that more than 40,000 professionals and technical personnel from the Northwest have moved to coastal areas since 1990.
> The brain drain has hurt the area's economic development.[49]

To counter such tendencies, poorer regions have been forced to offer preferential treatment to professional employees, further straining their already limited resources for economic growth.

College students now often complain of missing teachers and the neglect of academic institutions, which like all others, must increasingly find their own means of support, a haphazard process in which the business skills of administrators may count for more than the quality of research or teaching in the schools they head. For those who lose out in this scramble for funds, the consequences can quickly become dire. At the university where we taught, in the middle of the winter of 1993-1994, we heard that the pay of the Chinese faculty had been "delayed" for an indeterminate period, because the school had run out of the money needed for salaries. Such problems are occurring at all academic levels. "In some rural areas, teachers' salaries have been in arrears in recent years. Teachers sometimes found it hard to make ends meet."[50] In a striking parallel to what is happening in the countryside, many of those teaching in primary and high schools began to be paid in IOUs during 1992, with the defaults reaching 1.43 billion yuan or $250 million nationwide as of May, 1993, and 309 million yuan or $36 million owed as late as January, 1994. In an example of the new class divisions, "a county magistrate in Hubei Province sold 'his' luxurious car at 350,000 yuan ($60,000) to repay the local teachers."[51]

Thus, paralleling the geographic shift of professionals,

... educational institutions—high schools, colleges, and universities—
are also suffering from a "brain drain."
Statistics in Shanghai show that 1,500 teachers switched to other jobs in
the city in 1993. The number, however, jumped to 2,500 last year. Among
them, 1,000 were under 30-years of age and 954 had college education
background.
Some teachers left schools thinking their talent could be better put to use
in other occupations. A main reason for the "brain drain," however, lies
in poor treatment given to teachers.[52]

Over the past year or so, Guangzhou shows signs of having reversed
these trends, by raising incomes and living conditions for its teaching
personnel. But the national polarization may thereby only be exacerbated, as rich urban areas advance while less well-off neighborhoods
and especially poor rural regions fall further behind. Nor are teachers
alone leaving. Further paralleling the impositions on the peasantry,
illegal school fees and levies, even for such basics as exams or heat in
buildings, have been charged, to meet expenses and pay teacher
salaries. During the 1991-1992 school year, an estimated 2.1 percent of
primary school students and 5.8 percent of those in junior middle
schools dropped out because their families were unable to meet these
added costs. Among the dropouts, 70 percent are girls.

These conditions have been compounded by the growing practice
of parents pulling their young children out of school to work in their
family businesses, a consequence of the corrosive "get rich quick"
environment. In one township in Hebei Province, as many as one-third
of the students are said to drop out for this reason, and the high school
has been virtually abandoned. As a sign of the growing class divisions,
a prerevolution-type polarization is growing in the cities between
skinny and plump children, with some 20 percent undernourished or
anemic, while 5 to 8 percent are now obese as a result of the increasingly rich foods bought by their rich parents.

This widening gap extends even to preschools, which are facing a
national "crisis," since "local kindergartens can't keep up with soaring
costs and as enterprises try to streamline efficiency, the first things to
go are costly pre-schools and day care centres." Beijing alone lost over
1,500 kindergartens in the last six years, while those of preschool age
needing care rose 5.4 percent. With firms turning increasingly to
migrants "requesting [!] low pay and no housing subsidies, it is simply
inefficient to run an affiliated kindergarten with a small enrollment....
At the same time, private and foreign-funded preschools are filling
up—all for the low [!] price of 10,000 yuan ($1,149)." Some families pay
the entire income of one parent to these schools. The attitude which
surrounds these changes is expressed by Shi Guhao, director of the

Pre-School Education Department for Beijing: "'this means that our pre-school education has walked into the market economy.... We should realize that kindergartens are no longer welfare organizations.'"[53]

The situation is even more extreme at so-called "elite," "luxurious," or "Olympic" educational institutions, which some people even call "noble schools." Of the 629 nongovernmental establishments in Guangdong, thirty-one fall into this category, with tuition fees ranging from 150,000 to 300,000 yuan ($18,000 to $36,000) annually. The first such school, in Sichuan Province, "was considered by many as one for 'aristocrats.'"[54] Mainly middle and preparatory high schools, they serve the super-rich. More broadly, "in the past few years, schools and classes for gifted kids have mushroomed in China as anxious parents, eager to see their children become 'super talents'" demanded such programs, even though they "brought financial hardship to some families."[55] These developments in educational polarization have become a focus of growing official concern.

> Non-governmental schools are allowed to collect reasonable fees. But running schools is an undertaking for public welfare and they should never regard profit making as their purpose.
> However, "elite schools" make training elites as their purpose. Their educational principle contradicts the Party's educational guidelines.[56]

So serious has the problem become that the State Education Commission declared that "such schools must be shut down and courses for gifted students cancelled." But such crackdowns are typically hedged, to allow those already advantaged to keep their privileges. In Guangdong, a ban has been placed on the approval of new private schools, but "officials will examine and evaluate existing 'luxurious' schools with a view to strengthening their administration."[57] Thus whatever the restraints, educational polarization seems certain to continue to grow, as class divisions themselves widen.

At the top of the educational establishment are 1,000 or so colleges and universities, with their enrollment only 2.8 million—a tiny elite in a population of 1.2 billion. Here a similar set of policies is being implemented, to strip students both of their free education and of the job security which until now has been their guaranteed right. Already since the mid-1980s, the government had instituted a program of allowing those who scored lower on entry examinations to attend a university anyway by paying a fee, creating a dual track for wealthy families and enterprises, which could afford these charges. By 1993, 38 percent of the student body in Shanghai colleges paid their own way. The demand for such students as a source of revenue led to a lowering of academic standards and the displacement of those from poor families even if they had higher exam scores. Now this contradictory system is being "resolved" along marketization lines by instituting standard tuition fees for all students, in effect privatizing the costs of university education.

Introduced in 1994 on a trial basis, the system was being generalized by 1995, with serious social ramifications.

Paying for higher education is expected to be the trend of education reform. However, the tuition fees, which range from 1,000 ($118) to more than 3,000 yuan ($353) a year, are huge sums for many wage-earning and farmer parents.

Last year, the average yearly income was less than 1,000 yuan ($117) in rural areas. Half of the college and university students, however, come from the countryside.[58]

Despite a pledge to deal with the new barriers to participation in higher education by workers and peasants through work-study programs, loans, scholarships, and tuition wavers, the lack of trust in such solutions was evident in Changchun. As one student put it, "In the future in China, if you come from a peasant family, you'll have no chance to go on studying in the universities."

At the same time, the present right to look for work outside of the state system is being converted into a requirement to do so, by phasing out government-guaranteed jobs. Starting in the fall of 1994, those entering thirty-seven of the top universities not only had to pay a standard tuition of 1,000 to 1,500 yuan or $115 to $175, but they also will have to find their own employment after graduation. Caught between the higher costs of education and growing ranks of unemployed, new graduates are facing an increasing "squeeze." "As the reform is stepped up," one student declared, "especially after the bankruptcy and labor law were put into effect, the biggest problem college students face after graduation is unemployment."[59] The stakes in these changes is quite high. Speaking on the need to guarantee financial aid for poor college students, Zhang Tianbo, vice-minister of the State Education Commission, noted that it affects not only schools but "social stability."[60]

Increasingly, the growing competition for jobs is used to discriminate, especially against women, reversing recent gains in their labor force participation rates and educational and occupational opportunities. At a professional job fair in Beijing in early 1994, more than half the positions were "for men only." Such job segregation is growing more common, and in a form which heavily favors male employees. "Even occupations which are traditionally reserved for women, such as secretaries and teachers, are being taken by men."[61] The problem is growing worse, as "market efficiency" and ties to foreign enterprises

maximize the desire for male representatives, with fewer home responsibilities, or for single, young women, more and more chosen for their
physical attractiveness. Now female graduates at the University of
International Business and Economics are being told not to compete
with men for the best-paid positions or for chances to go abroad. "Girls
must lower their expectations," said an official with UIBE.[62] Women
are constantly urged by government officials to support the modernization reforms. But while in such pronouncements they may still be
said to hold up "half the sky," a promise of equality which was far from
complete even under the old socialist system, in the new China they
are increasingly excluded from holding even half the jobs or earning
half the pay.

These professional women have their proletarian counterparts in
the South, especially Guangdong, where the newer members of the
workforce are primarily female. They are among the most unprotected
and disorganized elements of the Chinese working class, isolated a
thousand miles from their homes, in unfamiliar urban settings. Generally poorly educated, they commonly lack even the basic knowledge
of what few social services and protections are available to them. As
young women in a society dominated by old men, they are especially
powerless and without social standing.

Similar conditions are spreading even to older, more established
industrial cities. But whereas in Guangdong and other centers of the
new market economy employers seek out young women to exploit,
elsewhere the tendency is to fire experienced female workers. This
process is accelerating with marketization.

> There are about 56 million female employees in urban China, which
> accounts for 38 per cent of the total workforce.
> As unprofitable State enterprises cut staff to raise efficiency, it is mostly
> women above 35 who are losing their jobs.
> In Liaoning Province—China's largest industrial base—a survey shows
> that 420,000 women workers have lost their jobs. That accounts for 56
> per cent of the total redundant workers.
> Conditions are more serious in some industries, such as textiles.
> In Jiangsu Province's 144 textile factories, 80 per cent of the 95,000
> laid-off workers are female.[63]

Though in Liaoning, according to one local activist, most fired women
are skilled, their "plight has been further aggravated by management's
discrimination against them" in favor of the men.

> An iron and steel manufacturer in the province even adopted the rule
> "ladies before gentlemen" to decide who should be laid off although the
> male and female workers had equal skills and capabilities.

Many enterprises are reluctant to hire childless women because they know they will be forced to grant them maternity leave at some point.[64]

Since unemployment benefits were not yet being provided by the government, most of these women were left without any income.

Adding insult to injury, the new "marketization" ideology insists that the blame lies largely with the female workers themselves. Wang Jun, vice-director of the All-China Federation of Trade Unions, typifies the attitude taken toward the fired women.

> It is also necessary for the surplus workers to change their mentality moulded by the planned economy when looking for jobs and receiving retraining, Wang said.
> Some women are accustomed to finding cradle-to-grave jobs. When laid off, they depend upon the State to solve all problems, added Wang.[65]

In Shenyang, capital of Liaoning Province, similar sentiments were expressed by the head of the provincial federation of women.

> Women, who used to stay at home started to join the large heavy industrial labour force in the city in the late 1950's, after late Chairman Mao Zedong called on women to get out of the home and strive for equal status in society.
> They enjoyed an equal-pay-for-equal-work policy advocated by the central government....
> Having been molly-coddled by the planned economy for decades with secure jobs, medical care and free housing, these women naturally now have difficulties re-adjusting to life in a free-market society.
> Overly optimistic, many have simply waited and waited for their former corporations to point them in the direction of a new job. But the corporations, trapped in debt, cannot afford to help them.[66]

Virtually none of these women, having grown up in the half century since the revolution, could have known anything other than the "molly-coddling" socialist economy in their work lives. So the entire concept of "readjusting" to "marketization" is a distortion. Thrown for the first time on their own resources, they now often feel "inferior to their husbands because they are not breadwinners. They were looked down upon by other family members." Some face divorce, like the woman "who thought of committing suicide when her husband wanted to leave her for losing her job."[67]

Many end up on the streets, feeding the growing prostitution and pornography trades, which flourish especially in the South, and where the women face further official discrimination and repression. A two-month crackdown in Guangdong alone in 1993 rounded up almost 33,000 prostitutes—there is no indication male customers were arrested. With prostitution have come sexually transmitted diseases. Guangdong alone has reported over 226,000 cases since the illnesses reappeared in the province in 1980, that is, simultaneously with the advent of marketization. The incomplete total for 1994 was 58,000 new incidents of infection, almost one quarter of the total for the entire past fifteen years, and at a rate 23.9 percent higher than in 1993. Guangdong by itself accounted for one fifth of all such cases nationwide. Thus female ex-workers often not only become prostitutes, but are ravaged by disease and hounded and arrested by the authorities.

Even more drastic is the situation of many peasant women, with the revival of such feudal institutions as the forced sale of wives, a development directly linked to the marketization reforms and the ideological pressure on individuals to "get rich quick." According to confidential documents presented to the national legislature, in 1990 alone 18,692 cases of women sold against their will were investigated, and 65,236 persons were arrested in 1989-1990 for involvement in such acts. Many more such incidents presumably go unreported or unpursued, and it is reasonable to assume this form of "trade" has only grown in the five years since. Because cadre and party members are sometimes implicated in this criminal activity, enforcement is often lax.

> The partial emergence of a market economy has reinvigorated this variation of slavery, as travel becomes easier and peasants accumulate enough cash to purchase a bride....
> The sale of women disappeared during the first 20 years of Communist rule, and slowly reappeared during the 1970's and 1980's. The number of cases has risen sharply since 1985, the documents say.
> In rural areas, a bride's family traditionally will insist on a wedding ceremony, and these days the cost of weddings has soared, as neighbors try to outdo each other. That has created a strong incentive to buy a wife and save the cost of the festivities.[68]

The documents from the national legislature report conclude that, "the criminal activity of the kidnap and sale of women more and more has come to resemble the slave trade."

In one such case, eleven kidnappers were sentenced to death in Anhui Province, part of a gang of forty-eight, seventeen of them women, of whom some had previously suffered kidnapping before turning to such activities themselves.

> The criminals kidnapped 102 young women from 32 counties and cities in Sichuan Province and earned 250,000 yuan ($29,411). They sold them as wives for 800 yuan ($94) to 4,500 yuan (about $530) each to farmers in poor villages in Anhui, Shanxi and the Inner Mongolian Autonomous Region.
> The kidnappers lured the women from railway stations and labour markets in Chengdu City and other counties to nearby hotels first, and then transferred them to the poor villages with promises of assigning them to work in medicine and clothing businesses....[69]

Speaking at an "anti-kidnapping meeting" held in Guangzhou in mid-1995, Zhang Shenqin, Deputy Director of the Guangdong Public Security Bureau, indicated the scale this has reached.

"Women-abducting and child-stealing have become more and more serious in Guangdong and have caused great disorder to local life," Zhang said.

Most of the women and children are from outside Guangdong Province and are sold in different parts of the province.

Some women are forced into marriage and prostitution.[70]

This "trade" is directly related to the conditions of migrant labor and the pressures of the market on poor families—who largely provide the supply of women and the demand from men.

A good part of the abducted women are young, most in their 20s, from Hunan, Sichuan, and Guizhou provinces and Guangxi Zhuang Autonomous Region.

These women, not familiar with local situations, are often tricked into abduction by those who promise to give them jobs.

They are sold mostly in the remote west and east of Guangdong to be wives of poor local men who cannot find a local wife.

Kidnappers are increasingly nationally organized and brutal.

The provincial police chief says the crimes are becoming more serious and professional as local rings collude with those in other provinces.

The kidnappings involve more and more violent methods, he said, but did not elaborate on the number of cases or types of violence.

So serious has the problem become and so vast the scale that

investigation, door-to-door if needed, will be carried out in the province, especially in affected rural areas, to track down the criminals and the trapped women and children.

Outposts will be set up along the main roads and entrances of villages known to be danger areas.[71]

In such ways, rural China, the birthplace of reforms and the model for entrepreneurial "riches," sinks into barbarities not seen since feudal times, reaching the most extreme levels in Guangdong Province, the very heartland of the new marketization. The effects of reform, therefore, are an increasing degree of polarization not only in society as a whole, but within the work force itself, along lines of region, class, and sex. This is producing not just capitalistic phenomena, but feudalistic ones as well. These conditions undermine the new policies from within, becoming most pronounced in the very areas that have been the model of marketization. They give the lie to the concept that under conditions of still high levels of impoverishment Chinese "modernization" can be achieved by capitalistic means, without producing at the same time a reversion to the worst premodern forms of oppression and exploitation. So too, even as China prides itself on its newly reformed and "modernized" legal system—that is, corresponding more closely to Western judicial norms—lawlessness in the society as a whole grows exponentially. As a result of these deepening contradictions, the advocates of market socialism are likely to face increasing opposition not only from those strata whose interests were from the start injured by their policies, but from within the ranks as well of those who had earlier been favored by marketization.

V. Macroeconomic Control

Having moved to destroy the main pillars of the socialist system as it has existed in China, and having gone a long way toward recreating the social divisions of the prerevolutionary period, what the government does mean by "socialism" today seems to be mainly what it calls "macroeconomic" guidance and regulation of the emerging market. The idea is that national ministries will still help to direct investment patterns, especially to underfinanced sectors such as infrastructure development, and will work to correct the worst abuses of a freewheeling market system, but without intervening in the daily management of enterprises, even those which continue to be state-owned. Though individual firms are thus increasingly free from control by central planners, the overall economy is still shaped by public investments and the directing of foreign funds into areas most in need of capital. The nightly TV news is filled with an endless round of conferences and meetings in which the highest state and party leaders discuss with lower-level officials and managers the shape and progress of economic plans, often with the promise of more governmental assistance.

Typical of such public funding are plans to invest over 700 billion yuan or $80 billion into 400 transportation projects, to be completed by the turn of the century. Another major program of the government now is to redress the growing gap between the booming southern and coastal provinces and the left-behind northern and interior regions. Such redistribution from more developed regions to those lagging behind includes, for example, a 2.1 billion yuan or $362 million development plan in Tibet for farming and irrigation. Many provinces, and even smaller localities, adopt similar policies, for instance in Fujian Province, where urban centers have been "twinned" with poor rural countries to provide financing and other forms of support. Programs like these also attempt to address such major sectoral imbalances as rural underemployment and falling peasant income, through expanded investment in the upgrading of farmland, reforestation, and so on. Included is a program meant to raise out of poverty the 70 to 80 million poorest peasants, with incomes below 320 yuan or $38 annually, by the year 2000.

Price controls are also still being exercised to some degree as a form of macroeconomic control. For instance, higher base prices were announced in the spring of 1993 for grain, cotton, and other major crops, along with lower charges for agricultural inputs. State purchasing agents were also encouraged to release more of their reserves of food stocks and other farm products in order to counterbalance manipulation of prices in the free market. But the problem here is that government marketing of agricultural goods has been largely replaced by private traders and, exemplifying the difficulties of reversing this situation, state purchasing centers had themselves attempted to recoup their loss of market share by holding back supplies in 1993, thus driving prices higher. Though Premier Li Peng condemned such practices, they have become endemic in all sectors of the economy as public agencies are forced to compete with private owners.

By the spring of 1995, twenty-nine out of the thirty-five larger cities had reintroduced coupons, allowing residents to buy state-subsidized wheat flour and rice in government stores at below-market prices, "because of the unstable fluctuations in the grain and edible oil markets.... Higher prices have squeezed the purchasing ability of some urban dwellers."[72] Grain coupons had earlier been fazed out, and had been eliminated entirely in mid-1993. But soaring prices forced their revival. Unlike the former national program, the decision to issue them is now up to local authorities. As a government official stressed,

> Issuing grain coupons again in some cities does not signal a rolling back to the old planned economy but is merely a temporary means adopted to facilitate transition to a market economy....
> But, he said, grain coupons may be used again in the future, as the government narrows the coupons' distribution to people with low incomes, poor regions and the jobless, as part of the social security system.[73]

Nevertheless, the necessity of returning to the use of coupons as a means of containing inflationary food prices in those large cities which are the very focus of marketization, points to the new difficulties arising even for the better-off urban residents.

Perhaps even more critical to the efforts at macroeconomic control is the government attempt to increase and solidify the role of township enterprises, which are seen as the key to absorbing the massive numbers of peasant underemployed. These generally small village-based firms are already the most rapidly expanding sector of the economy, with an average growth rate of 50 percent during 1991 to 1993. By 1992 they generated almost two-thirds of rural income, up from just one-third a decade earlier, and they accounted for about 62 percent of the increase in farmer incomes. Township enterprises already account for 32 percent of national industrial output value, and the goal is to increase their proportion to 50 percent. This is seen as critical to preventing an overwhelming number of "floating" rural poor. Such enterprises now have some 100 million workers, only slightly less than those working in state-owned firms, and the employment goal is another 50 million workers by the year 2000. A drive has even been launched to attract foreign investment into this sector.

But despite their enormous growth, rural firms are increasingly seeing their role challenged by the competition of high-tech urban enterprises tied into global marketing systems. Like the peasants themselves, the small township production centers are finding that early rapid gains made after reforms were introduced are now being lost with the deepening economic contradictions of marketization. Despite sweatshop-type exploitation, their ability to compete is limited, as urban-produced goods and foreign imports flood the markets. In a typical example, "publicly-owned township enterprises in the south of Jiangsu Province, which have proven a huge success ... have been increasingly challenged by Sino-foreign joint ventures and exclusively foreign-funded enterprises." As a result, "more enterprises are opting for capital investment rather than taking on new hands."[74] In 1993, such rural firms hired only 50 percent of the number of workers that would have been taken on under previous practices. Yet even at the projected expansion rates, township enterprises will be able to absorb only one-half the vast increase in "excess" labor which it is estimated will be generated in the countryside this decade. Moreover, regional distribution is already very uneven, with 66 percent of rural firms in the East, 30 percent in the middle of the country, and only 4 percent in the West. Largely due to such inequality in the rate of development, the eastern 10 percent of the country creates five times the GNP overall of the Western 70 percent.

The same pressures faced by township enterprises are increasingly being felt by state-owned companies, which are rapidly losing their predominant status in the economy. Forced to compete in global markets for which they were never organized, and increasingly denied the governmental support on which they had previously depended, many are caught in their own "price scissors" between rising production costs and falling incomes. Raw material and transportation prices have soared, driven by the over-heated boom, while the price which can be charged for finished goods remains relatively low. For example, though crude oil has been allowed a big rise in prices, petroleum products have remained more or less frozen, in particular to prevent a further squeeze on the agricultural sector. In addition, much more of the revenues of state-owned firms now goes to the service sector of banks, insurance companies, and advertising agencies than before. With productivity still far below that of the leading industrialized nations, marketization has seen a rapid reduction in efficiencies of scale, with the number of industrial enterprises multiplying some 80 times over, from 100,000 to 8 million, during the past decade, but production rising by only three to four times. There are now 120 auto plants, none large enough to meet competitive global standards, though a plan to consolidate them into three giant groupings has been announced. Even First Auto in Changchun, with an output of some 200,000 cars and trucks per year, only produces one-fourth the vehicles of a typical Western plant.

At the same time, in an attempt to survive under these conditions, many firms have been forced to invest in new technology and equipment, and have fallen heavily into debt. Under these kinds of pressures, it is hardly surprising that at least one-third of state-owned enterprises nationally are running in the red, costing the government some 60 billion yuan or almost $7 billion in 1992 in subsidies, up from just 31 billion yuan or $3.5 billion in 1991. To escape from the budgetary expenses needed to support unprofitable firms, while promoting the efficiency of its enterprises, the state has encouraged foreign investment or takeovers for failing plants. In one typical example, Liaoning Province in 1989 auctioned off thirty-three bankrupt firms to investors from abroad. The other common technique used to salvage unprofitable enterprises is their merger with more profitable domestic businesses, but these officially encouraged acquisitions often merely weaken the previously stronger partner.

Increasingly, therefore, firms are acquiring others simply to obtain their equipment and real estate, without any concern for continued production or the work force. In 1993, the first ever hostile takeover occurred, creating a sensation on the Shanghai stock market. Other enterprises are simply allowed to go into bankruptcy, with their assets often sold off at greatly reduced prices, leaving their workers stranded, or with only a small and temporary subsidy. Regardless of the form of acquisition or purchase, the initial act of the new owners is thus likely to be the "rationalization" of the work force, which is estimated to be 20 to 30 percent "surplus" labor in the average enterprise. But even large-scale firings have not been sufficient to salvage the position of many firms. Under these conditions, the share of industrial output of the state-owned sector has fallen from 77 percent in 1978 to just 53 percent in 1992, and the drop is accelerating. As a result, the State

Statistics Bureau has warned that government firms are in danger of losing their position as national industrial leaders.

The losses suffered by many state-owned enterprises, especially those producing finished goods, have not, however, restricted merchants from reaping enormous profits from these same products. In February, 1994, consumer prices in thirty-five leading cities were 26 percent higher than a year earlier. With retail pricing totally arbitrary and chaotic, some new department stores sell consumer goods for up to ten times their value. The papers are full of complaints by gullible customers taken in by these fancy outlets. As a result of inflationary pressures, the State Statistics Bureau found that the living standard of people in leading cities actually declined as much as 40 percent in 1993, with those on fixed incomes suffering the most severe losses.

In an attempt to control inflationary pressures, which are seen as the greatest threat to social stability, an even more drastic measure has been to put a limit on investment in fixed assets. These grew by 47 percent in 1993, while production increased by only 10 percent. In August of that year, the government "closed 1,000 of the nation's 1,200 economic development zones. These zones were set up by local authorities to attract foreign and domestic investment, and they often offered tax breaks and special incentives that violated national policy."[75] The government also contracted the money supply in 1993, but with so much construction already underway, this mainly affected working capital, further squeezing enterprises. Moreover, the new limits on investment were widely ignored or evaded, and the policy was quickly relaxed. In 1995, the overall growth rate did slow slightly, rising "only" 10.2 percent, compared to 11.8 percent the previous year, while the critical fixed-asset investment rate cooled off even more sharply, dropping to just 20 percent. Inflation also fell by almost a third, from 21.7 percent in 1994 to 14.8 percent in 1995, though this is still barely under the official goal of 15 percent or less. Moreover, these deflationary measures have other less desirable impacts. Thus, during the same period, the debt-to-asset ratio of state enterprises rose to 80 percent, up ten percentage points in just over a year, far in excess of the 50 percent rate considered to be a "normal." Such contradictory results indicate the basic weaknesses of macroeconomic control.

New measures were also introduced in late 1993 in an attempt to control rampant speculation in luxury real estate development.

> Pressing ahead with its clampdown on runaway economic growth, the Chinese Government has banned new golf courses and announced that work on some luxury hotels and villas will be halted even though they are already partly built.
>
> A seven-point directive issued by the central Government reflects its

efforts to regain control over the real estate industry from local developers. Thousands of small property companies have been making huge profits by "chao di," or "stir-frying property"—buying and reselling in a speculative frenzy.

The new controls included imposing strict limits on the leasing of land for development, and even converting some of the luxury complexes and country clubs "into standard apartments, to ease the housing shortage, and into regular commercial buildings." There were also threats to close down the "stir-fry" companies. "The Government will sternly punish those who engage in speculative activities with the aim of making quick money rather than a long-term investment," the New China News Agency declared.[76]

In the case of real estate, the government has also introduced credit controls, to limit the money which state agencies were directing into speculative investments instead of more productive purposes. The new policies succeeded in dampening some of the uncontrolled speculation in this sector of the economy, which was absorbing approximately one-quarter of all new investment, and flooding the markets. Beijing alone, for example, had a backlog of some 20,000 unsold luxury housing units. But some local and regional governments and economic departments are continuing to invest heavily in real estate, even in violation of national policy. Moreover, as leading Hong Kong investors noted, their activities have been left unaffected by the new monetary controls, since they are backed by their own banks, not those on the mainland subject to the new regulations. Thus it is primarily the domestic government enterprises which are subjected to control, and as a result even attempts to introduce some degree of "socialist" regulation of the market tends only to increase further the advantageous position of the foreign capitalists.

Partly in response to this ability of investors from abroad to escape regulation, as well as in reaction to the disaster at Zhili in Shenzhen, which generated strong protests from the trade unions and the threat that unofficial labor actions would increase in the Special Economic Zones, the government announced that the exemptions and privileges offered to foreign-funded enterprises would soon be reduced. In theory, these firms will be forced to accept changes in the areas of taxation, labor relations, and management practices, creating greater equality between them and other sectors of the economy. Any modification of the behavior of the enterprises based on capital from abroad, however, is marked by hedging and lax enforcement. In the area of taxation, for example, the government has pledged to equalize rates between domestic and foreign firms. But shortly after the new tax policy was announced, a high official stated that despite such formal changes, a way will be found to continue giving investors from abroad lower taxes, through rebates or other financial manipulations. By late 1995, there were indications once again that the tax on foreign investors would be raised. But such claims have been made—and proven premature—before.

Macroeconomic control has thus proven to be a tricky business, in which Peter is constantly robbed to pay Paul, and the forces of the market continually escape the limits which the government tries to impose on them. Much of this effort has been little more than a catch-up game. Until now, the common practice has been to release the forces of marketization, virtually without regulation, and only then to try to introduce some element of legal control and economic discipline. In effect, this has meant a series of efforts to lock the barn door long after the horse has fled. A lengthy list of measures has been issued in the last two years in every area of the economy, but these "cures" often produce consequences almost as bad as the conditions they were meant to address, or exacerbate even further the imbalances they were supposed to correct. Especially in the case of foreign investors, macroeconomic control has so far done little to restrain their free hand, and even reinforced their privileges.

"Socialism with special Chinese characteristics" is also supposed to mean, however, that even if the state cannot fully control marketization, it will buffer the effects in such a way as to prevent the contradictions historically associated with the development of capitalism, especially in the Third World. But much of what is meant by this "socialization" is little more than an effort to force enterprises to work through the "normal" methods associated with capitalist exploitation, rather than earn their profits by fraud, corruption, and speculation. In the last few years, so rampant have corrupt practices become that entire industries have been at least partially undermined. Most notably, the still small domestic auto production has been limited by the massive smuggling of cars into the country, estimated to have brought in hundreds of thousands of vehicles since 1990. In Yunnan Province on the Southwestern border,

> "Corruption is a problem because the police and military are paid very poorly and they see the entrepreneurial sector moving ahead of them," said Richard Dickins, a drug enforcement specialist for the United Nations Drug Control Program regional office in Bangkok.
> During a five-hour drive from Kunming to Pingyuan in October, a caravan of dozens of brand-new cars without license plates could be seen driving north from the Vietnam border, part of the car-smuggling overseen by military and provincial officials, a former police official said.[77]

The infrastructure is also badly affected. In recent years a virtual growth industry has developed among peasants in poor areas who steal power and communication equipment, resulting in losses of some 24 million kilowatt hours of electricity in 1993.

In some places, the scale of such operations is so vast as to constitute a complete breakdown of centralized national power.

> A frenzied and chaotic gold rush is under way across vast expanses of rural China, where newly wealthy "gold lords" and the peasants who toil and fight for them are challenging the authority of the state.[78]

Working illegal private mines, entrepreneurs—many of them with underworld connections—take over entire mountains, guarding them with private armies. "'Even if the Government wanted to control us, we are stronger then they are now,'" said one boss, "'and our guns are normally much better than the ones carried by the Public Security Bureau.'" Local police are often either afraid to intervene, or actively collude in the operations, which include evasion of environmental laws, resulting in massive damage.

> The chaos here is part of a broader breakdown of Government authority in large parts of the country as Beijing has relaxed its rigid controls and millions of people have joined the scramble to get rich....
> China's top judicial authorities have warned that security problems in rural China "are escalating enormously."

Or as one Communist Party employee put it, "What is really legal or illegal out here?"

For the peasant miners, life is rapidly coming to resemble the semi-slavery of the prerevolutionary and feudal past.

> For tens of thousands of peasants dreaming of wealth, the reality of the gold rush means only the chance to work for $1.25 a day in biting cold and at high altitudes, conditions so harsh that many try to flee only to be captured and returned to work in leg irons for the duration of their contracts.[79]

Others die in pitched battles for bosses fighting over turf, as entire rural areas fall under the sway of such modern bandits, who despite their cellular phones and Land Cruisers, are starting to resemble the brigands of Chinese history, who for centuries based themselves in mountain redoubts, preying on those below.

Even more threatening historical scourges are also reviving. In the early years after Liberation, China "had eradicated the country's longstanding opium habit." But once again, just as in the early nineteenth century, drugs are flooding into the country, especially in Yunnan Province in the Southwest. From there they are spreading in the countryside, and even to the large urban areas, where they are used especially by the Westernized business class.

> "Over the past several years, more heroin has been seized by China than by any other country," the State Department's top official for international drug control policy, Robert S. Gelbard, told Congress in July after touring the region....
>
> While 80 percent of China's drug seizures and more than half its registered drug addicts are in Yunnan province, the problem is far from confined.
>
> In the nightclubs and discos of Beijing, Shanghai and other cities, heroin is increasingly popular among young merchants and entrepreneurs, and they can be found injecting it or snorting it or smoking cigarettes laced with it.[80]

The number of known hardcore addictions jumped from 250,000 to 380,000 in just over one year, and estimates run into the millions of users, while "given the growth rate, China could have the world's highest number of heroin addicts in a few years." With the drugs have come armed battles over turf and between traffickers and outgunned police, official corruption, and wide lawlessness of all kinds, as well as a growing AIDS population, previously extremely small.

> The greatest danger for China may be the level of addiction among Chinese in their 20's and 30's, many of whom are rootless and disenchanted with the post-Communist system.
>
> "Maybe for some people it is because they have nothing to believe in, or for some it is just because they have more money," said Shen Qiongfen, 50, an office worker in Kunming, who was visiting her brother in a detoxification center on a recent morning. "If you have money, you can afford drugs," she said. "It's as simple as that."
>
> With China's population growing by 15 million a year, and the number of unemployed and underemployed expected to pass 200 million by 2000, a future of drugs, crime and instability is alarming to leaders in Beijing, who are obsessed with stability.[81]

Thus at both poles of the society, addiction is likely to continue spreading, contributing to the growing climate of social dislocation and criminality.

Such crime is increasingly a burden of daily life even in urban areas, after decades in which "the Chinese would not steal a pin."[82] In Hangzhou, burglaries have become such a problem that the public security bureau has installed the first automatic alarm system in the city, at a cost of 450,000 yuan or $54,000 for one district alone. "'We have resorted to science to upgrade our alarm facilities and strengthen our capability to respond quickly when criminal cases arise,' said Chen Wei, a local PSB official."[83] But such "scientific" advances are costly: individual residential alarms range in price from 2,000 to 6,000 yuan, or $241 to $723, with a 200 yuan or $24 monthly service fee, more than the entire income of many families. Across China, car stealing has become so common, rising 47 percent in just one year to 73,200 units nationwide, that the Public Security Ministry demanded that drivers fit their cars with anti-theft devices. Guangdong alone, not surprisingly, accounted for 26 percent of the losses.

The impact of crime is altering the relationships of the Chinese and the very manner in which they view the social order.

> China's growing affluent society, marked by an increase in luxury goods appearing in households, is bringing about a booming personal-security market in China....
> Observers said that protecting property and people is a new concept in China, where the improved living standard is encouraging and enabling people to invest in security.[84]

But this "new concept" is not just a function of the wealth of some, it is a measure of the growing impoverishment, at least relatively, of others, a polarization unknown since Liberation. The contradiction of greed at the top and desperation at the bottom, far from "encouraging and enabling" increased security, means that even the moderately well-off must protect their homes, while the "new rich" live under constant fear of personal attack.

> Armoured doors, priced from 300 yuan ($36) to about 1,000 yuan ($120), have become an indispensable part for many urban families, although some users still doubt whether the steel doors can really prevent theft....
> A reinforced door may be enough for an ordinary family, but some people living in villas or luxury apartments, expect costly household alarm systems to help them protect their property. A household alarm system can be installed for 10,000 yuan ($1,200).

"Women, who increasingly have become victims of crime," prefer electric batons and miniature alarms worn around the neck.

> Wealthy businessmen can find anti-violence helmets and bullet-proof documentary bags on the market.
> Another by-product of the increasingly safety-conscious nouveau riche is a burgeoning demand for bodyguards and the appearance of security services.[85]

One Beijing company served 2,000 such clients in 1994 alone.

The whole development program is threatened by such distortions. In early 1995, the national legislature was considering a law to raise the maximum punishment for financial manipulation from life imprisonment to the death penalty.

> The bill is aimed at safeguarding the nation's financial order....
> With the financial sector starting to play a growing role in China's economic advances, financial irregularities have increased over the past

few years and the sums involved have escalated to huge figures.
In some localities, more than half of the major crime cases were con-
nected with financial culprits.[86]

The kinds of crimes cited included counterfeiting, setting up unauthorized banks, cheating people out of deposits, and forgery. These had
become so widespread by 1995 as to threaten financial markets, a
growing source of funds for economic development, thus requiring
legal intervention at the highest national level. But what passes for
macroeconomic control is at times little more than imposing some
limits on private profiteering and manipulation, similar to those restrictions introduced in most of the leading capitalist countries after
their earlier "robber baron" stages. Corruption, however, has become,
in many cases, not an aberration, but the very way the system works,
deeply imbedded in the government itself. The same kinds of extrale-
gal fines and charges, forced "contributions," and purchases of un-
needed goods levied on peasants have commonly been used by
authorities to extract funds from the enterprises under their control,
supplemented by outright bribery. In a kind of pyramid structure, a
portion of these moneys is used to pay off those higher up in the state
and party. Provincial governments in 1993 canceled 5,227 such illegal
levies valued at 7.3 billion yuan or $839 million. So too, a recent
regulation has been issued against moonlighting by officials to supplement their incomes, which often allows them to take advantage of
their positions to gain business deals and privileged market ties. But
despite major anticorruption drives and even the use of the death
penalty against serious offenders, major cases doubled in 1993, and
more than 40,000 Party members had to be disciplined in one four-
month period alone. The atmosphere of "money by any means" is
rapidly becoming all-pervasive. Some journalists have taken to skew-
ing their reporting in return for a bribe, while even some papers are
encouraging the practice to supplement low salaries.

   Despite efforts to control corruption, indications are that the problem is still growing—threatening a revival of the social instability of
the 1989 Tiananmen movement, which made corrupt officials one of
its main targets. In early 1995 Premier Li Peng

   linked the struggle against corruption to the future of the Communist
   Party and the Chinese nation as a whole.
   The task of fighting graft must never stop during the course of building
   socialism, Li told a State Council meeting....
   It must be noted that some of the work has not gone well, he said,
   particularly that dealing with crimes in the economic field, including
   embezzlement, bribery, and others.
   The practices of abusing power to make illegal profits, trading power

for money, and arbitrary charges by law-enforcement and supervisory personnel have aroused resentment among the general public because they are very serious, he added.[87]

The government has now introduced "hot lines" to report corruption and consumer complaints, in an attempt to enlist the masses of Chinese people in its program of macroeconomic controls. These services have been heavily used, and have led to the cracking of some major cases involving corrupt officials. But the palliative effect of such expedients is indicated by the simultaneous pronouncement by the Central Committee of the Communist Party that no mass campaigns will be encouraged or even allowed as part of the anticorruption drive. Rather, "the struggle should be carried out within Party and government institutions, judicial departments, administrative and law-enforcement departments and economic administrations."[88] This allows the authorities to focus on only those cases which they choose to expose to the light, normally at lower levels, while the actions of the highest officials, most notably the massive enrichment of the families of many leading party and state officials, goes untouched. It also means that no mass participation will be allowed to interfere with, or expand on, the implementation of these "socialist macroeconomic controls."

The limited form of the anticorruption campaigns, however, has begun to weaken the control of the state itself. Many companies have been expanding their assets through joint ventures, without changing the book value of the parent enterprises. These firms can then generate profits from their new activities which are essentially "off the books" as far as the government is concerned. Others create phony front firms with foreign capitalists, in order to obtain tax breaks and other preferential treatment, going so far as to send funds abroad to be "invested" back in China. There are estimates that as much as two-thirds of all "overseas" investments in the Chinese economy today fall into this category. The scale of such hiding and diversion of property has weakened the entire public sector, and subjected it to widespread privatization through illegal means.

> The loss of State properties has been an impediment to the country's efforts to invigorate its enterprises in past years.
> Due to loosened controls, State enterprises tend to transform State property into individual or group interests in every possible way.
> Many launched new businesses with State properties, but defined them as non-State ones. Some undervalue the assets when selling them or when being changed into shareholding companies. Some simply hide part of the assets from the State.[89]

Some state-owned enterprises have also turned their assets to unauthorized uses, or converted to ownership by cooperatives made up of the former managers and employees, and others have simply divided up their resources privately, without paying for them. Such practices have seriously eroded the asset base owned by the state, which in turn undermines government revenues. Though oversight has been tightened, even where a proper evaluation is made, it may be disregarded by officials eager to develop their own regions, regardless of the effects on government as a whole.

The loss in asset value from these fraudulent practices and "market" forces have been staggering. Non- or under-evaluation of joint ventures alone is estimated to cost the government 30 billion yuan or over $3.4 billion per year. Over the past decade, the total of state assets lost by all means now amounts to some $500 billion yuan or $57.5 billion, despite overall growth of the public sector. In addition, particularly widespread practices have been to award state-owned shares less dividends and bonuses than private investors. These forms of fraud have been compounded by a growing epidemic of outright tax evasion and non-reporting of income, practices that are estimated conservatively to be costing the state 100 billion yuan or $17.2 billion a year. Furthermore, the vague question of ownership rights means that a chaotic situation has arisen over who controls the income of enterprises, and for what purposes it will be utilized, resulting in lost revenues at all government levels.

Even these losses in state revenue are penny ante compared to the massive diversion of taxes from the central government to lower bodies as a result of the decentralization which was implemented at an early stage in the reforms, largely to help break the power of national ministries and their related public enterprises. In particular, the provinces and townships have now become largely autonomous economic units, retaining taxes for their own purposes without sending them on to the national government, or granting tax breaks, in an attempt to attract investment and build up their regional economies in competition with surrounding areas. Some regions have even gone so far as to limit exports and imports, erecting a protective barrier around their own emerging industries. There has also been widespread falsification of economic data. Such policies have helped to generate a looming crisis, in the form of a massive deficit for the central government and inaccurate plan estimates, and even the threat of national disintegration and the growth of a form of regional "warlordism," uniting party and state officials, business investors, and the local military leadership, the recurring nightmare of Chinese history.

A major concern at present for the top state and party leaders is, therefore, how to reassert national control, how to divide the money generated by enterprises into profits and taxes, and which portions will be retained by the firm and by the local, provincial and central governments. This is the principal goal of the new economic regulations issued in November 1993, which included a shift from government dependence on a share of profits to a more tax-based system, and a more even distribution between the center and localities of the revenues generated by taxation. But regionalism has already become so far advanced, and the ties between local government officials and enterprises so close, that there is great resistance to changing the present system, and the decline of national authority may simply not be reversible by the belated top-down attempt to reassert control from the center.

As a consequence of these developments, while in 1981 the share of revenues going to the central government was 57 percent, by 1993 this had dropped to under 39 percent. Thus the national state bodies of "socialist" China are greatly underfunded compared to the United States and Japan, the leading capitalist countries, where the percentage of taxes going to the center is 55 and 70 percent, respectively. At the same time, the Chinese budget deficit has soared from 2.6 billion yuan or $442 million in 1981 to 23.8 billion yuan or $4.1 billion in 1992, a ten-fold increase. If debts are included, the figure rises to 90.5 billion yuan or $16 billion, equal to some 3.8 percent of GNP. It is this massive loss of revenue that has fueled the almost desperate drive to cut government responsibility for social security, health, and education, and to force all state institutions to make their own way economically. But it has also meant that the government increasingly lacks money for the investment programs of the reforms themselves, thus exacerbating the dependency on foreign funding. Perhaps most significantly in the long run, underfunding of the center has undermined the ability of the state to use the very macroeconomic financial methods on which it depends to control the market, and thus to maintain its claim to socialist goals.

VI. "Market Socialism" in One Country

Together with the still high percentage of public ownership and the continuing direct investment by the government in expanding enterprises, the use of the state for regional and sectoral redistribution, and the degree of macroeconomic control, the Chinese point to their attempt to find ways to combine public and private ownership as indicative of socialism. At the same time, any resemblance to the "guided capitalism" of Japan and other Pacific Rim nations is hardly accidental. These countries, with their rapid rise to global economic prominence, clearly serve in many ways as the model for much that is happening in China today. There is even talk of Guangdong catching up with the "four dragons," Hong Kong, Taiwan, South Korea, and Singapore. Yet even here, the reformers stress that their system will remain distinctly socialist, with it own unique "Chinese" characteristics.

Even if they were able to keep in check the internal contradictions of their system, the effort to build "market socialism in one country" seems likely to have an even shorter life expectancy than the earlier Soviet model. In the first place, whether the "cancer" of largely foreign-funded capitalist development, intentionally introduced by the government, can be controlled, or whether the most powerful figures in the current leadership even want to control it, is a fundamental issue today. From this perspective, the only question is whether there will be conversion to a totally private form of capitalism, and how long such a process might take. No doubt a complete reversion to a capitalist system is the goal of many within the burgeoning privatized sector, while some elements within the government, especially those most closely tied into foreign ventures and joint enterprises, must share these ultimate aims. The All-China Federation of Industry and Commerce, for example, has called for the creation of private banks, which it says are needed to finance the growing privatized business sector, since state banking institutions still favor government-owned enterprises. Partly in response to such "market" needs, the government has allowed foreign banks to open Chinese branches for the first time. In such a climate of increasing "big" bourgeois class pressure, the question naturally arises whether there is the will or the way to resist full recapitalization.

At the same time, as China becomes ever more deeply tied into the global economy through both investment and trade, it becomes subject to the vagaries of the world market, with consequences that are increasingly felt down to the local level. Already, peasants are feeling the competition of imports, and workers are being fired because their factories cannot meet international capitalist standards. Even the central purpose of the Special Economic Zones, to fuel the export market, has begun at times to turn back on itself. Foreign-funded enterprises imported $42 billion in 1993, some 40 percent of the Chinese total that year, and 59 percent more than in 1992. This compares to exports of only $25 billion, up 45 percent, and just 26 percent of the total. Thus the trade gap of firms capitalized from abroad was equal to twice the national export-import deficit of $9 billion in 1993, the first since 1989.

All this is happening in boom times. But the market cannot sustain endless growth of the kind China has achieved during recent years. When the inevitable downturns or even a crash come, the dismantling of the older socialist system will have left tens and perhaps hundreds of millions of Chinese without any buffer against the devastations of rationalization. As one indicator of the dangers now spreading throughout the economy, out of at least 4 to 5 million unemployed, "only 2 million of the workers have taken part in industrial insurance and 500,000 have taken the pension insurance" as of 1995.[90] This despite efforts to expand coverage to the growing legions of those employed in the foreign-funded firms in the South, where the problem of nonparticipation is most severe. Already deeply in debt and running annual budget deficits, and unable to provide unemployment insurance for all of the still relatively small proportion of jobless workers or to find work for underemployed peasants, it is virtually inconceivable that the Chinese government would have the resources to meet the social dislocations caused by a major economic crisis.

Moreover, in the logic of international capital, success may be almost as deadly as failure. For with a rise in incomes in China or an attempt to improve working conditions will come disinvestment on the part of those multinational investors who are always ready to move on to the next low-wage country free from labor regulations and high taxes. In early 1994, foreign investment was already slowing down or shifting northward to escape rising wages and new controls. Even more fundamentally, the effort of the Chinese to raise over one-fifth of the population of the globe even to lower rank "second world" economic status presents its own barriers not experienced by smaller countries. Such a large segment of the international labor force cannot enter the capitalist global system at a considerably higher level without altering the entire balance of power of the world economy as it is now organized. The full productive potential of more than a billion Chinese cannot be absorbed without displacing significant portions of the present leading economies of the globe. Thus the United States, Japan, and other dominant global powers are already torn between the attempt to capture the expanding markets of China on the one hand, and to prevent it from emerging as a major competitor on the other. Many of the tensions which are presently surfacing between these countries, such as the conflict over human rights, can be traced to this ambivalence over how to both exploit and contain the Chinese economy at the same time.

In this increasingly hostile global environment, as China attempts to define and implement "market socialism with special characteristics," it has before its eyes the example of the former Soviet Union, with its disastrous abandonment of any remnants of the former socialist system, leading to near collapse of the economy, social anarchy, and regional fragmentation. When the Chinese government speaks of maintaining socialism, therefore, whatever its definition of that term, it means first and foremost avoiding the kinds of dislocations and loss of national coherence now experienced in Russia. In this effort it finds widespread support among the Chinese people, who fear the breakdown of their own society, however much they may chafe at the same time beneath the repressive policies of the state. But the promise of continued "socialist" stability cannot be maintained without raising popular expectations which the program of market reforms is increasingly unable to meet. While the name of the system may have little effect on its actual practices, therefore, it continues to represent an ideological force among the masses of Chinese, who will not lightly abandon their revolutionary claim to socialistic goals for the sake of "order" alone.

That a tension still exists on the popular level between the two systems of social organization is indicated in many ways. While the salary level of employees in joint ventures are generally higher than in fully government-owned enterprises, for example, this does not alter their closer resemblance to private capitalist firms in their methods of operation, and gains in income there are largely cancelled out by the lack of benefits and greater work load. Thus the Volkswagen-affiliated plant in Changchun pays at least one-third higher than the fully state-owned First Auto Works, and one does not see there the same number of excess workers lounging around waiting for something to do. But the VW workers complain of long hours and demands for overtime, and the greater intensity of work on the line. Some who were eager to take jobs there have even left and returned to the more leisurely, if less well-rewarded employment at First Auto. Similarly, many of those who have gone South have learned that their higher salaries have been quickly eaten up by soaring costs of living and the necessity to pay privately for all forms of social security, and not a few of them too have returned home, no longer so enamored of reform.

In other ways also, the limits of "market socialism" have increasingly been recognized. Even in the peasant areas where it all began, there is a growing understanding that the extremes of individual entrepreneurship that were forcibly adopted have begun to reverse back upon themselves. As farmers face the difficulty of competing in a national and even international market, they find that their ability to succeed is undermined by the limits on their knowledge and technology dictated by micro-agricultural methods. A move has therefore begun back toward forms of cooperative investment and labor, backed up by local and regional marketing and information networks, to escape the bounds of individual enterprise. These are not, of course, a revival of the communes. But they reflect the increasing tension between marketization and the reality of a China still locked to a large degree in third world conditions.

However, any such movement toward cooperative farming, even if encouraged by governmental action, pales beside the plans now being promoted for the massive displacement of peasant families.

> The real crux of the problem lies in the irrational system of allocating cultivated land, which tends to lock farmers to farmland.
> Therefore, a new way of allocating farmland is badly needed.
> That in turn means that the country's land system also needs reforming and perfecting.[91]

This "irrational system of allocating cultivated land," however, is nothing less than the very cornerstone of agricultural reforms in the countryside that launched the entire marketization program. What is being admitted, in other words, is the inability of the current policies to resolve the problem of fragmentation of the land among too many individual families. The new proposal is to reconsolidate farmland, but only by "unlocking" even greater numbers of peasants from their lands.

> China is considering a sobering measure to put its arable land under contract to a few farmers instead of the on-going rural household contract responsibility system.
> The Ministry of Agriculture has submitted a proposal to the State Council for approval to push over the majority of field ridges between fields. These have taken shape for a decade in the countryside due to the responsibility system among China's 900 million rural residents.
> The ministry believes agriculture will be more effective if not as many farmers contract farming in large areas to ease current difficulties in sowing, fertilizing and management.[92]

In other words, the destruction of large-scale communal farming, which had allowed for the growing use of mechanization, and the creation instead of what William Hinton calls "noodle" fields—thin and fragmented strips of land separated by earthen dikes—so avidly carried out in the name of reforms, is now proving to be a burden on the technological development of agriculture.

To overcome this block, farmers will be encouraged "to put together the country's farmland for a few farmers to cultivate" and take up "contract farming in moderate-sized land."

> Some examples from experimental areas under the ministry show contract farming in large-sized fields, instead of the current contract responsibility system in small land parcels, has increased per capita grain yields and improved farmers' income.

The plan is also "to encourage farmers in underdeveloped areas to go to comparatively-developed regions to contract fields for farming," quite possibly leading to further abandonment of poor lands. Others are anticipated to move into new urban areas.

> The government also is expected to accelerate urbanizing existing towns
> and counties in the countryside and to extend the control over farmers'
> efforts to move into these towns and counties to seek jobs.
> Since they are settled in small towns or counties, these rural residents
> should abandon their contracted farmland. They also should be taken
> care of by local governments with an insurance system for pension,
> health care and unemployment....
> To put together the country's farmland for a few farmers to cultivate
> should, first of all, encourage surplus rural residents to move to the local
> small towns and counties to make a living.

Thus the growing problems of Chinese agriculture, brought on by
extreme fragmentation of land and production, are to be solved not by
collective development, but by an even more complete turn to the
market, and greater polarization of the rural population: a few farmers
permitted to become large-scale operators on one hand, and on the
other, the generation of a peasant proletariat for work in local industry
and as hired hands on the very lands from which they were driven. To
help absorb the displaced peasants, by the end of the century 3,000
townships have been slated to be expanded and renovated, and many
smaller urban centers upgraded to city status, so that the number of
cities is expected to increase from 622 in 1994 to 1,003 by 2010.

In theory, these changes are to be on a voluntary basis, in an attempt
to limit their overall disruptive effects on society.

> But, ministry officials noted, it should not be a compulsive measure to
> force farmers to give up their contracted fields because such a move will
> worsen the current influx of surplus farm labourers into big cities.[93]

Yet the history of the enforced breakup of even prospering communes
after the death of Mao offers little reason to believe that "encouragement" will not soon turn to government fiat here too. Even if this does
not happen, given the already vast release of labor from rural areas
under the current household contract responsibility system, it is difficult to conceive how its replacement by an official policy intentionally
structured to drive farmers off the land can lead to anything other than
the further explosion of the numbers of such "floating" population.
With peasants thrown on the mercies of the market, it hardly requires
a specific "compulsive measure" to encourage them to leave the farms.
Economic forces will provide the compulsion, even without the extra
pressure of official expulsion orders. As more and more peasants are
no longer "locked to farmland," and become dependent on the vagaries of rural enterprise development for survival, with only untested
local social security systems to protect them, it is thus virtually inevitable that the tens of millions now crowding into large Chinese cities

in search of work will soon be joined by even greater numbers of displaced and increasingly desperate poor.

Such fundamental transformations, which completely dissolve whatever restraints remain on the revival of class divisions in the countryside, continue to be carried out in the name of a "socialist" system. Yet rural China today clearly exhibits the limits of market socialism in its attempt to balance private enterprise and social needs, as the individual responsibility system proves increasingly unable either to provide sufficient income for most farmers or security of future food production for the population. The growing necessity of a larger scale to agricultural operations can be met, however, either by a return to a higher level of mass collectivization or by the promotion of a rich farmer class controlling ever greater tracts of land. Apparently it is the latter "solution" to which the government is now turning, as it has in all cases chosen the market over a strengthening of socialism under the reforms. Of course, even these new wealthy farmers may also practice some degree of cooperative operations, but only to better solidify their hold over the land and their private profits. For the rest of the former peasants, the one "collective" experience they will have is as common laborers in local enterprises, or as members of the reserve army of labor seeking work in the cities. Only the rhetoric of "socialism" remains to remind them of the past, and as an effort to obscure the full meaning of "marketization."

On the highest official level too, even as they are implementing the dictates of the reforms, administrators feel compelled to explain how they will prevent them from undermining the old system. Announcing the new policy of university tuition fees, the vice-chairman of the State Education Commission declared that the higher fees "must be set according to the exact costs for each student as well as the resources of students' families and local economic conditions."[94] Similar appeals to socialistic goals have been made by housing officials, who demand that more attention be paid to building apartments for low-income workers, and less money wasted on luxury villas. In field after field, the costs of domination by the market are being felt in ways that are often bitterly resented, not excluding the arts, where public support flounders.

The "slowness" with which the reforms have been introduced in China, in contrast to the wholesale and rapid recapitalization carried out by Boris Yeltsin in Russia, have thus worked to both the advantage and disadvantage of the market socialists. They have delayed the full impact of marketization being felt until now, and thus put off the final reckoning between the two poles of the current policies. But this has allowed the Chinese people to continue in their belief that market reform will not mean the same thing that it has elsewhere in the former socialist bloc, and to learn from what has happened to those societies, as well as from their own personal experiences. Below the calm surface there are increasing signs of a gnawing fear and resentment, and an explosive atmosphere, even among those who have been beneficiaries of the new policies in various ways, and still support the reforms to a large degree.

The first major clash resulting from the growing resistance to the effects of marketization, and especially the rampant corruption, was of course the uprising of 1989, led by students and intellectuals, though joined by many workers as it proceeded. The response of the government in the aftermath of Tiananmen seems to have been to accelerate the reforms, in order to present the Chinese masses with a *fait accompli*, to "complete" marketization while Deng Xiaoping was still alive to guide the process, and to overwhelm the country with a form of consumerism that would bury opposition beneath a mountain of newly acquired goods. At the same time, a large breach was opened in the dike which had previously kept out "bourgeois pollution" imported from abroad. This has led to an almost ludicrous ambiguity in the cultural and ideological images presented by the government. Thus state-run television stations in the winter of 1993 to 1994 would sometimes cut directly from movies exalting the revolutionary struggles of the early Communists to a fashion show runway with long-legged Western models strutting in the latest luxury wear or to foreign rock bands performing Michael Jackson numbers. To an extent these "bread and circus" policies have succeeded in diverting opposition, especially among those urban elites and rural entrepreneurs best positioned to take advantage of them, and among those too young to remember what China was like before marketization.

But the ever-accelerating pace of reform has come at a mounting price, which is being paid most heavily by the working classes. Though surveys claim wide support among peasants and workers for the current line, and many people in all sectors are said to be enjoying their new freedoms in the market, it is just now that the harshest consequences of these policies are beginning to be felt fully by the broad masses. It is only today that tens of millions of workers must face loss of their jobs and social benefits, and that hundreds of millions of peasants must give up all hope of ever again farming. They are joined by the elite of university students who will soon realize that they must now pay their own way through school, and the millions of graduates who no longer have guaranteed jobs, but must find work in the private market. For each of these groups, the promise of the reformers to maintain a balance between the old system and the new is vanishing, and they are faced with the stark reality that marketization means a total transformation of their lives.

The results of these transformations are increasingly catastrophic in just those terms that "market socialism with special Chinese characteristics" was meant to avoid. A spate of peasant disturbances led to the crackdown on illegal fees and charges in 1993. Shortly thereafter, Minister of Agriculture Liu Jiang warned that "Charging farmers randomly is not only an economic issue but also a political one ... closely related to rural economic development and security."[95] It was in May, 1994, that a top judiciary official announced that social order had begun to break down in large areas of the countryside, the result of uncontrolled crime and the rapid growth of a rootless and impoverished segment of the population. Reports surfaced that in the spring of 1992, "the Government was deeply worried by a series of wildcat strikes and attacks on change-minded factory managers."[96] In industrial Wuhan, with its long revolutionary history,

> irate workers have already demonstrated what they think of lay-offs. Several workers killed a factory manager who had laid them off.
> There are more and more reports of such violence. When an electronics factory in Beijing laid off several hundred workers over the last several months, some smashed an Audi driven by the factory manager.[97]

More than 200 riots were said to have occurred in 1993. In the cities and in large-scale enterprises, labor resistance is mounting, with 6,000 strikes reported that year, leading to disruptions in production and the threat of wider and more radical forms of struggle.

Growing worker complaints led to a 52 percent rise in arbitration cases before labor boards from 1992 to 1993. In Beijing alone, 1,043 such cases were initiated in 1994, 2.6 times those in 1993, and almost equal to the 1,146 in the six previous years. An "increasing number of infringements upon employee rights," and better knowledge of the law, drove the figures up.[98] One third of the disputes involved failure to pay the minimum wage of 210 yuan or $25 per month and refusal to reward overtime. Especially in foreign-owned enterprises, disputes and walkouts are increasingly common, accounting for 24 percent of the cases in Beijing, and even more frequent in the South.

But even among those parts of the population who have bought in most completely to the reforms, concern is growing at the vast polarization developing in Chinese society between rich and poor, and the threat of foreign domination represented by multinational investment. These developments awaken the deepest fears in the Chinese, who still speak with great anger and shame over the subordination and carving up of their country by the imperialist powers, and continue to revile Chiang Kai-shek for the era of corruption, wasteful luxury, and deepest poverty, and Japanese invasion over which he presided. It was this loss of national control and the growth of regional warlordism that was the main historical trigger of the revolution which brought the Communist Party to power in the first place. This threat, more than any other, still has the potential for releasing renewed social upheaval, tying together resistance to imperialism and domestic exploitation.

Like the imperial dynasties of Chinese history, modern China has moved through a kind of cyclical oscillation, though now greatly contracted in time. This pattern has resulted from mass reaction to the contradictions which flow from the policies of each of the class forces which have contended for power. Only some fifteen years separated the revolutionary triumph from the vast and cataclysmic showdown between the two lines of Mao and his opponents which gave birth to the Great Proletarian Cultural Revolution. Another period of the same length ended in the rise of Deng Xiaoping and his market reforms. Now another decade and a half has passed, and China is again at the brink, facing a fundamental choice as to which path it will take. Despite the current domination of marketization, the claim that the system is and must remain socialist is not simply a matter of official rhetoric. It is advanced by many Chinese, who reject the idea that the country is or should become fully capitalist, which is widely viewed as a pre-scription for disastrous social chaos under the present conditions of China, with its more than 1 billion people. It is therefore necessary to try to understand how much of a basis still remains for a movement once again toward a more revolutionary system of socialism, and which of the two tendencies may prove strongest in the end.

Three main possibilities seem to present themselves. It is of course conceivable that market reform will continue with a more or less unbroken development, leading the Chinese into the world economy as an equal with the other major international powers. But the factors weighing against such success are extremely heavy, and the costs even of succeeding will most likely be excessively high for significant portions of the population. If, on the other hand, China tries to pursue its present path and fails, the country will for the first time since the revolution face the prospect of truly joining the third world, which is not simply a level of economic development, but a subordinate position within the world market and the extreme polarization of classes which always accompany that status. The other possibility, therefore, is that the Chinese will pull back from their current headlong rush to private marketization, and restore at least some of the most crucial elements of the previous revolutionary socialist system. As Deng passes from the scene, it appears extremely unlikely that these oppos-ing paths will be negotiated without another massive eruption between the two main class forces which have struggled for control of the Chinese revolution.

In the event of such a clash, it seems certain that the top leaders, including major segments of the military, will try to crush their opponents, with the same kind of brutal force that was used in 1989 against the Tiananmen Square movement. The student-based and peaceful demonstrations in Beijing and elsewhere that precipitated that crisis, however, are likely to pale before the scale and violence of any renewed struggle, in a country where the peasants have for centuries produced leaders, often from their own ranks, to organize revolts, and where the proletariat has as revolutionary a history as any in the world. These classes would almost certainly be joined, not only by the hard-liners who are said to still exist even at the highest levels of the party and state, including within the military, but by significant numbers of lower level officials and professionals, who even as they carry out the reform, express their ambiguity toward its consequences and mourn the loss of older values.

Even should such a struggle arise and succeed, however, the massive effects of the genie of marketization cannot be put back in the bottle. China has been fundamentally transformed, from the look of its cities to the relations between its people. If the Chinese once again move away from the policy of reform, they will be able to do so only by absorbing both the positive contributions and the negative lessons of market socialism. This will require a new mix, in which the spirit of Mao Zedong will once again no doubt be more strongly felt, with a renewal of social egalitarianism and collective efforts, but only by moving forward from the plateau of massive economic growth and openness to the world which marketization has reached.

In the China of today, it is hard to imagine a rapid reversal of direction once again. But no country has been more full of surprises in the recent past. In the rest of the world, the vision of a billion Chinese buying foreign goods may dance through the heads of the capitalist class, a recurring dream for at least a century. In China itself, however, there is fear that the nightmares of the last hundred years, class polarization, regional fragmentation, and domination from abroad, may be recurring. In the face of growing social divisions and global contradictions, other dreams may be forming that are very different from the plans being concocted in the boardrooms of multinational capital and their Chinese friends. The mass of workers, peasants, and intellectuals have yet to be heard from, and when their voices are finally released, China may once again surprise the world.

OF TIME AND THE CHANGJIANG: CHINESE HISTORY PAST, PRESENT, AND FUTURE

It is in places like the Zhuge Liang Shrine in Chengdu, Sichuan Province, in the West, and the Tomb of Yue Fei, in Hangzhou, in the East near Shanghai, that one begins to understand what history means in China. Zhuge Liang, or the Marquis Wu, was a great military strategist and statesman of the Three Kingdoms Period, from 220 to 265. Yue Fei was a hero of the Song Dynasty, who defended China against the northern invaders in the twelfth century, and was treacherously denounced and executed in 1142. It is not simply that memorials to such past leaders, long since semideified, have been maintained, and often rebuilt several times over, for hundreds and even thousands of years—thus the memorial to Zhuge Liang was not even begun until four hundred years after his death, and was reconstructed most recently in the last prerevolutionary dynasty, the Qing, which began in 1644. That alone would not stand out, in a country where things built during the past 350 years are virtually "new."

Rather, what makes the Chinese approach to history so extraordinary, is the attitude reflected in the young English-language teacher who accompanied us around China. She is a very modern woman, a well-educated representative of the new professional stratum helping to "open up" the nation to the outside world. Yet though she had never travelled to these parts of the country before, she knew at every stop the story of those historical figures. Standing before their often larger-than-lifesize images, she would not only repeat in great detail their life stories, but would point out how "this one is very popular with the

Chinese people" because he resisted the invaders, or "that one is greatly respected" for his statesmanship and learning. It was as if these long-dead scholars, officials, and generals had fought their literary, political, and military battles a few years ago, so fresh was the feeling which she conveyed of the relevance of their struggles for today.

The verdict against Yue Fei was reversed twenty years later due to popular reaction, and opposite his tomb and that of his son, murdered the day he was executed, are statues of his four accusers, kneeling to ask his forgiveness. As a 1993 guidebook notes, these images are spat on even today. Cultural differences apart, it is hard to imagine people in the United States still spitting on the grave of Lee Harvey Oswald, much less that of John Wilkes Booth. Yet those who killed Yue Fei carried out their bloody deeds exactly 350 years before Columbus landed in the Western Hemisphere. As for Zhuge Liang, according to another guidebook, Mao sent new cadres to his memorial to study his writings, by then only 1,700 years old. Even a revolution to overthrow the millennial Chinese system could not be made without learning from those who had built up China almost two millennia before.

Mao constantly drew on historic incidents, even from earliest Chinese society, to illustrate to the masses the kinds of actions they must carry out today. Commenting on his uses of history, "a foreigner privileged in conversation with Mao Zedong spoke of 'losing all sense of time in his presence'—as events of the last century, this century and the next were 'criss-crossed' with those of yesterday and today."[1] Mao, in turn, was attacked by his enemies through literary allusions to incidents in the imperial dynasties, and one such play served as the actual trigger of the Great Proletarian Cultural Revolution. Certain factions of the young Red Guards mobilized by that movement, in a further twist, destroyed historical monuments, including severely damaging the memorial to Yue Fei. As if to expunge this violation of the past, rebuilding began almost as soon as the Gang of Four were overthrown in 1976. This sense of history as a living power, a battleground, a contemporary factor in the struggles of the present, as well as a guide for the future, has a depth and breadth in China which goes beyond the usual descriptions of the ancientness of its civilization. It is not just that Chinese culture is older and more continuous than that of any other modern society. It is the living contemporaneousness of its historical past that is so striking.

Western parallels are hard to find. True, the educated in the West once looked to Greece and Rome for lessons by which to guide modern life, but this use of ancient history has long since died out, along with the classes which drew on the classics to legitimate their power. Few today, even among the intelligentsia, could cite a single event from that historical era as a lesson for the present. More popularly, the Bible served as a source of ideas for all social morality, but only through the screen of religion and by parable. Perhaps the closest remaining Western parallel is the Jewish Seder, when the flight from Egyptian slavery is recalled as if it were yesterday, and the struggles of an entire people are linked to long past events. But in China, this history still exists everywhere, in stone and plaster, and most of all in writings and art. It is a constant presence, informing literature and culture, but also politics and economics.

Even when it is meant to be hidden, it seems inevitably to live once again. The army of lifesize pottery figures buried outside Xian near the tomb of Qin Shihuang, the first unifier of China and builder of the Great Wall in the third century B.C., was only rediscovered by accident in 1974. Yet the ranks of 8,000 soldiers and charioteers meant to guard him after death are so perfectly modeled, and express such individual personality, that even today they seem ready to come to life and march forth once again at the snap of a finger. History in China is not just something remembered, it is felt. It is an example of what Mao meant when he said that ideas become a "material force" once they are absorbed by the people. Thus Chinese history is more than a remembrance of things past. It lives among and in the masses, and is a basis for present-day action and future plans. No analysis of China can be complete if it ignores the people's profound refusal to forget.

Chinese themselves often stress how "old" their society is compared to the "new" United States. Yet more is involved for the people of China than a historical comparison. It is all too easy for Westerners as they move around the country to be overwhelmed by the Chinese past in all its richness, and to view it in isolation from modern China. But for the Chinese, the stakes are very high as to how history itself will be interpreted and used in the struggles of the present, for the examples of historical figures and the remembrance of past events resonate with implications for the direction as well of contemporary Chinese society. Those who control the way in which history is viewed today strengthen their hand in modern contests for power and gain a weapon in the shaping of public attitudes. This accounts for the bitter struggle that occurs between the contending leadership factions over their interpretations of history, as new meanings given to the past serve as an ever-shifting basis for the legitimation of those currently in power. Yet at the same time, the historical record so deeply imbedded in popular culture has also remained a well of lessons learned and battles fought which can be drawn on over and over again in the class struggles of each new generation. It is a constant force among the masses, reminding them of former leaders who "served the people," and providing a basis from which to resist current policies and programs they find oppressive and exploitative.

Thus Zhuge Liang and Yue Fei are not simply popular figures from the past, but represent two recurring themes of Chinese history. The first, and one of the oldest, is the scholar-official who refuses to put personal gain before service to the nation and the people. In a society which virtually invented administrative government bureaucracy and raised it to the highest level, the incorruptible officer or advisor to the realm was a revered counterbalance to the ranks of opportunists who from time immemorial have used their positions for private profit or to rob those beneath them. At a time when corruption is once again rampant in China, these historical defenders of a righteous social order have renewed contemporary resonance. They serve as constant reminders that there have been periods of history, including the early revolutionary years, marked by simplicity and service to the people, rather than by the greed and opportunism increasingly rife today.

A second major theme of Chinese history is the resistance to foreign attack and control by outsiders, which has been a threat to China virtually from the beginning of its existence as an organized society. The Great Wall, which faces north, the source of the main historic enemies, in time proved less needed than fortifications to defend China from the seaborne imperialists of the West and Japan. But though the enemy changed, the underlying concern has never faded, that those from outside would conquer the Chinese and force them to do their bidding. This possibility provides a dark contemporary undercurrent to the celebration of the new "opening up" of China to the world. Engagement with other nations, sometimes voluntary, at other times enforced from without, is a recurring cycle of Chinese history, but has always produced in time a renewed turning inward, and often a great counterreaction, in which the heroic figures were those who first warned of the dangers and then led the efforts to repel the foreign invaders.

Never before has the leadership of China itself so openly invited and welcomed those who would penetrate it from without, a gamble of enormous consequences in a society whose deepest fears have for millennia been associated with control by outsiders. Whether in the form of foreign investment, four-star hotels built with capital from abroad, or the culture of McDonald's and hard rock music, the current invasion from abroad deeply challenges Chinese control over their own resources, both contemporary and historical, and threatens the integrity of China as a society. It is almost certain to be met with a new phase in the reassertion of national identification, reacting against the outside world.

But it is a third theme of Chinese history that may weigh heaviest in the balance when the contradictions of the present "reform" period fully ripen. This is the aspect developed by the Communists themselves, since it could never conform fully to the interests of any of the premodern ruling classes of China. Throughout Chinese history, there has been a record of rebellions perhaps unequalled in any other society, not only in their number, but in their influence over the course of events. As part of the historical dynamic of virtually all the dynasties, one hears of peasant disorders, growing with the rising greed of officials and the closely related dislocations of production that so often marked the rule of each imperial family. Such uprisings almost always accompanied and often contributed to the fall of the dynasty and its replacement by a new group of rulers, at times drawn in part from among the peasant leaders themselves.

Of course, these early forms of popular revolt could not change the overall structure of the class system. That was a task which remained for the modern revolutionaries, and especially the Communists, to accomplish. Yet Zhu De, who together with Mao founded the Red Army, recounts how one of the first things they did was to seek out the veterans of the Taiping Rebellion, which lasted from 1850 to 1864 and took control of vast regions of southern and eastern China, in order to study the lessons of the past in making modern revolution. From these old anti-imperial warriors they heard of the positive and negative actions which first created and then undermined the greatest of all the uprisings among the peasantry, and the one which raised the clearest social program.[2] The constant presence of the threat of peasant and worker rebellion, and the knowledge that historically this has accompanied the overthrow of most of the ruling groups in Chinese history, tempers the analysis of social stasis which Marx attributed to the "Asian mode of production," and makes the heads of the rulers of China rest uneasily on their pillows.

In this respect, Mao was virtually unique among ancient or modern Chinese leaders in his embracing and encouraging "great turmoil under heaven." He called for recognition of the heroism and the historical struggles of the masses, while debunking the classical writings which treated oppressors as great figures. As Mao biographer Han Suyin described, he insisted that history must be viewed as the outcome, above all, of the class struggle, that most ancient "heroes" oppressed the people, and that it was the life stories of the common worker or peasant, and their acts of sacrifice for the collective good of society, that must now be made the central theme.

The "four histories"—personal and individual records of poor peasants and workers and what they endured, the story of their region or factory or village, the story of struggles for liberation, and the national history—must be assessed again, with priority given to the history of the down-trodden, the slaves, those who really made history.... This new sifting of what history really is Mao Tsetung called "establishing the family tree of the proletariat." Accepted "heroes" were often tyrants who had suppressed revolts, while the "wicked people" were indeed revolution-aries.

History conditions and molds awareness. It was necessary to reorient history away from emperors and Confucian "good" heroes, towards the real bone and blood of creation, the people.[3]

For Mao, the past itself must be reinterpreted to reveal the struggle of the masses and inspire revolutionary actions today.

Added to the themes of incorruptibility among some of the old scholar-officials and heroic resistance to foreign subjugation, the historical record of these popular struggles constitutes an explosive mix. It is this combination of integrity at the top and rebellion from below which provides a contemporary meaning to history, a potential for new social alliances that lies just below the surface of the current "reforms." This shared historical experience gives one the feeling in China that struggle could break out at any moment, and that masses of people would know what to do almost without being told. There is in the West perhaps only one very rough parallel, and that is the tendency of the French to go the barricades on short notice, as if their revolutionary history were still alive—reflected once again in the massive strikes in the fall of 1995. But in China, that rebellious record extends back not just to the late eighteenth century, but for hundreds of years. It was enormously deepened by the revolutionary struggles of the modern period, and was reinforced once more in the 1960s, when the Cultural Revolution turned tens of millions of Chinese into social actors, however ineffective or destructive some of their actions proved in the longer run. This history provides a popular basis for the "right to rebel," drawing authority from ancient concepts in China, in which loss of the Mandate of Heaven by an imperial dynasty was interpreted as retroactive justification for those who overthrew a corrupt regime. Modernized by Mao, it has erupted again in the last few years in many times and places.

Both the forces around Mao and those who have supported Deng Xiaoping have tried in their own ways to use and at the same time to overcome this historical weight. For many Red Guards, aspects of the Chinese ties to history had become a burden, especially in the hands of those intellectuals and officials who turned to the past as a way to limit and contain the revolutionary struggle. They objected, in partic-ular, to the Mandarin-like elitism of the professors in the universities, who insisted that learning still belonged to a scholarly class, and looked down on those of peasant and worker origin. In cultural circles also, old forms prevailed, despite the efforts of Mao, beginning as early as the days in Yan'an after the Long March, to raise up a new generation of revolutionary writers and artists who would put the needs of the masses before their own individualistic "self-cultivation." Thus the Confucian ethic was a special focus of the attacks by Red Guards, since it emphasized obedience and strict social hierarchy, dominated by the class of scholar-officials, against the rebelliousness and egalitarianism that Mao advocated.

In the increasingly anarchic and sectarian drive to stamp out all remnants of the earlier system of thought, while raising up in its place the long history of peasant rebellion and other class struggles in China, certain young people who claimed to be supporters of Mao did carry out very widespread destruction. The results can still be seen in such places as the Lingyin Temple complex outside Hangzhou, where some of the hundreds of statues carved into living stone are headless or otherwise damaged, smashed by Red Guards. These actions formed the basis for some of the most damning indictments directed at the Cultural Revolution by the Chinese reformers and Western critics. However, such destruction, despite the loss, and whatever its actual political purpose, is hardly new in China. Historically, rampaging armies and the invading imperialist forces of England, France, the United States, and Japan, have over the centuries wreaked far greater devastation— most notably the burning by foreign troops of the Yuanmingyuan imperial palace in 1860, partially restored and destroyed again in 1900, with many of the most treasured art works and writings of former dynasties either looted or consigned to the flames.

Like the Red Guards before them, the new reformers have their own ways of selectively using history. The Cultural Revolution, in particular, is a virtual "non-event" in their historical reviews. When the hundredth anniversary of the birth of Mao was celebrated in December, 1994, for example, television was filled with long documentaries and semifictional reconstructions of his life, and photo displays and similar exhibits were mounted throughout the country. But the years of the Cultural Revolution, among the most dramatic and far-reaching in their impact on Chinese society, were all but ignored, being virtually skipped over, as if the decade from 1965 to 1975 did not really occur. This attempt to ignore the recent past, in favor of earlier, more acceptable periods certainly corresponds with much of the popular sentiment, especially among intellectuals and professionals. For the latter, the Cultural Revolution is widely seen as an era best forgotten, or spoken of only as one of loss and suffering. Among the graduate students at the university where we taught, most of whose parents come from the professions, disparagement of that period was all but universal. Some had heartrending tales to tell, like the quiet young man who one evening told of his father, a historian, whose books were burned and who died in exile in the countryside, where the family still lives. Then there are the faculty who lost years of work, or fled to Changchun to escape from turmoil and threats, never to leave again. Some of this middle-aged generation seem stunned into a deep silence by the events of that period and the many sharp reversals of policy both before and since. This has left them with an unwillingness to speak about their earlier years which they break only with great reluctance, and then just among close friends.

Yet the issues raised by the Cultural Revolution are beginning to haunt even those who most avidly oppose it or recall it only with painful memories. A nostalgia for the era of the "lost years" of the 1960s has begun to emerge, suggesting a tentative reevaluation of its positive as well as negative aspects. This has taken somewhat bizarre forms, as in the opening since 1992 of several "Cultural Revolution" restaurants in Beijing and other cities, often decorated with posters of Chairman Mao and other paraphernalia from that earlier era, and serving the kind of rough peasant fare that the students who went down to the countryside lived on during their years of hard labor. To some extent, this desire "to savour what we went through and deliberate about the dramatic changes that have taken place in our country and our lives" resembles the "Sixties nostalgia" that has emerged recently in the United States.[4] In part it may be based on a yearning for lost youth among the activists of that generation. At its worst, it can even degenerate into a form of radical chic and commercialism. Thus some of those frequenting the new restaurants, with their upscale prices, complain that the owners, most of them veterans of the 1960s themselves, are "trying to make a profit from our feelings."

Still, the emergence of such a phenomena at this time seems to have a deeper resonance. Some of the restaurants serve not only the regular peasant food of the period, but recreate the coarsest dishes, such as gruel made of chaff or cornmeal dumplings stuffed with edible wild herbs, which were the only foods the poorest peasant families could obtain. Such meals were at times fed even to urban schoolchildren in the late 1960s and early 1970s, to give them a literal taste of the hard life of prerevolutionary China. To want to eat such things again today, is as if veterans of the 1960s civil rights movement in the United States suddenly developed a longing, not just for soul food, but for the simplest kinds of meals which were shared by the poor Black families of Mississippi and Alabama with the young people from the North who came to live and work among them. One Beijing restaurateur serving such dishes admits that his enterprise "was founded to capitalize on people's yearning to recall some of their harsh past in a special environment."[5]

There is something here beyond simple nostalgia. The desire to rediscover roots in the hard work of organizing and building among the poorest and most oppressed members of the society, to feel once again the end to that terrible alienation which haunts the "yuppies" of every nation, to forget for a time the drive for position and consumption that has become the all-absorbing end of life, this too must be what moves those who seek again the values of their youthful years in the "Cultural Revolution" restaurants. Without denying the difficulties of that period, or the desire of many at the time to escape from the countryside, the era is once again being recalled "with a mixture of bitterness and sweetness." Many come to the restaurants hoping to find lost friends with whom they shared those years, and some establishments serve as an exchange post for old comrades to relocate each other and together "recall those days."

These attitudes are reflected as well in the feelings of twenty-two middle-aged urbanites, many accompanied by their teenage children, who in the spring of 1994 travelled back for their first reunion to Red Flag Ridge Farm, in the Great Northern Wilderness of Heilongjiang Province, bordering on Siberia. They went to renew their acquaintance with the rugged frontier families among whom they had lived and worked during the Cultural Revolution. Many had volunteered enthusiastically for rural service in their youth, others had been forced for political reasons or out of economic necessity to leave their families and careers and "go down" to the farm. Even before the 1994 trip, they had formed a network of those who spent time on the commune, and held several reunions.

Now mainly successful professional or administrative urbanites, they nevertheless felt the need to renew their ties to the rural community which for many of them was a valuable training ground, and for all a crucial episode in their lives.

> Back in those 'cultural revolution' years, we tried hard to escape from that wild place and return to our families in Beijing. But in retrospect we all look on the experience, although tough at the time, as valuable, memorable and rewarding.
> ... For sure we owe part of our success to those years of hardship when our characters were formed.[6]

Half of those returning had met their spouses among the fellow students on the farm, which undoubtedly heightened the emotion that they felt on coming back. "Several children saw their fathers or mothers in tears for the first time." For their part, those peasants who had been friends and coworkers in the 1960s turned out to greet the ex-students, "saying we brought about a jubilant, festive atmosphere to the farm they had missed for years." On both sides of these exchanges, even those who had felt the most bitterness at being forced to work on the farm, or most resentful at what they perceived as the imposition of unskilled and elitist students on a poor peasant community, often expressed a kind of love-hate relationship to this crucial era of their past and its lost values.

The picture which thus emerges qualifies the image so often projected in "revisionist" interpretations of the Cultural Revolution, of reluctant youths and resentful peasants thrown into a negative and unproductive relation. Thus one returnee to the farm "was touched that after so many years, we were still remembered and loved." Many farmers recalled the difficulties the commune had faced after the students departed. Wang Baotai, deputy director of the farm, spoke of how it took years for operations to recover from the loss of the "educated youth" who not only provided 60 percent of the workforce during those years, but filled many important positions in its administration.

> "But local people only came to realize the value of the educated youths as a result of the farm's paralysis, and regretted not having made better use of their talents when they were here," he said.
> Sun Hongwu, a veteran soldier and experienced farmer, agreed with Wang. "The Red Flag Ridge could not have developed the way it did without the talent and dedication of the educated youths," he said.
> He and many other leaders apologized to us for not paying enough attention to our health care and for working us too hard. Their words moved me to tears.[7]

The same "returning student" who wrote these words was relieved to find that "local people's responses assured me that there was no resentment" for the sudden departure of the educated youth decades ago. In part to assuage any such lingering feelings, and to express their own appreciation, often left unvoiced in the past, those coming back from the cities after so many years brought with them money raised by themselves and their children, as well as ideas for projects on the farm, which has been greatly expanded and modernized in the intervening years. The farmers in turn offered suggestions as to what would be most helpful in the way of assistance to their current drive to boost production.

On a nationwide basis, efforts are being made to pass along this spirit of exchange between urban and rural areas to a new generation, with the formation in the fall of 1994 of a China Students Voluntary Corps, part of a service campaign initiated by the China Communist

Youth League to mobilize college and middle school students to help the poorest farmers and failing factories. The effort is seen as an attempt to revive the lost values of the past. "The call for young volunteers comes at a time when helpfulness and generosity are increasingly overshadowed by egoism and materialism."[8] This volunteerism was revitalized by six students at Beijing University, who took it upon themselves to clear an especially heavy snowfall in the winter of 1993, and since then local chapters of a Society of Loving Hearts have sprung up on many campuses, undertaking projects large and small. The hope is that the dying spirit of social concern and responsibility will be revived among the youth. In 1994, a half million students responded to such calls, donating part of their summer vacation to voluntary community programs. In one such campaign, a million young people helped maintain order on transport during the 1994 Spring Festival. The next year, a similar number were enrolled in a literacy campaign, fanning out across the country to teach 4 million rural residents the 2,000 most commonly used Chinese characters. "It is not only teaching the farmers to read and write. We should also view the campaign as a move to spread culture and relieve the poverty as well as to educate the students," according to one organizer.[9] By 1995, 10 million youth, including both professionals and workers, were said to have participated nationwide in these kinds of activities. In a reprise of the experiences of the generation of their parents, many felt for the first time what those eating at the "Cultural Revolution" restaurants are also trying to recapture. "We have found our values up there in the mountains. We know we are needed and we can do something," said one volunteer medical graduate student.[10]

Such efforts find encouragement at the highest level. The top leaders of the government and party, including President Jiang Zemin and Premier Li Peng and forty ambassadors and their families, joined an estimated 2 million other local residents in planting trees in and around the capital in the spring of 1995, a practice going back to 1989. Volunteers are similarly expected to plant some 4 million of the total of 14 million seedlings in rural reforestation. These efforts are seen as extending the history of revolutionary self-sacrifice and voluntary concern for the collective good. On the anniversary of the May 4 Movement, the great anti-imperialist and progressive struggle of students launched in 1919, the president of Beijing University, Wu Shuqing, said that the school "upholds the goal of becoming a first-class socialist university," from which many have gone out to help the working classes. "As a tradition, the university's students today engage in social practices. Many do research in poor regions when they take part in work-study programmes."[11] Others have pointed to such figures as Dr. Norman Bethune, the Canadian doctor who died caring for troops of the Eighth Route Army in the 1930s, and Lei Feng, the young peasant soldier honored for his simple acts of selflessness that have been held up as an example for young people, since his death in 1964. Though the story of his life has been questioned in more recent times, his picture still hung on the wall of the classroom where our daughter attended school.

Emulation of such examples is found even at a very early age. One program, Hand in Hand, brings together children from rich and poor districts, through visits and as pen pals. Begun in 1990, it involves millions of students who get to know and interact with each other, with the better-off areas encouraged to assist poorer ones. But it is also a means for modern youth to learn about the lives of their parents and of the older revolutionary generation, and to revive some of the values of the struggles of that period.

> Until he met Yan Feifei, 12-year-old Zhang Peng could not believe his father's stories about going hungry....
> And then Zhang Peng's school invited several students from Hebei Province to visit Beijing during the summer of 1993 sponsored by "Hand in Hand." Zhang Peng invited Yan Feifei to go home with him.
> Yan told Zhang Peng that his family only had one vegetable dish every day.
> Now Zhang Peng no longer asks his parents to take him to the McDonald's Restaurant every Sunday.[12]

Such programs are seen as a way to educate the growing ranks of "spoiled" kids, especially those in single-child families who are fawned on as the sole progeny of two sets of grandparents. Thus

> Its six sponsors hope the urban youngsters, sometimes called "little emperors," can gain some feeling for poverty and learn helpfulness, thrift, hard work and friendship from their rural counterparts. The rural kids can also open a window to the colourful world outside their home villages.[13]

Through such exchanges, socialist concepts of even development nationwide, egalitarianism, and devotion to collective goals are instilled in the young.

In a similar program, primary school children from Taiyuan took a "long march" through rural areas of Shanxi Province, carrying their own food and bags over mountainous trails, and visiting the poverty-stricken villages and schools there.

> "These city children have tasted the major difference between them and rural children," said Chen Xiaowai, their teacher. "Thus they began a serious re-evaluation of their lifestyle and behaviour."
> On the expedition, they tried to prove they could become as strong-

willed as their country peers and they could overcome any difficulty. The youths refused help from their teachers who wanted to help carry their bags. Each time the teachers suggested a rest, the children said "no."

"We should be strict with ourselves since we want to harden our minds," one student said. "Our older generation of revolutionaries ate straw, roots, bark and even their belts during the Red Army's Long March. Ours is nothing compared to them."[14]

Thus even the youngest children relearn the lessons of the past, and the spirit of sacrifice of the revolutionary period.

For those turning eighteen, a spreading movement sponsors "Adulthood Rites," stressing "rights and responsibilities," and bringing thousands of high school students together at public ceremonies, sometimes marked by planting special trees. Beijing Information Management School, encouraging intergenerational exchanges,

suggested that parents write letters to their children, telling them stories from when they were 18 and telling them their hopes. The children were asked to write back.

"This is the first time I've written to my parents. I feel freer to express myself in the letters. My parents and I never communicated in this way," said Li, whose parents went to northern Shaanxi Province during the "cultural revolution" to cultivate the barren lands at the age of 16 and 17.

"I promised them that I would be as responsible and independent as they were at 18."[15]

Not only the struggles of the past in general, but the Cultural Revolution specifically, have thereby come to serve as inspirations. The new volunteerism is thus seen as upholding both deep Chinese traditions of helping others and revolutionary examples, forming a necessary buffer to the effects of marketization.

As the country is stepping into a market economy, many people are worried about whether traditional values, including the volunteer spirit, can survive market competition.

What the million young volunteers over the country are doing shows that there are people trying to answer the question positively.

It seems to me that as the country is in transition from a planned to a market economy, the spirit of volunteering should be especially treasured because it is an important virtue of the socialist market economy. No matter what form the country is going to take, valuable traditional virtues must be inherited. Only then can we claim to carry "Chinese characteristics."[16]

Some believe that this spirit can actually prevent the Chinese from succumbing to the dehumanization of marketization.

A market economy in China should not lead to cold and detached human relationships, one scholar said, adding that he believes China's new generation will carry forward the traditional ethics of the nation.[17]

In such ways, history itself is invoked to ward off the worst effects of reform, and to call the Chinese to self-sacrifice.

But despite such drives, it is the spirit of marketization that is sweeping China, overwhelming everything in its path, including traditional culture, revolutionary experience and historical legacies. Not that the reformers are not also turning to history as a rallying point for their efforts. Among their state-sponsored activities is official promotion of a revival of interest in the Confucian ethic, but now harnessed to the goals of market reform. Thus "China will promote the study and application of Confucianism to serve its modernization," through sponsorship of national and international foundations and conferences.[18] At the first major academic meeting on the relationship of economy and culture in China, Confucian concepts were evaluated as having both positive and negative effects on economic progress. Those attending also agreed "that various kinds of cultural festivals and other activities can play a role in promoting local economic growth, and their impact can be immense." In line with the current marketization policies, since the mid-1980s, a wide variety of "commerce-culture research societies, enterprise-culture research societies, and economy-culture journals have mushroomed across the country.[19]

Entrepreneurs and even the government itself have been quick to exploit the economic potential of the Chinese past. Selling its cultural heritage in the most blatantly commercial form, "a series of tour packages rich with the folk customs of China's fifty-six ethnic groups has been planned by the China National Tourism Administration (CNTA). The tours are called 'China Folklore '95'," with leading tourist agencies "adding folklore attractions to their itineraries."[20] This "folk" culture is becoming big business. In 1995 alone, "China is expected to receive 8 million overseas tourists and earn $8 billion by introducing a series of tourism packages with folk culture as their central theme."[21] For those in China most able to take advantage of marketization, there is also new freedom and money with which to travel and sightsee. At the same time, Chinese themselves complain that they are increasingly unable to afford visits to parks, scenic spots, and historic monuments, as ticket prices have risen as much as tenfold, and visitors are often charged at several points just to view a single vista or to climb to the top of a pagoda. "The entrance fee in some parks in Beijing, for instance, can be as high as 100 yuan ($12), one-third of an average worker's monthly earnings."[22] Thus as foreign tourism and "folklore" packages spread, and as the new rich gain the time and funds to travel at home and abroad, the Chinese masses, under the impact of marketization and declining governmental support for public institutions, have been increasingly excluded from access to recreational facilities and their own cultural heritage.

Others, however, find ways to continue using the history of China for profit. The burgeoning high fashion industry, which "has strode eagerly down the path of internationalization," is being led by designers such as Wu Haiyan, who, following her 1994 collection "that made use of the graceful Tang dynasty style ... maintained her consistent pursuit of the lingering charm of Chinese culture." In 1995 she offered a "'Tender Blue Silk Line' which intends to express the feeling of ancient Chinese women who lived south of the Yangtze River."[23] In such forms the past and its "charms" linger just long enough to serve as one more arena for profit-making and to feed the taste for luxury of both the new Chinese and the old global rich.

On a more popular public level there is a state-sponsored "historicism" in the form of elaborate pageants staged for major holidays, notably the annual celebrations of National Day on October 1, marking the Communist triumph. These historical extravaganzas include masses of dancers and young people dressed in traditional costumes, portrayals of ancient heroes and mythical figures, and musical and theatrical performances, all mixed together with commercial displays exalting the accomplishments of the revolutionary period, especially those of the decade and a half of reform. Thus the 1994 celebration took on a decidedly commerce-oriented tone in Beijing, which sets the official "line" for the rest of the country.

> Unlike previous celebrations, which featured mostly cultural activities, this year's focus was on economic events in line with the call by the country's reform architect, Deng Xiaoping, for faster economic development.
>
> The parks were turned into exhibition grounds and shopping centres, because the sponsors of the activities, especially invited provincial governments, took the opportunity to demonstrate their economic achievements and to sell their best products.[24]

In Changchun, the same mix of culture and commerce took the form of a fall Lantern Festival with very elaborate and costly exhibits, most of them with a Buddhist or mythical theme, paid for and built by the leading "marketization" enterprises.

These festivals are popular, as are the officially promoted folklore troops, continuing and reviving local and regional cultural expressions, especially those of the non-Han nationalities. This effort has included a revival of serious institutes devoted to preserving the historical record in music, dance, and other areas of culture. But on the popular level, there is an air about all this pageantry that smacks of superficiality, a kind of modernized pop rendition of historical themes. At worst, it resembles the "theme parks" which are also sprouting up around the country, converting history into a kind of gala spectacle to be enjoyed like any other form of tourist entertainment—not unlike the recently blocked effort in the United States to build a Civil War Disneyland near the Manassas battlefield. Typical of these is the "tourism zone" in eastern Guangdong Province, with a series of parks combining "water sports and religious pilgrimages," golf courses, and folk art villages.[25]

Indicative of the standards employed in this kind of "popularization," in a recent flood of "historical movies, soap operas and novels ... the limelight has always focused on emperors and their concubines." Even a "wise emperor" like Qianlong of the Qing Dynasty is turned into a "philander with consummate acrobatic fighting skills. His story, full of jokes, romantic affairs and fantastic adventures provides excitement and sensual pleasure for TV audiences."

> A number of critics who recently wrote a series of articles on the phenomenon believe that the history craze isn't historically based at all, in reality, it's anti-history.
> In most TV and film productions, historical themes have been simplified to such an extent that the finished products serve only to function as audio-visual entertainment....
> "History has lost the function of being a mirror of fact and was reduced to the status of a commercial product. It was processed into an entertainment snack providing sensual pleasure for the mass audience," Chen Taisheng, a film and literary critic, commented.[26]

But these historical "snacks" have an ideological impact as well.

> Some of the works reflect feudal ideologies of 2,000 years ago....
> "These movies and operas extol imperial power," said Zhang Zhongxing, an old scholar.
> "To say it kindly, people who have interest in these things can't make a distinction between right and wrong. To be serious, they still have not detested autocracy."[27]

"Common people are totally meaningless" to such imperial "heroes," according to the writer Wang Meng, expressing the mass line toward history and culture which Mao laid out at Yan'an and in the Cultural Revolution. "The more heroic they were, the worse life the common people suffered." As a result of this kind of "history," "culture's proper role of edifying and moulding people's character has been ignored." But the public is being "molded" by this kind of historicism—to consumer culture and the dominance of rich and powerful elites who exploit the masses, however masked by being presented in "historic" form.

What is most lacking in this present-day historicism is the blood and guts, the reality of class struggle, that made the building of modern China possible. That record cannot be grasped if ancient history is reduced to showy pageantry, and the struggles of the recent past are airbrushed away. Stripped of this deeper dimension, historical references become appeals to a superficial nationalism and serve only to selectively reinforce the policies of the status quo. They make of the masses of the people spectators to what should be their living history, denying them the depth of knowledge from which present and future actions can once again be organized. This promotion of nationalist sentiments, without the class element that was inseparable from the modern anti-imperialist struggles, is most evident on television, where there is a constant flow of programs recounting the bitter campaigns of the anti-Japanese war, but almost none showing the revolution of the poorer classes against the rich.

Such a duality fits the ideological needs of the leaders of the present marketization drive, as it promotes the national advance of China, while suppressing knowledge of the past polarization of classes, which the reforms themselves are once again rapidly exacerbating. The effects of this historical amnesia are already being felt among the younger generation. Graduate students at Changchun, who are themselves only in their twenties—members of a generation among whom a revival of interest in and respect for Mao is said to be occurring—complain that undergraduates now entering college are interested only in personal advancement, lacking both social concerns and knowledge of history. As a study by the Chinese Academy of Social Sciences confirmed, among many youth under twenty-five, there is a great disinterest even in the recent past, and it is not uncommon to find some almost totally unfamiliar either with the conditions of prerevolutionary society or with the revolution that Mao led.

So too, one already feels, travelling around China, that historical sites are becoming increasingly isolated islands of the past in a sea of modernity, reduced to the status of "tourist spots." Not that the tourism is primarily foreign. Despite the growing costs and other barriers, it is the Chinese themselves, drawn from every class and stratum of the population, who make up the overwhelming proportion of visitors to the Great Wall, Forbidden City, Summer Palace, and other major historical monuments in Beijing and throughout the country. Thus there have been major efforts to preserve and renovate these ancient complexes, including new rebuilding on the site of the Yuanmingyuan Palace. Yet throughout the country, historical sites, many of which only became open to the masses after the victory of the Communist revolution in 1949, are now more and more set apart from the surrounding communities, as a result of transformations being wrought by the new forces of the "market." Some of this is no doubt the unavoidable effect of modernization per se. But like everything else in China today, it is occurring in a "get-rich-quick" atmosphere, in which the past is disregarded in the rush for present profits. It is this far less intentional—yet for that very reason perhaps even more fundamental and insidious—form of the wiping out of Chinese history that is being wrought by the forces of marketization.

Outstanding examples of this process are the construction of highrise buildings and the erection of billboards on the edge of some of the most beautiful and historically significant bodies of water in China, disrupting their ancient and irreplaceable milieu. This includes the West Lake of Hangzhou, one of the premier centers historically for Chinese expressions of beauty and art. Fragile cultural relics are endangered even more drastically in many cases. For example, the 1,500-year-old Buddhist statues in the Longmen Grottoes of Luoyang, Henan Province, are being shaken by a recently constructed railway line, threatening to bring them down. The Yungang Grotto at Datong, Shanxi Province, carved from 386 to 534 A.D., is suffering from acid rain from nearby factories, eroding and discoloring the statues. In an official investigation of four provinces with some of the richest historic treasures, "to the surprise of investigators, numerous ancient buildings and cultural relics had been destroyed to make way for railway and highway construction and real estate development."[28] In the face of such widespread losses, Construction Minister Hou Jie declared in mid-1995 that "natural and historic treasures must not be converted to other uses under any circumstances.... The remark was made in the wake of a wave of scenic and historic destruction cause by the country's recent construction boom."[29]

A striking example in this regard is the new Guangzhou-to-Shenzhen expressway, in the heart of the Southern "marketization" region, built on a route that runs directly through Jingyuan Fort, used by the Chinese navy in the Opium War in 1840 in the effort to repel the invading British, "considered by historians as the beginning of modern Chinese history."

'According to law concerning cultural relics, builders of the Guangzhou-Shenzhen expressway should have tried to bypass the fort before construction began. But none of them even thought of the fort when designing the expressway's blueprint.'...
If the builders destroy the fort to make way for the expressway, departments

in charge of cultural relics will strongly protest. But bypassing it would mean heavy economic losses on the part of the builders....[30]

In such competitions between those pursuing short-term economic profits, and those concerned with preserving the historical record of China, it is the former who have most frequently won out, in many cases in collusion with local authorities who are eager to disregard master plans and authorize haphazard building, and who are under official pressure from above to speed up the pace of modernization.

In the hot-house atmosphere of market reform, not surprisingly, "construction units often have gained the upper hand."[31] Thus many ancient towns have had their centers gutted, governed only by the profit motives of those promoting development zones and the real estate market. Shanghai, in particular, is being totally transformed, as neighborhood after neighborhood of its distinctive old housing are ripped down to make way for multi-story apartment complexes and for soaring high-rises in the ubiquitous style of showy glass and steel that might be called "Asian modern." A massive television tower, the Oriental Pearl, complete with a hotel and condos affordable only by the richest of the rich, now looms over the city center from the Pudong development zone across the Huangpu River, a monolith so monstrous and out of scale with its urban surroundings that residents speak of averting their eyes to avoid having to look at it. So too, in the heart of Beijing, "in recent years, urban developers have disrupted traditional architecture by using all available space and maximized profits by constructing high-rise apartments over the height limit."[32] In other cities the ancient centers have been preserved and some even renovated, but only to serve the ever more commercialized tourist trade, converting what had been viable traditional communities into shallow show-cases.

As government officials are increasingly judged primarily by their ability to generate profitable investments, they most commonly ally themselves with the largest developers, to the neglect of all other societal values. Plans to raze the Science and Technology Bookstore in Guiyang, capital of Guizhou Province, to make way for a commercial plaza, have brought protests from leading cultural and scientific figures and even the vice-chairman of the National People's Congress. But across China "such a trend seems to be on the rise instead of being curbed."

Our attention is too frequently being drawn to news of bookstores being driven off the high streets into the alleys as property developers hone in on prime retailing locations....

Mostly built in the 1950s in downtown areas, bookstores in different cities are finding themselves targets of real estate developers. Such development projects usually are backed by local governments since they may bring much greater commercial profits. As a result, the interests of bookstores, which make little money or none at all, tend to be overlooked.

In deciding their stance in the tug-of-war between commercial interests and social responsibility, many of our leaders unfortunately give weight to the former. To them, economic development is a hard quota which tells the quality of their performance. Cultural and scientific prosperity, on the other hand, is something more abstract which they can just pay lip service to.[33]

In this way local officials and private developers, working closely together, undermine the broad base of history, culture, and technology among the masses of the people, even as a new educated and "modernized" elite emerges to dominate these fields.

As in all other areas of marketization, the government is belatedly scrambling to implement macroeconomic controls to limit the damage caused by runaway development, and to impose some rules for protecting historically valuable cities and monuments. The designation of historical and cultural urban areas has led in some cases to their protection or even renovation. Typical is Guangzhou, where the "government will review its decision on how to build a boulevard through the city's botanical garden without causing great damage to the plants there.... The road was to cut through ... the most complete collection of tropical and subtropical plants in China" and "now the only place where local people can come nearer to nature." Nevertheless, even if this park is saved, it is only "one of several events involving erosion of gardens and natural reserves by the city construction projects in Guangdong Province."[34] In a few instances, damaging intrusions such as the billboards on the edge of West Lake in Hangzhou, and even three large luxury buildings built there without proper permission, have been ordered dismantled, though elsewhere already-built high-rise complexes can hardly be as easily removed. In Beijing, plans have been made to allow only gradual increases in building heights in concentric rings around the Forbidden City, covering some 209 blocks, while acres of land with historic interest have been placed under government protection, and new construction is required "to combine traditional Chinese characteristics and modern style."[35] Such policies have been able to control or reverse some of the worst situations, and promise at least to take preservation of the historical record into account in future construction.

Nevertheless, Chinese experts have warned that continued uncontrolled building is having a devastating effect on the preservation of the history of the country, and it is by no means certain that the forces of marketization will not continue to overwhelm all efforts at restraint.

The commitment of governments at every level, when faced with the choice between the "hard quota" of rapid economic growth and further historical and cultural destruction, remains very doubtful. With corruption endemic, planning is often seen merely as one more restraint to be bypassed, and rules are broken almost as soon as they are issued. In Beijing itself, the much noted tearing down of the McDonald's outlet on Tiananmen Square was carried out to make room for a massive commercial center exceeding by a wide margin the height limits put on buildings in the vicinity of the Forbidden Palace—though the new complex is virtually within sight of the compound which houses the top leadership and the very governmental bodies which had created the legislation restricting such construction.

Such examples illustrate the increasing inability or even unwillingness of the Chinese authorities to control the forces they have released with market reforms. Not only in the more marginalized regions of the country, where the sway of the central government often breaks down first, but in the heart of Beijing itself, there is growing evidence of disintegration, historically a sign that those in power are losing their grip. This weakening is often a harbinger of coming social instability. Thus just as the devastation of ancient sites and materials was used by Deng and other reformers in the late 1970s to condemn the goals of the Cultural Revolution, today it is in turn a basis for opposition to marketization, not only because of the actual losses involved, but because it adds an historic dimension to all the modern damages being inflicted in the name of "progress"—uncontrolled and massive corruption, growing class polarization, a "floating" population of tens of millions without regular work, and dismantling of social securities in the areas of housing, medical care, and education enjoyed by the masses for decades.

It is on the Changjiang (Yangzi or Yangtse) River that the most profound clash of modernization and historical preservation is coming to a head. Passing at night through the last of the Three Gorges, the magnificent passageway of water between towering cliffs that is one of the geographic wonders of the world, it is shocking to come across the bright lights of the all-night crews building the massive dam—the largest ever constructed—that will destroy this natural marvel. The project will raise the level of the river until the mountains become mere molehills, "making the gorge a gorge no longer."[36] It is as though, in the United States, a decision had been made to build a dam across the Colorado River, flooding the bottom of the Grand Canyon, and cutting by two-thirds the height of its walls—an idea for which there actually were serious proposals in the 1960s. Yet even were that to happen, it would be for most only the destruction of a natural beauty spot, however wondrous, since except for the Indians who have inhabited it for centuries, the Grand Canyon has little historical meaning for most people in the United States.

Such is not the case with the Three Gorges region. It lies, both geographically and historically, at the heart of the Chinese cultural orientation toward rivers and mountains, an inspiration for centuries of artists and writers, a center of folklore and toil. The region has some 8,000 historical sites, among them relics dating back thousands of years, to the first settlements spreading out from the fertile flood plains along the river. These will all be lost behind the dam, except for what can be salvaged before the waters rise. The situation is not unlike that which occurred in the Upper Nile Valley of Egypt in the building of Aswan with the giant reservoir rising behind it. About 1.2 million people will be displaced in the Three Gorges region, with twenty counties, several sizeable cities, and 140 towns in two provinces all or partially submerged. Some 1,600 factories will have to be transferred or abandoned. The project was to cost an estimated 100 billion yuan or $11.6 billion, 30 percent of which will have to be raised from international and domestic money markets. But estimates are already rising, ranging from over $17 billion to as high as $30 billion. The entire complex will not be completed until 2008, a fifteen-year period that is as long again as the entire reform era under Deng Xiaoping. It "spans such a long time that more than 300,000 Chinese who have not even been born yet are among those counted to be relocated."[37]

This alone makes the project extremely risky, given the potential for economic downturns and political reversals over such an extended time. While the damming of the Changjiang in this region is said to have first been proposed by Sun Yat-sen, the founder of republican China, and endorsed by Mao, the glory or failure of the undertaking will fall on the current leaders.

> A go-ahead for the dam would be a political triumph for a leadership that for 40 years has sought to rally support for a structure it hopes will symbolize the 'superiority' of socialism.[38]

Yet the Chinese hope to attract at least $1 billion in foreign contracts for construction of the dam, and twice that amount for building of communities for the relocated population. Vice-President Zou Jiahua estimates that resettlement of those displaced by the project alone may cost up to 30 billion yuan or $5.1 billion. But with a recent further short-fall of $3 billion in projected financing, even larger dependency on funds from abroad seems probable. So this symbol of socialist superiority can only be built with a heavy influx of capitalist financing.

But that is just one aspect of the ties between the Three Gorges project and global capital. The goal is to turn the "once-impoverished area around the proposed site" into "one of China's richest regions."[39] In 1994 alone, 131 overseas-funded enterprises were established in Yichang, the major city in the region of the dam, raising the total of such firms to 501, drawn from nineteen countries, with $1.3 billion in capital. The local government has a long-range plan to attract $3 billion in investment from abroad, involving 3,000 companies. Upstream in Sichuan Province, a traditional temple celebration in the spring of 1995 was merged with a trade fair to attract businesspeople and tourists into the region, "to lure more overseas funds for proposals related to the Three Gorges water conservance project."[40] To help attract foreign funding, the national State Council "will classify the area as a new economic development zone by granting the kind of preferential policies that were adopted in the coastal provinces."[41] This means that the full effects of marketization and of foreign capitalization will be welcomed into the very heart of China, no longer centered primarily on the South and East Coast, the traditional gateways to outside penetration. In this way, the dam would not only lose any hoped-for value as a symbol of the superiority of socialism, but the Chinese interior itself would be converted from a potential base of resistance to global capital into one of its most advanced outposts.

That the Three Gorges dam constitutes a battleground for the future direction of social organization in China is indicated by the refusal of Washington in the fall of 1995 to offer subsidized loans for contract bids on the project by U.S. corporations—a highly unusual stance by the pro-foreign business Clinton administration. The reasons given were concerns over human rights issues and environmental impact, as well as "doubts about the dam's financial viability."[42] Despite its otherwise enormous assistance program in China, the World Bank has also refused to provide funding, most likely under U.S. pressure. Such opposition strains even further the financial basis of the project, raises its costs, and makes it subject to foreign pressures, not only in the economic sphere, but as a bargaining chip in political and social areas as well. Thus the Three Gorges dam is not just another domestic project, but the centerpiece of the entire marketization program, and the ultimate test of the value for China of "opening to the world."

It is this which gives added weight to the fate of those who must be moved to make way for the dam and its ever rising waters, a process which has already begun, with the evacuation of the first peasant farmers in September, 1993: "It was harvest time. The villagers chopped down their fruit-laden trees with tears."[43] Even though their numbers constitute only one tenth of 1 percent of the total Chinese population, the loss of their traditional lands and familial burial sites resonates with greater import—so much so that Premier Li Peng himself said that "success of the Three Gorges Dam project would depend upon the success of the relocation programme."[44] The record here is not especially good. Of 10 million people who were moved in previous years to make way for a series of smaller dams, some one-third are still suffering from poor living conditions and the effects of the disruption of their lives as a result of having been torn from their ancestral homes. There have been riots over compensation claims among those resettled earlier, and similar problems are emerging at Three Gorges.

> In Wanxian, where a third of the city's 300,000 people must move to higher ground, thousands of residents who are part of the first phase of relocation have been living in tents. The local government's promise to provide jobs for farmers pushed off their ancestral lands has foundered on a shortage of money to start construction on the chemical plant that was to employ 20,000 of them.[45]

Some of those being moved from the Three Gorges region have already staged demonstrations, broken up by police. As tensions mount, the new evacuees could become a living symbol of the long-term social costs and growing class polarization wrought by uncontrolled modernization and the policies of marketization.

There is no simple or easy solution to the needs of China for more power and the desire to finally gain control over the floodwaters of the Changjiang, which for centuries have devastated the plains below, with enormous loss of life and property. But concern over the historical, social, and ecological damages of the Three Gorges project is nevertheless widespread.[46] Environmental engineers in Chongqing have spoken with surprising openness and frankness about the dangers of silting, and how "local and national leaders have no money to treat the 265 billion gallons a year of raw sewage and industrial waste that they say will flow into the impounded waters." They accuse officials "of shortsightedness and of misleading the public about the potential threat."[47]

Dai Qing, a prominent opponent of the dam who has been jailed for her outspokenness, expresses the fear that, far from promoting development, the massive resources needed to build the project will only serve to set China back even further.

> "I still have some hope that the Three Gorges Dam won't go ahead.... If we devote so many resources to the Three Gorges, then everything else will have to wait. Education and science spending will slow, and China's backwardness and burden on the world economy will grow."[48]

From an advance in socialist modernization, the project can potentially turn into one of economic weakness and international dependency, typifying the modern relation to global capital.

As in so many other areas of public policy today, the destruction at Three Gorges touches deep chords among the Chinese people, and there is a barely suppressed uneasiness over the vastness of the dam and the radical transformation of central China that it will bring. As far back as 1990, resistance from those being displaced contributed to the project being delayed, and already "anticipated problems with resettling the residents ... have deferred the filling of the reservoir to its full capacity by another decade, to 2019."[49] But in the aftermath of the crushing of the Tiananmen movement in 1989, the opposition of local people, environmentalists, and others was suppressed, and the government pushed forward once again with the plan. Even so, deep-seated and widely felt nervousness about the dam was reflected in an unusual split vote in the National People's Congress when the project was formally approved in April, 1992, with almost one-third of the delegates either voting against or abstaining.

Every year tens of thousands of Chinese, including the poorest peasants, make the riverboat trip through the Three Gorges. Though many do so simply as a means of transportation, others make the journey to see the sites and experience the great river in all its power and majesty, almost as an act of pilgrimage. Their numbers have increased with the looming loss of this natural wonder, as those both from within China and from abroad seek to experience the Three Gorges before they are reduced to a mere memory. This act of physical and historical disruption may potentially, therefore, serve as a focal point for all those who are increasingly disturbed with the direction of modernization, for it combines in a single project all the contradictions now haunting the reform policies. Built to feed the seemingly bottom-less maw of marketization, heavily dependent on foreign financing, disrupting the lives of millions of workers and peasants, destroying a priceless natural and historical region, and wiping out one of the premier tourist attractions in China at the very time that that industry is being promoted as a major sector of the economy, the Three Gorges dam is the greatest gamble of all by the reformers.

If the project succeeds, it will become the physical and ideological capstone of "modernization." But should the endeavor fail, or the cost turn out to be insupportable, or the sense grow stronger that it is a monument to the uncontrolled forces of the market, bringing deepening dependency on foreigners, and vast social, historical, and environmental destruction, then it might even become a flashpoint for the renewal of the class struggle in China. If there is a single action that could raise the economic and political contradictions of the reforms beyond the breaking point, construction of the Three Gorges project could well play that role—and it must be reversed quickly, if at all.

"Over the next twenty-four months, the project may well pass the point of no return," according to Yang Guowei, a leading scientist in the state body planning the project.[50] The social pressures linked to the damming of the Changjiang mount every day, not unlike the relentless rise of waters behind the dam itself.

There is a precedent for the massive scale of the Three Gorges project. The woman who served as our escort around China had recently read a book which recounted the history of the building of the Great Wall. In her reaction to the construction of this historical symbol of the creative power of the Chinese lay all the contradictory emotions which surround massive modern projects such as the Three Gorges dam as well—though she herself did not raise this parallel. On the one hand was her pride in the vastness of the accomplishment, and the knowledge that no other society on earth had erected something of such enormity, utility, and beauty all in a single object. For her, the Great Wall stood as a historical monument to the greatness of the Chinese people, and their determination never to fall beneath the sway of any foreign power. Yet she could not help but express at the same time her horror at the cost in human life and social wealth which had gone into its construction. She spoke of the women whose husbands and sons had gone off to work on the Great Wall, never to return, of families forced to spend their entire lives slaving in its ever-lengthening shadow. Finally, she concluded, the horrible suffering could not be forgiven, yet without it the legacy of Chinese history would have been greatly diminished, and some of the tremendous contribution of those of the past lost to present generations.

There was in the complexity of her feelings more than an echo of the current dilemma facing China. The glories and lessons of the Chinese past still live in the present generation, which in turn both destroys and builds on the historical record, all in the light of that modern revolutionary knowledge which understands the costs of progress for the masses of the people, and the role which the class struggles of workers, peasants, and intellectuals play in it. The issues raised by these historic contradictions are not easily resolved. In moving forward, the record of the past, and its preservation and destruction, will be powerful factors in China, today and tomorrow. As opposing class forces contend for control, and the masses of people begin to assert their power once again as the ultimate arbiters of social development, history will continue to be employed as a guide and a weapon in the struggle to shape the future of Chinese society.

OF HUMAN RIGHTS
AND WRONGS:
CHINA AND THE UNITED STATES

It should hardly have come as a surprise that the March 1994 visit of Secretary of State Warren Christopher to Beijing, calling on the Chinese government to improve its human rights record under the threat of denying it renewal of Most Favored Nation trade status, ended in fiasco. The attitudes and conditions observed while teaching and travelling in China make clear why the U.S. human rights policy toward that nation was virtually certain to be rejected. Conversations with Chinese, most of whom were students, showed that the effort of Washington to act as the enforcer of universal standards in their country is meeting not only with official rejection, but with very strong popular opposition. An understanding of this reaction requires altering the perspective from which the issue is commonly approached in the United States, and questioning the very definition of human rights that prevails there. To do so reveals that the U.S. government and people have as much to learn from the Chinese in this area, as vice versa. These "lessons" for the United States regarding human rights are similar to the ones being voiced across Asia, from Japan to Singapore. But in China, they draw not only on deep historical and cultural differences, but on the experience of decades of socialist revolution.

The 150 or so graduate students that my wife and I taught were from the very "Tiananmen generation" that filled U.S. television screens with their antigovernment protests in 1989, which ended in the terrible events of June 3 and 4 and the continuing repression of dissidents down to today. These young people keenly felt the restrictions placed on their ability to communicate freely and to influence the policies of their country. It was all the more striking, therefore, that among these students support for the Chinese government in its showdown with the United States over human rights was both widespread and intense. In our many discussions of this issue both inside and outside class, not a single student voiced anything but opposition—often with great anger—to the prospect of Washington applying economic sanctions to China. Indeed, it was on this subject, more than once, that the most passive and seemingly apolitical students, or those most attracted to Western culture, suddenly spoke up forcefully. Given this indication of popular backing of official policy among the very group where it might be expected to be weakest, it was virtually a given that China would stonewall the U.S. administration on this issue.

To understand the apparent anomalies of this situation, it is necessary to look carefully at the Chinese attitude on human rights, especially in relation to the United States and the world community. Most treatments of this question in the U.S. media, paralleled by the stand of leading organizations active in this area, simply parrot the administration's position that the Chinese government is a major violator of international standards, with the only debate being over which forms of pressure are most appropriate and likely to bring about necessary changes. This view assumes that the United States stands for universal values, and that it has the right to serve as their global enforcer in China. By extension, much has been made at times of the supposed "conflict" between the U.S. government and certain multinational corporations, who are said to put business interests above the need for human rights in dealing with the Chinese. That the United States might actually have something positive to learn from China on this issue does not even arise for those who start from this perspective.

The occasional effort to be sensitive to opposing Chinese attitudes on human rights usually takes the form only of noting that China does not have a history of Western-style political democracy and individual liberties. But this still leaves China defined in essentially negative terms, as simply lacking what we have. Even more infrequently, the Chinese assertion that national sovereignty and economic justice must also be part of the human rights agenda is mentioned. But these are almost never explored in depth, the implication being that such issues are of lesser value, and perhaps advanced by the Chinese government only as a cover, to deflect attention from its problems with "real" human rights. The corollary, sometimes stated openly, at other times implied, is that the U.S. quarrel is only with the authorities in Beijing, it being assumed that the people of China share opposition to their government on this issue and would welcome intervention from outside.

Our Chinese students did indeed voice human rights complaints, the most frequent of which concerned the lack of greater freedom of speech and of a nongovernmental press. The vagueness of available information could indeed be quite striking, exemplified by the faculty member from a university in Changchun—obviously well informed and erudite in most respects—who felt the need to ask us, almost five years after the event, whether it was true that tanks had really crushed demonstrators at Tiananmen Square. Even reports of local events from that time were sparse and sometimes wildly at variance. Students were also clearly distressed that there were no regular channels through which government policies could be openly criticized, much less changed. In all probability, these concerns overlay even deeper fears that were not necessarily exposed to us as temporary foreign visitors. But these students nevertheless offered strong support for the three primary objections raised by the government of China to the U.S. attempt to impose its human rights conception on others.

First is the problem of a double standard. Leaving aside U.S. creation of and support for some of the worst violators of human rights in the world, such as the Guatemalan military regime, the Chinese question the United States in its own practices. Tiananmen? How about Panama City six months later? Tibet? What about Puerto Rico? Refusal to accept universal international standards? But the United States itself stonewalled the World Court ruling to pay reparations to Nicaragua. Police repression? All our students had seen Rodney King beaten on TV and the widespread destruction that followed. Political dissidents? A short list for the United States would have to include those imprisoned, murdered, or driven into exile, such as Leonard Peltier, Puerto Rican *independentistas*, and the black victims of the FBI counterintelligence program COINTELPRO. Prison labor? While we were in China, the press was reporting on the growing U.S. export of goods produced by prisoners. None of these parallels are exact, and any given student was usually familiar with only some of them. But all knew enough about these and other similar situations that, whatever their own attitude toward Chinese human rights, they believed strongly that the United States comes with filthy hands, hypocrisy, and arrogance to the role of global enforcer in their country.

Our students in China also insisted that national sovereignty is just as much an issue of human rights as are individual liberties. Thus the very attempt of the United States to impose its will on the Chinese is seen as violating their human right to self-determination. As an immensely old and proud culture, now attempting to regain its position as a global leader, China sees the current human rights pressure from the West as just one more attempt to "civilize" the Chinese, right in line with the missionaries, opium, and gunboats of old. Thus our students were deeply suspicious that the human rights issue is being used as another imperialist weapon to keep China down. They put it in the same category as the denial of the Chinese bid for Beijing to host the Olympics in the year 2000, under pressure from the United States and Britain, and expressed particular outrage that the U.S. House of Representatives, referring to human rights issues, passed a resolution opposing their Olympic request. They found equally hypocritical the sudden last-minute passion of the Hong Kong authorities for "democracy" after 150 years of appointed colonial government and just three years before reversion to China. Citing as well such conflicts as the *Yinhe* freighter incident in the fall of 1993, in which the United States falsely accused the Chinese of shipping military chemicals to Iran and interfered with free passage of the ship in international waters, many spoke bitterly of the self-appointed U.S. role as "global police."

But the most critical and basic issue is the question of what kind of "human rights" are considered universal standards. We lived in a northeast Chinese industrial and university city of 2 million people, only now beginning to feel the full effects of the marketization policies of the government. Still following earlier socialist principles, workers in the local auto factories were paid approximately twice as much as most of the faculty at our school, while the population as a whole enjoyed high levels of collective welfare and relative egalitarianism. Despite a very low general economic level there were no public signs of homelessness, and in four and a half months, we saw two people with physical problems begging at the local temple, and what seemed to be a single "bag lady." When the weather turned bitter cold, a couple more adult beggars showed up in the downtown tunnels. But we never saw a single child beg, or so much as ask a stranger for candy or chewing gum. There was practically no crime, and women walked freely alone at night. Having lived in and around New York City, I was particularly struck by the way people moved down the generally dark streets without checking out who was approaching them, even from behind. Our students enjoyed a virtually free education, including at the graduate level, and looked forward to guaranteed jobs, with health care and housing—all remnants of the socialist system. Indeed, about half of them came directly to the university from work units, to which they frequently made return visits even during the academic year.

Despite the emphasis from a U.S. standpoint on governmental domination of China, we began to feel there what "civil" society means. For those living and working in such an environment, the idea that the United States—a vastly wealthy country with several dozen billionaires, but in which many millions are unemployed and without

health insurance and hundreds of thousands live homeless on the
streets, and strangers are shot just for knocking on the wrong door—
could serve as the global enforcer of universal human rights, seemed
simply ludicrous. For these students, however, what was hardest of all
to understand was why African-Americans and Latinos have to periodically burn down the centers of major cities to call attention to their
never-ending oppression and poverty. Over and over, I was asked why
the U.S. government does not do something to end these conditions.
While their own view of the Chinese treatment of minority nationalities was undoubtedly too rosy, their attitudes at least reflected the
official line that the non-Han peoples are equals and that their regions
should receive special economic advantages on the road to development. Raised in a system with a socialist conception of governmental
activism and a media that constantly presents positive images of
minorities, the idea that any society would allow a problem like the
U.S. inner cities to fester endlessly without any serious attempt to
address it on the national level was beyond their ken.

    In trying to explain this gap in social perception and policy, my most
effective method was to read them a *New York Times* article from a few
years back concerning a court ruling that the homeless in Grand
Central Station had the right to beg, but only because they were
protected under the free speech provisions of the First Amendment.
As it turned out, even this freedom proved less sacrosanct than the
right of corporate commuters not to have to look into the faces of the
human wreckage the U.S. capitalist system produces, and the decision
was soon reversed. My students, nevertheless, got the point: that in
the United States there is no human rights guarantee against starva-
tion, homelessness, unemployment, or lack of health care, only the
political freedom to protest—sometimes—that one is starving, homeless, jobless, or dying. Or as the plaintiff in the begging case himself
put it after his temporary victory, "It's wonderful.... It's not just for me.
It's for everybody that's panhandling." But still, he conceded, "It's
hard to get real excited about winning the right to beg."[1] As much as
they themselves yearned for greater freedom to speak, write, and
complain freely, the U.S. "trade-off" of political for economic rights did
not strike these Chinese students, either, as especially exciting, and it
certainly did not represent for them a standard of universal justice.

    In this same vein, when I once remarked to one of my classes that I
felt much freer talking openly about socialist concepts with them than
I ever had in a classroom in the United States, one student replied, only
half jokingly: "At least in China, we can discuss both socialism and
capitalism." Still, many of them made clear that they envied the human
right to speak relatively more freely that, as a U.S. citizen, they believed

I enjoyed. I assured them that, having accepted the teaching position in China in large measure because I lacked regular employment and adequate health coverage for myself and my family in the United States, and that I would soon return to the same conditions (as indeed I did), the envy flowed both ways. The idea that the freedom to complain about joblessness and no medical coverage is a fundamental human right, but that jobs and health care are not, seemed ridiculous in China.

The attitudes of our students affirmed on the popular level the official Chinese response to the annual global human rights review issued by the U.S. State Department. China objects especially to the self-appointment of Washington as world judge.

> At present, the United States is the only country which publishes a report every year to pass judgments based on the concepts of value and human rights of its own upon human rights conditions in each of the more than 190 other countries and regions in the world. The US State Department has never justified itself for this; what countries or what world meetings have ever granted the United States the "global Judge of Human rights" status and empowered it to place itself above all other countries of the world.[2]

The Chinese point to numerous conditions and incidents in the United States which exemplify its hypocrisy in this area. Citing U.S. State Department allegations of the imprisonment of religious activists in China, the official response notes the example of the "Family of Jesus" in Shandong Province, whose leader, a la David Koresh, was accused of financial corruption, imposing group marriages, and allowing poor living conditions and sanitation, malnutrition, and "children ... deprived of parental care." It contrasts Chinese actions with those in Waco.

> In dealing with the cult, the local government did not follow the example set by the US Government which sent armoured cars to attack a Branch Davidian Sect manor and burned more than 80 people there to death. Instead, it banned the cult in accordance with law and the demand of the broad masses of the people and with regard to those who had been cheated, it educated them and helped them go back home, leaving only the so-called "chief of the family" to be dealt with by the public security authorities for his violation of the law.

Through such comparisons, people in China become well-versed in the brutality with which Washington deals with its own misfits, and its hypocrisy in citing abuses by the Chinese authorities—however valid those accusations may be in their own right. Given U.S. social conditions, China has no lack of reasons to object to Washington sitting in judgment on others.

> As a matter of fact, the United States itself has grave human rights problems. The US Government admitted last year that the homeless in

the country numbered 7 million, of whom 2 or 3 million lived on the streets.

China estimates it has only 150,000 without homes, despite having almost five times the U.S. population. Chinese observers also note the rising poverty rate in the United States, 15.1 percent in 1993, and 22.7 percent for children. They point to the Department of Education estimate that 21 percent of U.S. high school students are armed with guns, and that "Americans' lives are threatened, the number of people killed or wounded by bullets exceeding all other countries," with Washington, D.C., in particular, known as the "capital of murder." They stress the 1.3 million prisoners in the United States, giving it the highest rate of incarceration in the world—though it may since have been surpassed by Russia—while China claims to have only some 1.2 million imprisoned, despite five times the population. As the U.S. government points to the poor quality of Chinese prisons, it ignores this abysmal quantitative gap, which China attributes to its own rehabilitative approach and low recidivism rate, which it claims is 8 percent versus 41 percent for U.S. repeat offenders.

But it is above all the racial situation in the United States—exemplified by the one third of young black males either in jail or in the criminal justice system—that the Chinese authorities highlight as indicative of both the depravity and hypocrisy of Washington, even as it casts stones at the record of others. Noting the prevalence of racism in all aspects of U.S. life, the official response continues:

> If the US government is sincere about human rights, it should do its utmost to improve the abominable human rights conditions in its own country, rather than covering them up by attacking others on the issue.[3]

In the Chinese view, the very imposition of U.S. standards on other people is an extension of the racism of its domestic society: "Such a practice is a new form of racial discrimination in current world affairs."[4] But as a Chinese delegate to the UN Commission, Peng San, noted, racist policy in the guise of human rights "is more 'deceptive.'"

> "With this protective facade, the abhorrent racism turns into the embodiment of justice, hegemonists into saviours, and interventionists into human rights defenders. Victimized countries and peoples, on the other hand, all become human rights violators."[5]

In this respect, China calls attention to the failure of the United States, as of early 1995, to ratify UN Conventions on racism, as well as those addressing women and the treatment of prisoners—even as it violated a 1981 General Assembly resolution explicitly opposing the use of human rights to intervene in the internal affairs of other states.

Through such selective and arbitrary application of international standards, in the Chinese view, the United States tries to assert hegemony, while covering up its own violations.

> The basis, prerequisite and core of human rights are equality. Human rights within a country should ensure that everyone is equal while human rights within the international community should first of all ensure that all states are equal.[6]

All differences can be settled without difficulty, "so long as dialogues are conducted on the basis of full equality and non-interference in each other's internal affairs." However:

> If confrontation is conducted, pressure exerted, and the human rights issue used for political motives or as a pretext for changing the economic, political and social system of other countries, such practise of hegemonism and power politics will only bring about disasters to the cause of human rights in the world.[7]

Thus if some countries claim the role of global cop in this area, it can only lead to worldwide conflict and chaos on the issue.

The U.S. use of human rights to pressure China is seen as just one aspect of a larger agenda: "Is there anyone who is not clear about the political motives in this?"[8]

> China is firmly opposed to clique politics, hegemony and exploitation of human rights for political purposes because these represent a continuation of the Cold War mentality and serve only to hinder dialogue.[9]

What the United States cannot accept, in the view of the Chinese, is the right of each people to their own social, economic, and political system.

> Zhang Hongyi, a professor with Beijing Normal University, said the real aim of the US Human Rights Report is to deteriorate the ideological system of China.
> Due to American animosity and anxiety toward communism, the US would set many obstacles for the Chinese Government.[10]

Not human rights per se, therefore, but the remnants of the socialist political and economic system of China is the target.

As the Chinese emphasize, there is nothing new about any of this. It is simply a continuation of historic imperialism.

> Some of the co-sponsors of the anti-China resolution still owe a debt to China because of their own past actions. But now they pretend to be defenders of human rights and improperly criticize China's internal affairs, which will undoubtedly spark indignation among the Chinese people.[11]

These hegemonic relations extend to the UN Commission itself, where the United States relies on third world client states such as Nicaragua, El Salvador, the Philippines, and Egypt, to protect U.S. interests—for example, to reject a Cuban call in 1995 to condemn racism in the United States.

> In an effort to force the adoption of this year's draft resolution against China, its main co-sponsors, particularly the US, vigorously lobbied and even unscrupulously attempted to coerce some members of the Human Rights Commission.
>
> Such a behaviour has laid bare their true nature of hegemonism and power politics.[12]

That the human rights pressure on China is just one part of a larger U.S. global strategy is evidenced by its own selectivity.

> The United States has co-sponsored a human rights resolution on China every year since the 1989 military crackdown on the Tiananmen Square democracy movement, with one exception. That exception was in 1991, when the Bush Administration was seeking China's support for a Persian Gulf war resolution.[13]

Thus in its effort to keep control over the third world in general, the United States must sometimes ease pressure on the Chinese. But this only exposes further its hypocritical posturing, and the larger strategic goals which lie behind its actions in this area. Writing in the early 1980s, James Petras and Morris H. Morley noted the cynicism in the uses of this issue as part of U.S. imperialist strategy.

> In recent months the initial hostility toward the Carter human rights program has been modified in one particular respect: Reagan policy-makers have come to appreciate the utility of the rhetoric both in neutralizing opposition to the new military posture and in promoting an anti-Soviet, Cold War strategy. A memorandum on human rights prepared by the State Department and approved by Secretary of State Alexander Haig in early November stated in part:
>
> " ... 'Human rights'—meaning, political rights and civil liberties—conveys what is ultimately at issue in our contest with the Soviet bloc."[14]

Though the memorandum also discussed the need to oppose "serious abuses" even by "our friends," such policy statements make clear the underlying U.S. position on this issue. "Human rights," in this perspective, are reduced to nothing but political and civil freedoms. But this narrow conception also serves as a perfect cover to obscure, not reveal, the "ultimate issue" in the struggle against socialism, since economic relations and social conditions are completely ignored. It goes without saying that this "anti-Soviet, cold war strategy" has now been transferred, virtually without alteration, to undermine what remains of socialist China and any challenge by it to U.S. "hegemony."

Our students, like the Chinese government, therefore raised yet a fourth aspect of human rights in arguing against the U.S. position, perhaps the most crucial of all in their eyes at the present time. This is the right of third world countries to rise from the poverty and subordination to which the imperialist economic system has consigned them. For China this is the essence of human rights for those still trapped near the bottom of the global economy. In this view, the issue is not only the role of the individual, but collective social development as well. As Chinese delegate Liu Zhenmin told the UN Commission:

> It is hardly possible for one to enjoy all the human rights when a man does not have food or clothing, he said.
> Due to "unreasonable" international economic order, Liu pointed out, most developing countries are suffering from heavy debt, deteriorating trade conditions and lack of financial sources; people there live a nightmare of hunger and poverty.
> Agreeing with some Western countries that "the human person is the central subject of development," the Chinese delegate meanwhile stressed that an inalienable human right, the right to development, is individual and collective. Individual development cannot be isolated from that of a country or a society.[15]

From this standpoint, the recent economic surge in China is itself a major advance in the human rights of its people.

> Thanks to the economic reform during the past 15 years, the living standard of Chinese people has been greatly improved. It has epitomized the improvement of human rights in the country.[16]

For China, this has become an overriding goal, in the pursuit of which other rights can and must for now be restricted. They speak of greater political democratization emerging in time from an expanding economy, in a mirror image of the U.S. claim that all economic problems can ultimately be solved through the normal channels of politics. Both positions may be equally specious. But there is no fundamental reason why either claim should be privileged over the other as a basis for global human rights standards, and China refuses to recognize any such arbitrary assertion. According to Jin Yongjian, head of the Chinese delegation to the 1995 UN Human Rights Commission:

> "China does not oppose the principle of universality of human rights, but we do oppose the attempt to impose on others the so-called universally recognized values of one country or group of countries, totally disregarding the differences between countries and regions in tradition, culture and level of economic development...."[17]

From our experience in Changchun, any idea that the rapidly expanding Chinese economy might have to be slowed down to accommodate political democratization did not have much appeal, and attempts to enforce such a view from outside were once again met by our students with suspicion that they are only meant to hold China back. Almost without exception, these young people insisted that the Chinese system is still socialist and that it should remain so. While they generally expressed support for many of the current market reforms of the government, and were eager to participate in the new consumer society, they at the same time indicated deep misgivings about the growing economic polarization in China, and the massive invasion of foreign investors. With over 1 billion people, and a GNP per capita still at third world levels, they believed that a move to full capitalization of their society would be a disaster, generating dislocations completely beyond social control. Added to this was a nationalist pride and a determination to see China once again become a powerful world player, which fueled resentment at any foreign effort, political, economic, or cultural, to keep the Chinese forever "second rank" within the current global system. This tempered any appeal which Western human rights norms might have had.

Nor, least of all, do they view what is happening in the former Soviet bloc as a model. Contrary to the widely-held image of Chinese students in the United States, the only time I sensed real terror in their voices was, not when they talked about their own government, but when they spoke of the possibility that their country might slide into the economic collapse, social anarchy, and regional conflicts of the former Soviet Union. Much of the support they expressed for the official policy rested on this deeply rooted fear of a breakdown in society—one as ancient as the period of disintegration, warring states, and anarchic conditions which produced the Confucian concept of social order 2,500 years ago, and as recent as the Cultural Revolution. The idea that outside forces, such as the United States through its human rights pressure, might help push their country too into such a state of turmoil was completely abhorrent.

Only against this background must the sometime "conflict" between the U.S. government and business community over the issue of human rights in China be approached. In the eyes of those Chinese who express critical support for a system they still see as socialistic, this is a falling out among thieves. Both the U.S. government and business community have exactly the same goal, the destruction of whatever remains of socialism in China and its conversion into a Western-dominated capitalist country. They are equal in their determination to undermine the economic securities and elements of social justice that are the human rights legacy of the socialist revolution. They only disagree on how to do it. In fact, the U.S. administration itself is primarily caught between two sets of conflicting corporate interests: those who are motivated by the short-term greed for profits through doing business with the Chinese, versus those who fear the growing economic power of China and are driven by the desire to destroy a potential rival, a goal in pursuit of which the human rights issue is just one more convenient tool.

The only "human right" which either the U.S. government or business community has ever consistently fought for is the freedom for some to make capitalist profit off the exploitation and misery of others. Toward this end there is no violation of human rights they have not been willing to commit or condone, no democratically elected government they have not been prepared to overthrow, no socialist society they have not striven to destroy. Only when it fits this larger agenda does the issue of political freedom and civil liberties get raised, and then only very selectively at that. Perfectly expressing this relation, a "compromise" position was floated by the Clinton administration and some in Congress, and backed by exiled dissidents such as Fang Lizhi, in which only state-owned enterprises in China would be subject to trade sanctions, to "'encourage the private sector'... and reduce the impact on American business and on places like Hong Kong and Taiwan."[18] Given the hypocrisy and cynicism of this approach, it is hardly wild speculation to suggest that, should China become fully capitalistic, "human rights" of any kind there would rapidly disappear as a U.S. concern.

Faced with such a choice of "friends" in the United States, many Chinese adopt a "curse on all your houses" stand. They are concerned with making their own society, which today at least is still officially socialist, work better. This certainly includes developing new forms of democratic expression and decision-making. But there is no reason to believe that the best forms of the latter for China are those which were developed in parallel with Western capitalism. As that country knows only too well, any attempt to achieve the simultaneous implementation of human rights in the areas of political freedoms, economic development, and social justice is extremely difficult. The Chinese have had as much and as painful experience with these interlocking struggles as any people on the globe. It behooves the rest of the world, including the United States, to approach them with an attitude of respect and humility, and in the posture of student as much as teacher.

The Chinese government is itself now moving rapidly to dismantle those human rights in which it has hitherto excelled: including full employment, guaranteed housing and health care, and a free educational system through the university level. Travelling from Changchun in the Northeast to the Southern areas which have gone furthest in marketization starkly revealed the effects of this abandonment. The peasant-worker families living in the open and the packs of begging street children around the railroad station in Guangzhou, attest to the "success" of these "reforms." But no whimpers of disapproval will emanate from Washington or Wall Street over this kind of violation of human rights. They will instead greet such phenomena as welcome evidence that China is moving toward a "free" labor market, which is the *sine qua non* of capitalist exploitation, and that the Chinese government is rapidly accepting "Western values," at least in its economic system. Indeed, the 1995 UN Resolution sponsored by the United States on China "praised the Government for improving the lives of its people through economic and legal reforms."[19] By this it no doubt meant the introduction of a market economy and the framework of Western-style laws needed to implement it, the very policies which are devastating former social securities.

Yet, here too, recognition must be accorded to the deep poverty still evident in much of China, and the success in gross economic terms of the current marketization policies. The difficulty of achieving rapid development while maintaining social justice is a contradiction which the Chinese must also be free to sort out by themselves. As they do so, they ask only that the United States and the rest of the world approach the issue of human rights in a spirit of mutual respect and learning. For the U.S. government, on the other hand, the right to define which human rights get stressed and enforced is the essence of what it means to be the dominant global power, one more tool in its control of the international system. It is no more willing to accept an equality of exchange on this question than in any other relation to China or the rest of the world.

As valuable as the form of political freedoms and civil liberties advanced by the United States may be, they represent at most only "one-fourth" of a truly global human rights agenda, which must also include national sovereignty, economic justice, and racial and sexual equality. There was once a time, beginning with the Declaration of Independence, when freedom for the nation as a whole was recognized as coequal with and inseparable from political liberty for its people, at least in theory. But the United States has long since become the most consistent and universal invader of the national sovereignty of other countries, and has lost any claim to represent human rights on this issue.

As for economic justice and an end to class exploitation, it never was, and never can be, part of the U.S. agenda for human rights under its present system. Imagine Washington cancelling Most Favored Nation status for Brazil because children there have to search for food in garbage dumps in order to survive. The idea is too laughable even to contemplate. For the U.S. government, freedom from being tortured in prison may sometimes be considered a "human right," but the daily torture of poverty and hunger is just business as usual. Even more beyond the pale is the idea that China or any other country could successfully use trade rights to force the United States to show "overall, significant progress"—the measurement which the U.S. government employs for the Chinese—in providing every adult worker with a decent job or guaranteeing inner-city children the same opportunities as others in the society, much less ending its imperialist intervention in other countries. To truly implement such changes, with all that they imply, would be as basic a threat to those who run the U.S. system as human rights critics claim political democracy would be to the authorities in Beijing. It is questionable if even the democratic practices of the United States itself would survive any serious attempt to bring about such a fundamental revolution in its social order.

The idea that "human rights" can be reduced to political freedoms and civil liberties is to denigrate humanity itself, and says infinitely more about the U.S. social system than it ever can about China. Yet people in the United States have been taught their whole lives that they are "free" because of these limited conceptions, which do not even include such basic democratic powers as control over the corporations that completely dominate their economy. The Chinese experience teaches once again that there is more than this to humanity and a decent society. Nor are such lessons limited to China. After the 1994 murder of two Japanese students in a carjacking near Los Angeles, a television commentator in Japan was quoted as saying: "It's a great thing that the U.S. raises human rights issues in its diplomatic policy. But the most important human right is not to be killed."[20] Until the United States is willing to accept alternative concepts of human rights, from Asians and others, it is bound to fail in its attempts to influence China, and the efforts to address the needs of its own society will end in even greater failure. From the Chinese, in particular, there are aspects to be learned from Asian forms of societal organization, with their emphasis on collective responsibilities and supports, merged with and transformed by socialist revolutionary practice.

If tomorrow word came that the students that we taught were out on the streets in a new wave of protests, it would not be at all surprising. As the contradictions of reform deepen, there is a rising tension in China, under the apparently calm surface. But despite Western presumptions, it is just as likely that Chinese students, workers, and peasants would be out fighting against the loss of human rights most of us in the United States in particular have never had, as to win those we sometimes have and they lack. Indeed as history has amply demonstrated, China may come up with revolutionary answers to its social problems that go far beyond anything people in the West can even dream of at this time. The lessons in human rights we should be learning from the Chinese, even now, may in the near future be added to in ways that break new ground not only for China, but for the United States and the rest of the world.

MEIGUO, ZHONGGUO:
"AMERICA THE BEAUTIFUL"
VERSUS "CHINA THE CENTRAL"

I. Heaven and Hell

In late fall and early winter of 1993, millions of people across China were captivated by a riveting television series, "A Native of Beijing in New York," which follows the lives of a Chinese couple trying to adjust to life in the Big Apple. The drama was an eye-opener for many in China, including students in Changchun. Through it, they had their first in-depth look at social conditions in the United States—even if in a form which seriously distorted the reality of daily life for most Americans. The main character in the series, a highly accomplished cellist from Beijing, is at first shocked to find that as a new immigrant he must earn a living washing dishes in a Chinese restaurant, while his wife, a doctor of traditional medicine in China, works in a garment factory. But in typical "American Dream" style, the husband quickly establishes a liaison with the restaurateur who is his boss, and she gives him the money to set up his own apparel business. Soon, like her, he is living in a beautiful house, enjoying "the good life," having risen from "rags to riches" with an ease that would be the envy of most of the U.S. middle class, not to mention the average worker, much less a recent Chinese immigrant.

Up to this point, the series could only serve to confirm the image of the United States widely held in China, as a land of instant wealth for all who manage to reach its shores. For over a century, this U.S. mirage has drawn Chinese immigrants, and the numbers are once again on the rise. The growing ranks in China of those without work and others seeking opportunities for economic advancement or advanced degrees have generated increasingly desperate attempts to emigrate to the United States. Not only many poor peasants and workers, but professionals too, are joining the exodus.

The character for the United States in Chinese, *mei*, also signifies beauty, and for many of the students we knew in Changchun, as for others at all levels of the society, the idea of "America the Beautiful" had real meaning. They constantly spoke of how "new" the United States is, and asked how such a recently developed country could have obtained so much wealth and power in such a short period of time. These students were already vaguely acquainted with the riches of U.S. life, as television programs increasingly bring them images of wealthy Americans and other foreigners, with their fancy cars, large houses, fashionable clothes, and other material goods. Such consumer items, even those that are common in the United States, appear as luxuries to many Chinese, living as they do in cramped dorms or small apartments, on meager budgets, going everywhere by foot or bicycle, or crammed into old, overcrowded buses and vans.

For many of the students, in particular, U.S.-style consumerism, so recently introduced into China itself, has great appeal. But despite glimpses of the consumer culture, the extremes of life in the United States remain largely beyond the knowledge of most people in China. When I showed my students the mansions in the real estate section of the *New York Times Magazine*, for instance, it bespoke a level of wealth and luxury that was completely inconceivable in their experience. Even the pictures of typical middle-class houses, in the weekly flyer from our local newspaper in upstate New York, appeared as virtual palaces. So too, the relative freedoms of U.S. life, especially for the young, shine for many of them as a kind of lodestone, representing a form of individualistic liberation that was not allowed in traditional Chinese society and has been officially restrained throughout most of the period since the revolution. It is only recently, and then to a very small extent, that such strictures in personal relations have been somewhat relaxed.

Thus for some young people, the greatest hope for the future is to be able to travel to the United States, to live and study, or even settle permanently. It was hard to disabuse our students of the image projected by "A Native of Beijing in New York," or to convince them that while not impossible, the rapid acquisition of wealth depicted there was improbable even for immigrants with professional backgrounds, and certainly did not represent the typical experience of the majority of Chinese-Americans. They were skeptical not so much of the series, but rather of our critical reaction to it. The lure which the United States held for these students was evident in the stream of requests from them and from other young professionals, often among the most intelligent and best-trained, for help in applying to schools there. Still, U.S. visa restrictions, which limit student applicants from China to those who can demonstrate full financial support, make the goal of study or immigration unobtainable for all but the wealthiest or luckiest of these young people anyway.

But the outflow of talent to the United States and other foreign countries continues in spite of such limits, resulting in a serious Chinese "brain drain" over the past decade, a source of deep concern. Among the 1994 graduates from Beijing University, the preeminent institution of higher education, the top five postgraduates in physics and all eight in physiology and biophysics were studying or working outside China as of early 1995. At Qinghua University, another leading school in the capital, of 150 graduates in its renowned architecture department, 60 percent were employed abroad that year.

> The country's brightest are draining away at such a high speed that ever since August 1987, more than 200,000 people have pursued advanced studies abroad. Although most are presumed to have finished their studies there, only 70,000, some one-third, have come back.
> This happens against a pressing background of the aging of the country's current contingent of senior talent.[1]

It is the loss of these young professionals that is the most damaging to China, and the most wounding to its patriotic pride as a growing power in global competition with other world leaders. Young Chinese professionals well know the attraction of working and living conditions abroad, compared to the limitations they face at home.

> Nonetheless, it is really a pity to see intelligent people who have been trained at home dedicating themselves to other countries when they are needed most by their motherland.
> "Flower blossoms in a courtyard sends fragrance beyond the wall." Can this situation be changed and forceful ways to keep both the "flowers" and "fragrance" at home be found?[2]

The government, which sponsored some 40,000 of those in foreign study, now finds itself unable to attract many of them home, especially after crushing the student movement of 1989. In 1992, in an attempt to reverse this situation, Deng Xiaoping himself issued an appeal for the return of all students abroad, after completion of their studies, "regardless of their past political attitude," pledging that they would be well-treated, and appealing to their patriotism in helping to build up China. Since then, both the state and some leading schools have taken steps to try to attract the scholars back, with housing and salary incentives, promises of research facilities, and patriotic appeals. In

Shanghai, enterprises set up by returning students are granted the same privileges as "overseas" firms funded from Hong Kong, Macao, and Taiwan. But despite some successes in this regard, it is the values promoted by the market socialist economic system itself which are driving more and more students to seek individual opportunity abroad, and the return flow, which has drawn many nationals and especially professionals of other Asian countries home to work in the rapidly expanding economies of the region, seems not yet to have swept through the communities of Chinese living in the United States.

On a more popular level, the same growing pressures for emigration are also felt, and the attempt to obtain visas to the United States, so often frustrated, can take bizarre turns. One New York entrepreneur has been selling off square-inch lots in each of the fifty states for $29.95 to Chinese "investors." Though billed as a kind of fun fad, comparable to owning a "pet rock," the scheme took on more serious dimensions for those seeking to emigrate.

> In China, a limited edition sale of 100,000 immediately sold out and reportedly sparked riots, prompting criticism that Chinese buyers were misled into thinking that owning an inch was good for getting a visa. It isn't.[3]

Faced with this kind of desperation, the appeals of leaders in China to patriotic sentiments have a plaintive ring, especially when addressed to those living outside the mainland. Thus they too have initiated an "Own a Piece of Your Chinese Homeland" campaign, part of a national tourism program, in which 9.6 million certificates, each costing $100 and representing the ownership of a square inch of "homeland gardens" being built in each province, will be sold in overseas communities. In this "battle of the square inches," it is doubtful if such schemes will result in a large-scale return flow to China. But it is quite likely, on the other hand, that any attempt to cut back forcefully on the right to emigration, so recently relaxed, could cause social unrest on the Chinese mainland.

Even those who do not seek to emigrate often turn instead to trying to introduce into their own society more of the lifestyles and values they associate with the United States. Virtually all of our students expressed the belief that it was necessary for China to advance economically like the United States. Thus U.S. cultural and political values, its materialism and economic power, in some respects were a standard against which they were constantly measuring Chinese society as it seeks to "modernize" and "open its door" to the rest of the world. Viewed in this light, China can appear not only old but "backward," and some of our students did describe their own country in just such negative terms, contrasting its tradition-bound social order with the youth and vigor of the United States. The weight of the past lies heavily on Chinese society, and poverty, even after decades of revolution and marketization, remains the common lot of hundreds of millions. Even most professionals have a lifestyle which is only the faintest reflection of the middle-class lives of their Western peers. It is easy in such circumstances to make a connection, as some of our students did, between the drag of history and the lack of "development," to believe that its ancient ways of doing things have prevented China from emerging more rapidly as a modern industrialized country, open to the world and "ready for business." Such an attitude promotes efforts to learn from and imitate the ways of the West, and in particular those of the United States, not only in economics and politics, but in the cultural realm.

Yet even when they seemed closest to a Western lifestyle, these students exhibited, as measured by "international youth culture" standards, a kind of quaintness that more closely resembled the United States of the 1950s than that of the 1990s. Their ballroom-style dances—which also reflect Soviet influence—and parlor games and hand-holding couples were more reminiscent of the high school scene of my youth than of any recognizable expression of the current U.S. college generation. Even the occasional rock dance performed between more traditional numbers at student holiday celebrations seemed more like a 1950s talent show than a soulful rendering of modern pop culture. This imitative quality conveyed the sense that the West sets the cultural as well as the economic and political standards. For those who want to be "modern," as defined by the leading capitalist countries—the United States above all—China can only poorly and belatedly copy the world powers, an endless catch-up game in which the goal post is always receding. From this viewpoint, there was something rather discordant and disturbing in watching these vibrant young students trying to act like their Western peers.

Yet the Chinese reaction to U.S. society contains deeper and more complex contradictions. "A Native of Beijing in New York" itself soon takes a darker turn, especially in family relations. The leading couple in the series quickly breaks up, and the wife marries and then divorces her American boss. The restaurant owner too, for all her beauty and wealth, struggles to maintain a relation with the child of her own failed marriage. When she also tries to provide her son with the traditional Chinese medicine she believes he needs, she is met with the scorn of her former U.S. husband, and his white male doctors and lawyers, who turn her use of such "primitive" cures against her attempts to regain custody—though she is ultimately successful. But it is the arrival from China of the daughter of the Beijing couple, her distress at the disintegration of the relationship between her parents, and her rapid conversion into a typical rebellious U.S. teenager who ends up marrying the father of one of her schoolmates, that conveys the fullest image of the cultural clash and dissolution of social bonds, especially those of family, that marks U.S. society.

The bitterness of this portrait of familial collapse is inseparable from the overarching theme of "A Native of Beijing in New York," that there are Chinese and American ways of doing things that are fundamentally at odds. In the end, not only does the "hero" lose his family, but most of his money as well, as he is viciously outmaneuvered by the ex-husband of his ex-wife in the cutthroat world of New York business. The "moral," such as it is, is that in the United States nothing counts but making a fast buck, and families are as impermanent as wealth. Still, with typical Yankee spirit, the lead character picks himself up to start all over again, and the series ends on a hopeful, if unresolved and problematic note.

"A Native of Beijing in New York" thus confirmed for our students both their best hopes and worst fears about the United States. It reinforced the idea that quick wealth and luxurious consumerism are the U.S. norm, even if they can be easily lost and must be won over and over again. But that these riches could be bought only at such a high cost, especially to family life, came as a surprise and shock, and had a sobering effect, taking away much of their glamour. It illustrated for these students that "to get rich" like people in the United States may be "glorious," but it comes at a steep social price. For these young persons, most of whom talked of returning home after their university training was completed so that they could live near and care for their aging parents, "family values" still had real meaning, and the picture of complete familial dissolution conveyed by the television series was shocking. They were particularly appalled by the attitude of the teenage daughter, whose almost total lack of "filial piety" was deeply disturbing, even in this age of loosening social bonds. That the surface image of U.S. wealth and freedom could hide such widespread family breakups and social dislocations put a sharp edge on whatever yearning these students might have had to make China over in the "American way," and threw a different perspective on their own society and its accelerating rush to Westernized modernization.

Their misgivings were hardly unrealistic, given the breakdown of traditional familial relations already beginning to occur in China. One indication of this is the growth of a new Chinese occupation, *peilao*, or companion to the elderly—most commonly retired intellectuals—whose own children no longer live near them. The job is "increasingly popular in Shanghai," where rising numbers of young people have been leaving home to pursue careers opened up by marketization. In a typical case, "One elderly couple felt very lonely after retiring from their university posts. Their children had gone abroad and their eyesight and hearing were failing, so they hired a college student."[4] Companionship often deepens on both sides. But such "substitute families," based on cash, indicate the ways in which market forces are insinuating themselves even into the most personal relationships. It is against this growing background that our students viewed "A Native of Beijing in New York."

Deeper discussion of the United States made clear that whatever general knowledge these young people had about current conditions there was either grossly inadequate or had been largely suppressed in their eagerness to absorb the more glittering aspects of U.S. culture. Though they had some awareness of certain issues like crime and police brutality, the scale of the social pathologies of the United States was largely beyond their ken. They were all but stunned to hear of the extent of homelessness and desperate poverty, of middle-class families unable to afford even basic health care, of expanding sweatshop exploitation, much of it based on immigrant labor from China, paying as little as $.65 per hour for eighty-four hours of weekly work,[5] of the bottomless depths of racial and ethnic conflict, and of children with guns killing each other and anyone else who gets in their way. It reminded them that Chinese society too had once been deeply divided by class and region, with vast wealth at the top and deepest poverty at the bottom, and that becoming more like "America the Beautiful" today meant turning China again into a land riven by polarization of classes, regional divisions, loss of social stability, and threats even to family structure.

Nor did the glimpse of current U.S. ethnocentrism as seen in the television series—especially the view of Chinese medicine as backward and primitive—sit well with our students. They would arrive at our apartment at the first news that we were sick with little bottles of a traditional cure, the most potent ingredient of which was snake bile, and which proved to be very effective against winter respiratory problems. Many students continued to use the old-style medicines, though they complained that these were bitter to the taste and slow to work. Such methods are still very popular and widespread. The Cultural Revolution was fought, among other issues, over whether Chinese medical practices would be taught and used on an equal basis with Western-derived ones. Traditional care had been disparaged by the modern elite of urban-based doctors—though there were also cases in which it was attacked by Red Guards as being one of the "old things" to be suppressed. Largely as a result of the struggles of that time, the ancient cures are still a basic element in the medical system of China today, even in up-to-date and urbanized institutions. Thus the mother of one of our students, just like the wife in the television series, was a doctor in a municipal hospital specializing in traditional medicine. Across China there are 2,530 such facilities. Major hospitals in Changchun, as elsewhere, also often have separate wings for the practice of Chinese and Western-based methods. Patients choose which they prefer, and doctors frequently combine elements of each in a single course of treatment.

The issue of how the traditional medicines of China are viewed in the West is more than just one of cultural differences, however. It is at once a practical issue of international trade and a symbol of the growing clash between Asia and the U.S.-dominated global system. For the Chinese have not only become the second largest producer of "Western" pharmaceuticals in the world, after the United States, with exports of well over $1 billion annually, but they have also been pushing sales of the traditional cures, now a rapidly expanding indus-try, increasingly mass-produced under modern scientific and techno-logical conditions. A conference in April, 1995 in Beijing brought together some 800 doctors working in this field, many of them from ethnic minority regions, all winners of prizes for research papers. The meeting also promoted the compilation of a Chinese-initiated encyclo-pedia of worldwide indigenous medical practices. A national Acad-emy of Traditional Chinese Medicine operates clinics and promotes research, and since 1982 the government itself has sponsored a study in which almost 13,000 herbal plants and animal products were iden-tified as useful raw materials. It is common to hear reports of near-mi-raculous breakthroughs using such methods. New laws now regulate the production, prescription, and sale of these products. In one recent case, an employee in a pharmaceutical plant was charged with the crime of revealing "state secrets" for supplying a traditional medicine formula to three confederates who produced and marketed the cure on the black market.

Western disparagement of these ancient practices, as seen in "A Native of Beijing in New York," thus not only denigrates Chinese cultural tradition, but challenges the ability of the country to emerge as a leader in the modern world, using its past experience as a resource. Efforts by China to popularize its traditional medical techniques inter-nationally have met with considerable resistance. As a leader of the Chinese Chamber of Commerce of Medicines and Health Products Importers and Exporters, Cui Bin, noted:

> traditional Chinese medicines have encountered difficulties in tapping the world market....

> Because the principles of Chinese medicine differ from those of western
> medicines, meeting western countries' standards on imported medicine
> has been difficult.[6]

The growth in exports has been hampered, therefore, not only by the
differing cultural tastes, limits of knowledge, and greater inconve-
nience sometimes associated with some of these techniques, but by
insistence that traditional Chinese products meet the norms of Western
medical science. Yet it is their variance from such standards that may
make them so effective. Such differences limit the ability of China to
gain acceptance for its alternative medicines, and serve as a convenient
nontariff barrier to expanded exports. Thus, issues of culture, trade,
and Western-derived "universal" standards are all wrapped up in
even such a "little" conflict as that over Chinese medicine.

In raising such opposing worldviews, "A Native of Beijing in New
York" exposed not only the extremes of U.S. life—though virtually
nothing of its more common and drab daily existence—but many of
the basic contradictions of the relationship between Asia and the West,
and especially China and the United States. Referring to the lines with
which each episode opens—"If you love him, take him to New York,
because it's heaven; if you hate him, take him to New York, because
it's hell"—one commentator noted:

> The series does not take delight in telling a love triangle but focuses on
> conflicts between Chinese and Western culture, psychology and con-
> cepts of values.
> The series objectively reflects the two sides of the "Big Apple": skyscrap-
> ers and slums, luxury and poverty, fierce competition and tender feeling.
> Critics say that the series will help Chinese TV viewers better under-
> stand American society and remind those who entertain a rosy American
> dream to become cool-headed....
> Whether the United States is a "heaven" or "hell" is a "hard nut" left for
> viewers to crack. But one fact is clear: the United States is a battleground
> on which everyone has to confront challenges of different kinds from the
> womb to the tomb.[7]

Viewing Chinese society from the perspective of "A Native of Beijing
in New York," the issue of who is "advanced" and who "primitive,"
who the leader and who the follower, was a major theme underlying
the personal stories of the protagonists. Thus even as they were
attracted by the glitter of New York, students sensed behind the screen
deeper and darker issues, not only within U.S. life, but in the relation
of the United States and China as well.

The cultural clash which was so striking in the television series had
such power, therefore, because beneath the drama of what happens to
Chinese trying to adjust to the United States, there are larger implications,

raising basic questions about the direction which China itself should take, and its role within the present U.S.-dominated global system. In watching "A Native of Beijing in New York," Chinese were not only gaining new insight into the United States, but into the choices which they themselves must now make about their own society. With marketization bringing new-found wealth, but at the cost of ripping apart much of the traditional structure of their culture, they could glimpse in the series their own possible future, if they try to catch up with and imitate the leading capitalist power. At the same time, the series was a warning that with renewed attempts to "open to the world," China once again confronts old dangers in the reimposition of foreign values, and a return to a past of Western disparagement and even domination which it thought it had escaped once and for all since it "stood up" in the Revolution.

II. "China Century"

The same kinds of doubts and contradictions raised by "A Native of Beijing in New York" also riddled the image of the "new" United States, whose quick rise to power and wealth students in Changchun so admired. Just as in its domestic society, so too in its role as international leader, the U.S. experience presents a dual image to the Chinese, of successful economic "superpower" on the one hand, and as international cop and bully on the other. Of course these young people know that the achievement of global dominance by the United States, together with the European powers, followed by Japan, was accomplished only through centuries of imperialism and neocolonialism, not least of all in China itself. Yet teaching U.S. history to these students, it became apparent that they were often unfamiliar with the full extent of the imperialist basis for its speedy climb to wealth and power, accompanied by genocide, slavery, and a vast continental land-grab, and its predatory and exploitative rise to superpower status. From this perspective too "America the Beautiful" looked a bit more tarnished, and the inability of the Chinese to repeat its experience—even were the United States itself to be dethroned—was obvious. It reminded these students of what they already certainly knew, but many had repressed in their eagerness to embrace the image of the United States as a model of economic advancement and cultural modernism: that Euro-American and Japanese imperialism rose up only in the process of driving the Chinese people down, and that current international leaders, and especially the U.S. ruling circles, would not take lightly to the idea of China reclaiming its historic position as the dominant regional power in Eastern Asia, let alone its rise as a global force.

When viewed from this historical perspective, many Chinese expressed the belief that it was their own social order that was "new," and the United States that was "old" and tired, a worn-out and dissolute imperial power, attempting to cling to its role despite the pathologies of its own society—an attitude that is now widespread through much of the Pacific Rim. In the classroom, almost without exception, students talked of their personal projects in terms of achieving national goals, which were invariably defined in terms of building up China as a great economic power and a modern society, ready and able to reclaim its historic role and to challenge even U.S. dominance. For these young Chinese, there was a sense of unity between their own lives and the well-being of the general social order, and they expressed a strong dedication to its rapid improvement. Over and over again they stated their determination to devote their studies and work to the building of a modern and powerful nation, in which the advancement of both their own individual careers and of the country as a whole were seen as virtually inseparable, each naturally complementing the other. On the most personal level, this was evidenced in Changchun, as across China, by the vigor of the young people, who rose before dawn, even in the depths of a bitter winter, to run around the campus in groups or singly, passing their elders, who were themselves performing Taijiquan exercises in open spaces cleared of the snow. There was a freshness and sense of social unity, participation, and purpose in all this early morning activity that contrasts most sharply with the jaded cynicism that marks so much of U.S. life and culture today, especially among the youth.

In a similar vein, at holiday assemblies, these young people performed traditional folk dances with amazing skill and beauty, clearly delighting in the celebration of their past culture, in a way that would no doubt be dismissed as "boring" by the current student body at almost any U.S. university today. Thus in sharpest contrast with "Generation X," students in China seemed to know very well who they were and what their purpose in life was, guided by a moral sense, and in close linkage with the development of the nation and society as a whole—despite the confusion of values and social transformations which are rapidly altering their lives. These attitudes, which are not limited to mainland Chinese, are further reflected in popular "campus ballads," which began in Taiwan in the 1980s, and have titles like "My Deskmate" and "Brother Sleeping on My Upper Bed." As a newspaper report described, they have a "simple theme (love, friendship, and some immature thought to life and society), a simple melody and a simple instrument."[8] They reflect, according to Huang Xiaomao, the head of Dadi Music Company, "the sincere heartbeat of a college student. That's the most precious quality of the campus ballad, which is just what we need in a society charged with economic dynamics but lack of moral sense"—though here too, with the recent revival of this form on the mainland, "some music companies and businessmen obsessed with profit ... overexploited it frenziedly."

On the official level, this same approach is revealed in the constant meetings which occur at all levels, discussing the next steps to be taken to develop the economy or improve the society. One feels in China a universal determination to deal with the issues of their own social order, without the distraction of pretensions to world dominance that plague "the last remaining superpower." The Chinese are confronting the need to build up their own society with a single-mindedness which has all but disappeared from politics in the United States, where virtually all public discussion of social goals is intentionally obscured by the playing off of class, race, and sex divisions, by extreme assertions of individualistic freedoms, and by the "necessity" to maintain its position at the top of the global system, a goal which all but prevents any attempt to deal with its domestic needs. By contrast, even for those who oppose much of what is being done in China in the name of market reform, it is impossible not to be impressed by the dedication to collective social advancement that is felt at all levels of the society, and which informs the most personal activities. Even slogans such as "to get rich is glorious" won support in large measure because they were advanced in the name of building up the entire economy, and the most individualized pursuits still carry with them today a sense of participation in a great new national endeavor.

Despite their envy of the United States, our students thus also expressed a very strong sense that China was again on the move, rising together with the rest of Asia, and including a belief that the Chinese have both the right and the potential strength to challenge U.S. power, economically and politically. Many in the younger generation, in particular, see themselves as the heirs to past Chinese greatness, working to transform their country into a modern nation that will reclaim the historic position of China as the leading and dominant power of Asia and for centuries the most highly developed culture in the world. Their personal enthusiasm and energy was directly related to the conception of Chinese society as becoming once again the center of a resurgent Asian region, and even bidding for global leadership. It thus carries with it the possibility of a reversal of international roles, and a revival of traditional Chinese power, raising the spectre of future clashes between Asia and the West, and between China and the United States in particular. This potential finds expression in the determination of the Chinese not only to build up their own national strength, but to challenge the current Euro-American and Japanese-dominated system. In this light, it is easy to view the United States not only as a model of modernization, but at the same time as the main barrier on their path, the upstart newcomer who has for too long, but only temporarily, replaced the rightful role of China in the central global position. From this viewpoint, the ancientness of Chinese society could be seen once again in a positive light, as the historic basis for its claim to modern power and the right even to replace the current world leaders.

This concept of centrality, which is incorporated in the very name for China by the use of the character *zhong* or "middle," is not simply based on past glories, nor can it be attributed merely to present-day self-delusion. It derives from the "weight" of China in the global context, with almost one quarter of the population of the world, a wealth of still largely untapped natural resources, and a sense of geopolitical independence and cultural depth that is millennial and profound. It is seen in its international relations, not only historically, but to a remarkable extent in the modern world as well. For hundreds of years, the Chinese sat at the center of their known universe as the "Middle Kingdom," collecting the tribute and receiving the homage of surrounding lands, while they themselves focused their attention and energies within their own society. There were at times great Chinese explorers, and enormous naval expeditions, especially in the early fifteenth century, carried them at least as far as the Red Sea and eastern coast of Africa. But such adventures always proved to be short-lived, and were even viewed by the Chinese leadership as a threat, since they engaged the outside world in ways which might escape the control of the central authorities and lead to unwanted foreign entanglements. The Mongols, under Chinggis (Genghis) Khan, might conquer China and sweep west to threaten Europe itself. But for the Chinese, it was the great landmass of the Asian continent that was their natural environment, self-sufficient not only in its material resources but culturally as well, able to satisfy all their needs and desires.

In this fundamental sense, the Chinese did not need to go exploring, because they were already "there," at the center. It was others who came to them, and even the imperialists felt the need to reach China before they could truly claim to know and dominate the globe. The Western sense of excitement at being admitted into the presence of the Chinese leaders—which is at least as old as Marco Polo in the reign of Khubilai Khan in the fourteenth century and as recent as Richard Nixon meeting with Mao Zedong in 1972—is a remarkable testament to the historic strength of this "centrality." It affects even those, such as U.S. government officials, who are otherwise smugly certain of their own historic right to global domination. The rare return visits by Chinese leaders, such as that of Deng Xiaoping to the United States in 1979, from which the most enduring image is his donning of a Texan cowboy hat, are barely remembered, and seem weightless and insubstantial in comparison.

The recognition of this centrality, far from fading, seems to be growing. Thus in 1994 alone, "more than 40 heads of state and government leaders visited China, a record in the history of China's exchanges with other countries. It also was rare for Chinese leaders to have visited so many foreign countries in 1994."[9] President Jiang Zemin and Premier Li Peng have been unusually outgoing in their personal diplomacy, visiting many regions of the world and attending international meetings. Still, the "balance of visits" has almost certainly remained in favor of the Chinese, so that "Canadian Ambassador John Paynter noted nearly every week last year China received a head of state or government from other countries. 'That is extraordinary,' he observed."[10] Such visits are a source of national pride, and reaffirm for many Chinese their rightful place in the global order.

It is this traditional position that students in China seem determined to try to recapture today. Their attitudes are in turn merely an extension of the goals of the market reformers in their modernization drive. Though government officials are somewhat restrained, others speak openly. For the boldest of these, China will not only lead Asia and the third world, but the entire globe, and they fully expect it to displace the United States as the dominant international economic power.

> This makes Chinese economists believe that a "century" for Chinese economists is coming, with this country becoming a world economic giant next century.
> "China's hefty economic development will bring about a takeoff of economic theory," said Lin Yifu, director of the China Centre for Economic Research.
> The world's economic research centre has always been located where the economy is the most promising, he said.
> Before the 1930's, it was Britain. Since World War II, it has been the US.
> "China must be the next one, with East Asia growing to be the world's economic engine," Lin said.[11]

For those holding this view, the Chinese experience represents an entirely new phenomenon, that cannot be accounted for by previous Western ideas. "Although China reaped benefits in switching from a planned economy to a market-oriented economy, current economic theory can not explain such success."

A whole new theoretical school is therefore needed to understand the "miraculous" growth of "market socialism with Chinese characteristics."

> Economists from around the world will swarm to study the economic
> miracle China has achieved, which has aroused world interest.
> The conventional development of theory says that a large economy
> cannot maintain a sustained growth over 7 per cent for a long period of
> time. China, however, has generated an annual GNP growth rate of
> roughly 10 per cent since 1978, hence the miraculous turn.
> "Chinese economists who have grown up in the society will have
> advantages in this field," Lin said.
> He said his research centre, established last month in Beijing University,
> is preparing for the "China century."
> "It needs generations of work to make China's research influential in the
> world," Lin said. "But let's start now."[12]

The center will not only "analyze China's reform experience, with the
aim of providing examples or lessons for other developing countries,"
it will address such problems as inflation, regional income gaps, and
corruption, which "need a theoretical guide." But even here anomalies
and ironies abound. For it turns out that most of the researchers at the
facility are foreign-trained, and the center itself is financed by overseas
funds. Thus even those who are proclaiming the birth of the "China
century" and claiming to express its new and unique theoretical
foundation are dependent on personnel and money from abroad,
hardly a propitious start to the era of Chinese global dominance.

Such assertions of independent strength in the midst of growing
foreign dependency reveal the contradictions of China in the world
system. Even as it rises toward the place it held historically, it recreates
the entanglements with foreign powers which undermined that very
same role. The reassertion of the power of the Chinese is thus fraught
with historic tensions as well, and their bid to reclaim a central position
is a major source of current conflicts. In particular, even as China now
seeks to enter the global market, it at the same time often seems to insist
on "playing by its own rules," or rather by alternative ones to those of
the U.S.-dominated system. It has done so on the grounds that it is too
large, powerful, and independent to be subordinated to Western-derived standards, and that it has its own equally valid historic and
cultural norms, now reinforced by the development of "market socialism with Chinese characteristics." This has led to a revival of the
attitude that the world needs China more than vice versa.

From the very first modern contacts of the Chinese with the West,
the concepts of self-sufficiency and centrality created major contradictions, leading rapidly to growing clashes that ended in war and
conquest. There were the early attempts of the Emperors to treat
Britain, for example, as just another potential vassal state, expected to
send the usual tribute. As the classic 1793 Imperial Edict to King

George III expressed it, what could the Chinese possibly want or need from the Western "barbarians."

> As a matter of fact, the virtue and prestige of the Celestial Dynasty having spread far and wide, the kings of the myriad nations come by land and sea with all sorts of precious things. Consequently there is nothing we lack, as your principal envoy and others have themselves observed. We have never set much store on strange or ingenious objects, nor do we need any more of your country's manufactures....[13]

The Chinese attitudes toward self-sufficiency did not survive unmodified in the modern world, of course. But even after these illusions began to be shattered, and the unprecedented strength and challenge of the West came to be realized, the problem of what Europe had to offer China remained a basic dilemma.

In the Forbidden City there is a large room filled with an enormous and fabulous collection of European clocks, the kind of exotic toys that were imported by the imperial family from the West. Their very exoticism, however, makes them seem especially out of place in the middle of one of the central symbols of Chinese culture. But even as the Emperors were collecting Western exotica, from China at the same time flowed a vast array and quantity of valuable exports, most notably teas and ceramic ware, which flooded Europe and the United States, and became inseparable parts of Western culture, to such an extent that even today English royalty and workers alike must have their daily tea served in "china."

As such products became European and North American staples, they drew China inexorably into the expanding global net of the capitalist economy. But the inability of the Western powers to claim a similar loyalty for their products among the Chinese led to an enormous imbalance in trade. The result was to drain the English treasury to pay for imports, for which there was no equivalent exchange. It was this in turn which led the British to force opium on China, leading to the first major war with the Euro-American powers, and the beginning of the carving up of the Chinese mainland. In this drug trade U.S. merchants played a secondary but still significant role, with their profits being employed "back home" to help fund railroad construction, among other capital investments, as early as the 1830s, and before the Opium War. Thus modern economic issues cannot be reduced to export-import balances alone. Such trade conflicts have a very bitter history for China, as the West used them as a basis for forcibly "opening up" the country at the point of a gun, and imposing the most morally corrupting imports on its people.

These historical memories persist, and are constantly being reinforced—for example, by a major new film which is being produced on the Opium War, in time to help mark the celebration of the return of Hong Kong in 1997. Still today, in the eyes of many Chinese, nothing exemplifies better their relation with the outside world. They see themselves as a source of useful goods for the rest of the world, from which in return come corrupting and harmful products, notably in the form of drugs and cultural pollution, and money-driven social values, especially affecting intellectuals and youths. This perception takes the form of ongoing resistance to profit-oriented methods viewed as largely foreign-derived and seen as threatening ancient cultural patterns, but equally as undermining the gains of the socialist revolution, in the areas of art and literature, as well as those of economics and politics.

Such fears of pollution from abroad find expression in an article headlined "Culture needs money, but not a money-cult":

> "For some people, the opening-up policy and market-oriented economic reform seem to have made money the priority of society. Though the economy is growing rapidly, without respect to culture, such development will be only one-sided and can not go too far," said Wang Chengjun, vice-chairman of the Chinese Committee of Folk Art Collection....[14]

Under marketization reforms, tight budgets are hurting cultural activities, all the national museums are in financial difficulty, and "palace arts" take precedence over more popular forms. As a result, the historical memory of Chinese culture is undermined, opening the door even wider to the threat of foreign domination.

> Many other folk arts, like skills in making silver articles, are in danger of being lost.
> China's 5,000-year history boasts variety and creativity. We may ultimately face the danger of becoming dependent on Western culture if we do not keep on inheriting and carrying forward our own national culture, according to Wang.[15]

Faced with declining governmental support, Chinese art and cultural products of all kinds are being sold to the highest bidder, most often in the international market to rich private collectors. Even the leading dance company has threatened to auction off rights to its most popular ballet to foreign investors to meet rising expenses.

The atmosphere of "money by any means" is rapidly becoming so all-pervasive, and corruption invading so deeply every pore of Chinese society, that the cultural realm and its historical base are directly threatened, especially from abroad. Speaking of the growing entertainment industry, Culture Minister Liu Zongde stated:

> The major problems troubling cultural authorities are illegal publications, the smuggling of overseas audio and video products, pornography,

prostitution, gambling, rocketing fees charged by overseas pop stars, tax evasion and corruption of some cultural administrators.[16]

To combat such problems, Liu called for wider promotion of culture in the less urbanized areas, price ceilings to keep events affordable to the public, and policies to give preferential support to development of classical art forms.

But the "high" arts have been equally unable to escape from corruption, largely fed by the growing foreign demand for Chinese goods. Thus "one of the most important factors that cause disorder on the art market is the money cult.... Driven by the desire of making money, many painters rush to fake works by well-known artists."[17] As a result:

> Works by Chinese painters have been faked in such large numbers recently that many artists and critics are seriously worried that the Chinese art market could be inundated if faking isn't stamped on....
>
> "A Hong Kong art dealer came to a Beijing gallery in the hope of buying paintings. He was told that he could buy works by any famous Chinese artist he had in mind. But all the supposed works by famed painters were all fakes...."

Even those who do not engage in outright fakery are affected.

> Painter He Haixia said: "In the past, we painted pictures for self-appreciation. So qualities and genre were guaranteed. Now that economic gains are the main factors, inferior quality painting emerge in large numbers."[18]

The scramble for money increasingly corrupts every form of artistic or professional integrity. Even many journalists have begun selling their services to the highest bidder, accepting bribes to write favorable stories about investment deals or those accused of being corrupt, while some newspapers are said actually to encourage the practice to supplement low salaries for reporters.

The very concepts of beauty are no longer exempt. There are now some 18,000 local "Avon ladies" peddling Western cosmetics door to door in China. So far has the corrupting influence of Western culture gone that some Chinese are resorting to plastic surgery to alter their eyes, and even to enlarge their noses—the very symbol of the European "barbarians." This trend has reached considerable proportions: on a daily average, one hundred women receive eye operations and fifty of both sexes get "nose jobs"—in Shanghai alone. In such ways, there is a

> steady spread of Western goods and values to so basic a dimension of life as esthetics and love.
>
> "Many young people have very Western minds, and think that the Western look is very beautiful," a Shanghai beautician said. "So a lot of young men and women perm their hair and do other things to look more Western."[19]

Clearly out of the reach of average workers and peasants, such "pollution" is a sign that many of the "new rich" are abandoning any claim to historic cultural integrity, in an effort to join their Western peers not only economically, but even physically.

Expressions of concern regarding the degradation of its culture thus have a decidedly historical ring in China, not only recalling the era of imperialist domination, but also the efforts of the socialist revolution to reverse the money-driven yearning for all things foreign. Thus, in an address to the annual meeting of the Chinese Writers' Association, Zhai Taifeng, deputy head of the propaganda department of the Communist Party central committee,

> criticized some writers who have marketed commercial books of poor taste. "We do not like to see our people harmed by 'spiritual opium' in any form and will never sacrifice social wholesomeness for the sake of developing the economy."
> He demanded that writers be guided by the theory of building socialism with Chinese characteristics set forth by Deng Xiaoping, and that they stand away from the influence of evil cultural trends.
> Zhang Qie, a member of the association's secretariat, said the association's top priority is to mobilize writers to "do their utmost to boost the cause of socialist literature."
> Two slogans that for decades guided China's literature and art are still alive, he said. They read: "Let Culture and Art Serve the People and Socialism" and "Let One Hundred Flowers Blossom and One Hundred Schools of Thought Contend."[20]

Though unstated, the source of much of this "spiritual opium," like that of its physical predecessor, is clearly foreign.

Yet a basic contradiction arises here, for it is precisely the "theory of building socialism with Chinese characteristics set forth by Deng Xiaoping" that has opened the door to rampant commercialization, and with it the inevitable corruption by "evil cultural trends," especially from abroad, and the sacrificing of social wholesomeness on the altar of economic development. Thus even an editorial which cites Deng as calling for bringing up "a new generation with lofty ideals, moral integrity, profound knowledge and a strong sense of discipline," also complains, without any sense of irony, that "decadent ideologies, such as money fetishism and hedonism, have reared their ugly head in society again. Innocent young people are most liable to fall prey to them."[21] These youthful "innocents" must indeed wonder how they are to get "gloriously" rich while at the same time avoiding such ideological decadence.

Significantly, therefore, resistance to foreign profit-oriented values and polluting goods still draws on concepts from the Mao era, such as "let culture and art serve the people and socialism." This attitude dates back especially to the aftermath of the revolution, when a spirit of fierce self-reliance was added to the older patterns of Chinese centrality. Such an attitude was fed by years of isolation from the West, largely U.S.-imposed, but it also came from a determination to avoid any repeat of the history of imperialist subordination. This go-it-alone attitude was largely an expression of the form of socialism advocated by Mao Zedong, which stressed the necessity of China depending on its own resources (especially after the 1960s break with the Soviet Union), developing new social standards not based on monetary or elite interests, and, in particular, resisting the imposition of foreign-derived norms. While the policy never was simple isolationism—the Chinese remained heavily involved with other third world countries in particular—it did mean a turn toward self-reliance, and a determination to convert external boycott and attack into internal strength and development.

These attitudes too have carried over into the recent period of market reforms and opening to the outside world. Thus even as it has tried to expand its contacts and exchange with other countries, China has frequently clung to an attitude of doing things its own way and on its own terms. In the current trade tensions with the United States there are clear echoes of these sentiments. In this view, China by its very scale has less to lose by being isolated from the outside world, than those who would attempt to punish it for its commercial or human rights policies. Speaking of the U.S. threat to impose tariffs in early 1995 over the issue of ownership of "intellectual property," a spokesperson for the Chinese Chamber of Commerce typically stated:

> "While the US is bragging (about its potential victory over China in a possible trade war), everybody can see that by trade war the US will actually kill the goose that lays the golden egg....
> "Indeed, some exporters from China will suffer economic losses in the short term if the US carries out its sanctions, but it's the US that stands to lose the huge Chinese market in the long run."[22]

This was echoed by Zhou Shijian of the International Trade Research Institute:

> For US entrepreneurs, Zhou said, a trade war would inevitably delay their exploration of the Chinese market—"perhaps the last huge potential market in the world."[23]

This continued insistence that China has less to lose than those who would try to impose their standards on it and that it is more crucial to the survival of others than vice versa, finds powerful echoes abroad, including within U.S. business circles, which fear being excluded from the most dynamic global market today. This attitude found official reflection in 1993 when the trade representative for the Clinton administration,

Mickey Kantor, declared that: "America's future is increasingly linked to Asia.... We have got to look west to Asia."[24] He and others cited figures showing that 49 percent of U.S. exports were then going to the Pacific region, supporting 2.5 million U.S. jobs, and that trade with Asia was 50 percent higher than that with Europe. Even Secretary of State Warren Christopher declared that the aim of his policy was "doubling US exports to Asia, and the jobs that sustain them, in a decade."[25] Of the "big emerging markets" at the heart of the Clinton administration trade strategy, China is potentially the biggest. The Chinese thus see themselves as increasingly at the center of U.S. strategic goals, and of the means to fulfill them, giving them enormous leverage to pursue their own interests in their own way.

However, what was in earlier times an expression of a self-reliant and inward-looking spirit, and even insistence on playing by its own rules, creates serious contradictions when China attempts at the same time to be integrated into the foreign-dominated and global capitalist economy. Setting their own standards was one thing, when the Chinese were truly seeking a relative degree of autonomy from the world market and were developing new socialist concepts of collective production and exchange at variance with the methods of international capital. When, however, the goal is to generate profits in a manner indistinguishable from that of any multinational capitalist investor, and every effort is being made to expand commercial and financial ties around the world, such an attitude can only lead to major conflicts. In this case, the Chinese are themselves caught between their desire to hold on to an historic independence, which is seen as inseparable from the protection of national sovereignty, and their need for foreign investment and trade. In particular, increasing reliance on funding from abroad and the closely related necessity of expanding export markets puts China in a weak position, a tendency which can only be heightened as market socialism becomes ever more tightly linked to the world capitalist economy. An especially sharp contradiction thus looms between the reassertion of regional and global economic power by the Chinese, and their growing international dependency.

III. Who Do "Correct Ideas" Belong To?

As it seeks to reassert its role in the world system, China faces a growing collision between its historic self-sufficiency, reinforced by the socialist forms of organization and reliance on its own resources of the revolutionary period, and the demands of the international capitalist market that it seeks to enter. This was notably apparent in the conflict over the protection of "intellectual property rights"—and of the vast profits which such investments can yield—that in late 1994 and early 1995 was a central focus of the trade tensions with the United States. Here attention centered on the large-scale pirating by the Chinese of computer programs and video cassettes, a significant portion of which are exported, thus denying U.S. and other foreign corporate manufacturers royalties and sales not only within China, but abroad as well. In this one area, the United States alone estimates its sales losses at $1 billion annually. The scale of these operations is indeed massive. Within Hong Kong, which serves as the primary export outlet for mainland producers, U.S. sources claim that some 62 percent of software products are pirated, and a test version of Windows 95 was said to be selling briskly in early 1995, prior to the formal release of the program by Microsoft later that year. Similarly, a video version of "The Lion King" was selling in China long before it was released for sale by Disney. But even in attempting to measure such areas of conflict, there is vast disagreement. "Chinese officials denied the United States estimates that 95 percent of computer software used in China was pirated and asserted that it was closer to 25 to 30 percent," a figure that would actually be slightly lower than the 35 percent piracy rate that the industry believes prevails in the U.S. domestic market itself.[26] Thus the very dimensions of the problem are in fundamental dispute, and with it the question of whether the Chinese are being unfairly singled out for trade retribution and arbitrary actions by the United States.

Since 1983, governmental authorities in China have put numerous anti-piracy laws on the books, accompanied by mass education campaigns, insisting that they are very serious about the protection of intellectual property. In the early 1990s they further revised domestic regulations to bring them in line with international conventions. The Chinese also note that other countries have taken much longer to develop the kinds of legal framework that they have implemented in a few short years. To enforce this drive, there have been many well-publicized raids on factories engaged in mass production of illegal goods, and not only on those enterprises specifically named by the United States. In 1994, the Chinese authorities reported that at least 5 million pirated products were confiscated, including 1.58 million books and 2.2 million laser disks, and hundreds of producers and retail outlets were subjected to fines or even closure. On the other side, by the end of 1994, 460,000 trademarks had been registered in China, 70,000 of them from abroad. That year alone, new requests reached 136,000, of which 78,000 were accepted. This included some 5,000 foreign brand names, just under half of those who applied for trademark protection. Patent requests by 1994 had totalled more than 440,000, of which some 220,000 had been approved. The 77,000 applicants that year alone made China the tenth largest receiver of requests for patents in the world. Foreign applications, moreover, accounted for only 14 percent of the total.

As such figures indicate, and as Chinese authorities stress, protecting patents, copyrights, and trademarks is part of the marketization reform, in which domestic business needs, even more than foreign demands, are the compelling factor.

> "Our commitment to IPR [intellectual property rights] protection came about 15 years ago as a response to the call of the open-door and market-oriented reforms," said Guo Shoukang, a professor in the Law Department of the Beijing-based People's University.
> "There was no outside pressure when we launched a working group on March 19, 1979, to draft China's Patent Law," he said.[27]

So too, according to Zheng Chensi, a law expert at the Chinese Academy of Social Sciences, "It is China's building of a market economy, not outside pressure, that forces the country to protect copyrights.... China opposes pressure from foreigners as regards the solving of certain problems."[28] The technologically advanced Wuhan Iron and Steel Works alone held 147 patents on its own inventions, some of which have been leased to foreign producers. Trademark officials and patent authorities have handled many thousands of claimed infringements, the vast majority of them by domestic inventors and producers, despite a few well-publicized international cases. Some 80 percent of intellectual property claims brought before the courts have been settled.

It is thus the expansion of "business" in China itself that drives this legal reform. The Chinese computer software industry, for example, is expected to expand its output by almost one half in 1995 alone, and is already approaching 7 billion yuan or somewhat less than $1 billion in annual output. The development of its first supercomputer to reach world standards was recently announced. With some 80,000 researchers in over 1,000 enterprises, China needs its own copyright protection in order to profit fully from programs such as newly developed Chinese versions of DOS and Windows, and to make them competitive in the national and world markets.

> Foreign software companies can get back their investments from domestic markets, and their costs to develop Chinese versions are usually low, but to domestic companies, piracy is almost ruinous.
> If the problem can not be solved quickly, the survival of the fledgling domestic software industry will be seriously threatened, experts warned.[29]

Yet a dilemma arises for China as it tries to protect its young high-tech industries. Even with spectacular growth, the relatively small Chinese software manufacturers, most with fewer than fifty employees and collectively or privately owned, can only meet an estimated 30 to 40 percent of the rapidly expanding domestic market demand, leaving them highly vulnerable to global competition.

This opens the door to future domination of the computer industry in China by foreign-based multinationals, such as Microsoft, which saw its sales soar by 200 percent in 1994 alone, and expects to see a rise to $100 million annually in three years. The general manager of its Chinese affiliate vows to "make China Microsoft's largest overseas software development base."[30] The U.S. company AST already controls 26 percent of the Chinese personal computer market, in which it has held first place for five consecutive years, selling some 184,000 PCs in 1994. "China is AST's most strategic market in Asia," according to Safi Qureshey, chairman and CEO. "We will make China a base for us to march into other Asian markets."[31] Corporations like these, with their vast scale and resources, are leading the foreign drive for copyright protection. Microsoft itself has already brought several suits against domestic Chinese computer enterprises. "As the world's largest software company, Microsoft stands to gain most" in any agreement between China and the United States concerning intellectual property rights, because it "needs the Chinese Government's protection of its copyrights if it wants to be successful in China," a vice-president of the corporation stated.[32]

Microsoft has even announced that its first investment in China will be a $1 million training program, "to make Chinese customers understand more about property rights and help software engineers learn advanced technology and skills."[33] The 2,500 graduates, who will become Microsoft Certified Professionals, will no doubt form the entering wedge into the market in China, for example in the cooperative development of the Chinese version of Windows 95, for which the company signed a memorandum of understanding with the Ministry of Electronics Industry. Such developments lend credence to the claims by the government that China has as big a stake in the protection of intellectual property rights as do foreign companies, both to guard its domestic copyrights and patents and to attract needed investment. It also indicates that there is rapidly developing a stratum of entrepreneurs and professionals who share these legal goals. Yet at the same time, it reveals that control by China over its own production and markets is seriously endangered, especially in leading high-tech sectors.

Thus the struggle over patents and copyrights, and the issue of pirating, runs much deeper, raising basic issues of national sovereignty and of the very structure of Chinese society. This was illustrated in rather "amusing" form in Changchun. When we arrived there to teach, we were presented with multiple copies of a hardcover textbook on U.S. history which had been duly bought from a legal supplier. But there was also a pirated version of a new edition of the same book, reprinted on the college offset presses, which was missing all the pages indicating the copyright and publisher, and began abruptly with the first chapter. A work of similarly anonymous character served as the text for the technical writing course I taught. Such books did fill the need for English-language writing, almost impossible to find, much less obtain in multiple copies, outside the major cities. But even this blatant pirating proved to be merely the tip of the iceberg. Searching for other books in English to use in our classes, we located a Foreign Languages Book Store, which turned out to have very little that was of value to us. But it did have a back room, from which all foreigners were prohibited entry, where university students from all over Changchun could buy pirated texts. We even heard stories of Western scholars who gave Chinese associates papers they had written, only to have their work turn up some time later in a journal in China with their former colleague listed as the author. Similar and very insistent efforts to acquire materials from us were going on while we were in Changchun. Pirating has thus become ubiquitous and increasingly commercialized at all social levels, including the academic community. There is therefore some basis for the Chinese claim that they cannot gain control over the problem overnight, for those who pirate are dispersed throughout the economy and society as a whole, and there is clearly now a deeply ingrained belief in the right to appropriate the work of others for personal gain, without acknowledgement—much less payment.

As one consequence, the inflow of products from abroad, far from leading to a contraction of pirating, has seen the number of imitation products rise exponentially, as both demand and access grow, and with them an expanding market for cheap copies. Every effort to force open the Chinese market to foreign goods thereby produces a counterreaction of increased copyright and trademark infringements. Thus "counterfeiting in China ballooned" between 1993 and 1995, with pirating extending to everyday items like "razors, soap, and cornflakes."[34] Frequently this involves small local factories, closely tied to government bodies, which place U.S. and other foreign labels on every variety of imitation goods. Very often these operations are directly owned by or at least under the wing of the most powerful enterprises, public ministries, and political families in the country. Moreover, with the weakening of central authority, crackdowns on such pirating, as in all other areas of macroeconomic control, have been seriously hampered. A spot check in late 1994, at the height of the "intellectual property rights" tensions with the United States and the campaign in China to prevent copyright violations, found 1 million pirated CDs in a single

Guangzhou shopping center, the largest number ever discovered on the mainland. Even sincere drives to stamp out the problem are therefore highly unlikely to succeed without a more fundamental social restructuring, and marketization and "opening to the world" together become a two-edged sword, promoting both the legal sale of foreign goods and their illegal pirating at the same time.

Such global difficulties, however, still fail to reveal the most critical issue, for "intellectual property" gets to the very heart of the dilemma of market socialism and of the Chinese position in the world economy. When in 1963, on the eve of launching the Cultural Revolution, Mao asked "Where Do Correct Ideas Come From?" he went on to answer his own question as follows:

> Do they drop from the skies? No. Are they innate in the mind? No. They come from social practice, and from it alone; they come from three kinds of social practice, the struggle for production, the class struggle and scientific experiment. It is man's social being that determines his thinking. Once the correct ideas characteristic of the advanced class are grasped by the masses, these ideas turn into a material force which changes society and changes the world.[35]

The point Mao was making went beyond the philosophical observation that ideas, if they are to be socially valid, must not be based on "mere" thinking alone, but must be tested in practice, especially against the needs of the masses. He was also showing that all "correct" knowledge is a social, not individual phenomenon. Since no idea arises, nor can its validity be established, in total isolation, therefore it must also belong to society at large, and cannot properly be the private possession of those who claim to have initiated a given thought. In this way, Mao extended the theoretical basis of socialist ownership from the realm of material forces to what Marx and Engels called the "means of mental production" as well.[36]

As is so often the case with Mao, these concepts also built on more ancient Chinese philosophical ideas and social practices. Commenting on the history of "pirating" in China, Professor Julia K. Murray of the University of Wisconsin-Madison has pointed out:

> According to Confucian ideals, the "superior man" does not seek personal profit but strives to improve the world. Through writings, his wisdom is disseminated.
>
> Also, unauthorized reprinting of texts has been a practice of Chinese publishing since the 11th century. Government efforts to restrict it were driven by concerns about textual corruption and ideological control, rather than protecting profits.[37]

In the Cultural Revolution, the concept of social ownership of ideas was extended to all levels of society and applied in practice, to break the stranglehold of the educated elite over science and education, and even over economics and politics, through the process of mass participation and the requirement that the ideas of workers and peasants be recognized as equally legitimate as those of professionals. Through such actions, the conviction that knowledge as well as factories and land properly belong to society—not to individuals—and that they should not be used for private profiteering, became deeply rooted. It also came to be recognized that public control over the use of ideas was crucial to building socialism. Such beliefs, once they were widely accepted among the masses of Chinese, "turned into a material force which changes society and changes the world."

Few concepts are therefore as central to socialist property relations, especially as they were expressed in China during the Cultural Revolution, as that knowledge and culture belong to everyone and should be used freely for social development, not privately owned and exploited for profit. This has led to a conflict between the consciousness of the masses and the new social relations of marketization, and especially the legal restrictions needed to enforce them. Thus, "although China has established an advanced copyright protection system, the average person still lacks copyright awareness."[38] Before the Chinese adopted international standards of trademark and patent protection, this concept was extended to foreign products as well, as explained by Shen Rengan, deputy director general of the National Copyright Administration.

> Since copyrights are defined in strict accordance with the jurisdiction of corresponding legislations, laws of foreign countries are not applicable to China, nor are any world conventions unless endorsed by China. It is in this very sense that all use of foreign works by Chinese citizens or institutions did not constitute as illegal before June 1, 1991.
> So, legally, publication of foreign books or the use of foreign software in China before that date should not be regarded as piracy.[39]

The difficulty of reversing this socialistic approach, and the contradictions which it raises in an emerging market economy are further shown by Shen.

> According to my knowledge, copyright violators in China fall into two categories. Some of them have neither a sense of law nor the concept of the legal consequences of intellectual property violation. Others avail themselves of loopholes in the nation's infant market system to rake in exorbitant profits. Violators in each of these categories have received severe punishments.[40]

Despite the attempt by Shen to lump them together in this way, the two groups are at polar opposites. One is a product of socialist collective property, the other of emergent capitalism.

The attitude of the first group of "violators" reflects the belief—if only implicit—that ideas belong to everyone, and that China has the right to use the knowledge of the entire world, without paying profits to its foreign "owners." Yet this kind of socialism is completely incompatible, not only with the global forms of capitalist monopoly of intellectual as well as material goods, but equally with the present "get rich quick" atmosphere in Chinese society in which everyone, even including university faculty and cultural producers, must struggle to survive in the marketplace. As the expanding venality of the pirating we saw in Changchun so well demonstrates, any claim to common or socialistic ownership of the "means of mental production" becomes a mockery, and a source of corruption on the most personal level, if it is at the same time "marketized." It makes no sense to say that ideas belong to everyone, if those who make this assertion then turn them to individual profit. But to privatize knowledge totally is to abandon yet another of the most precious and hard-won forms of socialist relations, one that was gained at such high cost, especially during the Cultural Revolution.

Confronting the issue of pirating, therefore, not only requires the Chinese leaders to accept that massive borrowing from the West cannot be combined with traditional attitudes of playing by their own rules, it also forces them to choose in one more area of the economy between the market and socialism. Here again, global relations and domestic class conflict prove inseparable. For "opening to the world" can only be accomplished by increasing conformity to capitalist norms, yet giving in to the United States on pirating raises fundamental issues for Chinese domestic society and its resubordination to outside powers. As Murray points out, the issue of pirating therefore has deep historic implications in China, calling forth popular resistance. "Hectoring the Chinese will not shame them into giving up the practice. They will see our tirades as Western chauvinism, refusing to bow to them."[41]

Thus what appears in the United States to be just an issue of "trade," in China becomes a question of national sovereignty and the direction of social development. In this way, a "simple" clash over intellectual property rights comes freighted with all the historical weight of the struggle against imperialism going back to the Opium War. The Chinese are convinced that there is more to the U.S. position than trade alone. For them, this is merely an entering wedge for the United States to gain control over the entire economic, political, and social system of China, and an attempt to keep it "in its place" as a third world country. Thus the Chinese note that the U.S. demands included allowing for "independent" industry bodies—which are little more than a front for

leading multinational computer firms—to evaluate the future performance of China on intellectual property rights. As Ying Ming, the
Deputy Director of the China Computer Software Registration Center
protested: "What qualifications does an organization composed vol-
untarily of a dozen US software companies have to 'approve' registra-
tions worldwide?"[42] Such actions have led to claims of U.S.
interference in the Chinese legislative and judicial system.

The United States is also seen as going beyond its own regulatory
norms, raising threats to the sovereignty of China it would never
accept for itself, and violating world standards.

> Some of the US negotiators' requirements even surpassed their domestic
> practice. For example, they demanded trial of overseas-concerned IPR
> violation cases finished within six months in China; similar cases in the
> US sometimes last for three or more years.
> Chinese foreign trade ministry officials also called demands for regular
> reports on IPR progress to be submitted to the US government "undue
> interference" in China's sovereignty. That interference extends to US
> negotiators' demands to revise China's own judicial and legislative laws,
> the official said.[43]

U.S. claims are seen as both unfairly selective and hypocritical. "In
China, according to another American trade group, the Software Publishers Association, only 1 or every 50 copies of software is legal," the
New York Times reported.[44] But while attention focuses on Chinese
piracy, the situation in other leading countries is at least as bad and in
some respects even more extreme. In Russia, for example, intellectual
property losses are also estimated at some $1 billion, but there has been
no similar campaign of pressure from Washington there. During 1994
in Japan, lost revenues for U.S. and other companies in the software
industry exceeded $1.3 billion. Pirating in the United States itself, after
falling by nearly 50 percent from 1993 to 1994, was still $1.05 billion,
and appears ready to rise in the future, largely due to the wider
availability of the Internet and other easily accessible technologies.
With a remarkable similarity among several leading countries in the
total amount of pirated intellectual property—somewhere around $1
billion annually—China is therefore far down the list as measured on
a per capita basis.

What makes the Chinese situation unique, at least as compared to
the United States and Japan, is the alleged involvement of the government itself, or at least of those closely associated with leading party
and state officials. Thus China is singled out largely because its pirating still has aspects of socialistic organization, as opposed to the "free
market" pirates of capitalist nations, as well as because of its large
export of such products. Pirated goods thereby become just one more

handy club with which to batter the Chinese for their resistance to full recapitalization, part of the general public picture painted in the United States of China as a backward, incipient outlaw state, which must be specially isolated and punished for violating global norms. At the same time, just as in the "drug war," Washington focuses its attention on the mote of foreign suppliers rather than on the beam of the insatiable demand for illegal goods at home. To the Chinese, the U.S. attitude reeks of "great power" hegemonistic pretensions, an attempt to bully them into accepting standards it would never deign to adopt for itself, in a renewal of "big stick policies."[45] Thus the conflict over pirated goods is viewed as only one part of a general plan by the United States to dominate China, denying it the right to choose its own forms of social organization.

IV. The Balance of Trade and Investment

Even as the economic impact of China on the world grows, it attracts renewed attempts by the global powers, and especially the United States, to subvert its expanding strength from within. The result is rising tensions, as each points to different forms of advantage in their ever more contentious economic relations. The conflict between China and the United States extends even to fundamental disagreement over the dimensions of their trade gap, and the scale of the Chinese economy. According to U.S. figures, China has rapidly moved into second place as the source of its global export-import losses. As recently as 1986, the Chinese exported only $2 billion more to the United States than they received in return. But in 1994, when the U.S. overall merchandise deficit was $108 billion, China accounted for $29.5 billion, or over 27 percent of the total, and just under one half of the $65 billion loss which the United States suffered in its dealings with Japan. Together the two countries were the source for fully 88 percent of the U.S. negative trade balance. Even though China is only the sixth-largest trading partner of the United States, it is the fourth largest exporter to it. Thus while in 1994 it accounted for only 4.2 percent of total U.S. trade, its impact was out of all proportion, as the imbalance of imports and exports with the Chinese grew 30 percent in one year.

This situation has created considerable alarm in some U.S. quarters.

> In many ways, the deficit with China is more troublesome than the one with Japan because it is growing so much faster, and because the gap between America's exports and imports is proportionately much larger. Trade problems with China could soon dwarf the two decades of economic confrontation with Japan.
> "There is a profound sense in which the China deficit is worse than the Japan deficit," C. Fred Bergsten, the director of the Institute for

International Economics, said today. "To even the accounts with Japan, our exports there have to grow twice as fast as our imports. In the case of China, they would have to grow four times as fast as imports. That is almost inconceivable."[46]

Yet even these figures are by no means uncontested, for China claims that the United States includes products reexported from Hong Kong in its Chinese trade account, though much of the profits goes to entrepreneurs in the colony. There are similar disputes with Japan. Clearly, however, in such critical areas as high-tech goods, the exchange for China is heavily unfavorable.

Engineering and electronic products are the second biggest export product of China's and have experienced an annual increase of 38.5 percent from 1985 to 1993.

But these exports are not high-tech products which China still lacks. In 1993 China's import of engineering and electronic products was $49.5 billion, exceeding its export by $26.8 billion.[47]

Thus the Chinese economy, despite its apparent advantage in trade with the United States and other leading capitalist nations, exhibits fundamental structural weaknesses, especially regarding its future development and control of its own technological base.

Nevertheless, there can be little doubt that for now China occupies a position in relation to the West not unlike that which it held 150 years ago, as a vast supplier of cheap products, while still resisting imported manufactures. The Chinese themselves, in a recent poll, indicate a strong preference for Japanese products, rather than those of the United States or Western Europe. Of those goods with the highest brand-name recognition in China—a growing aspect of marketization—Japan produced six of the top ten, all of them from leading electronics or auto companies, like Hitachi, Toshiba, and Toyota. The United States, by contrast, could only score with Coca-Cola, Mickey Mouse, and Marlboro. The single Chinese entry in the top ten was Tsing Tao beer.[48] Resistant to many U.S. goods for cultural reasons as well as on more contemporary grounds of quality, still maintaining quite high protectionist barriers, and limited in its per capita purchasing power, China has little incentive or ability to reduce the trade imbalance. Its imports from the United States are largely big-ticket items like aircraft or machinery, and raw materials, grain, or fertilizers, often through sales requiring state-to-state negotiated agreements, and with little direct impact on the average Chinese. China, in turn, exports primarily consumer products to the United States. Thus while the $10.7 billion in U.S. goods which it imported in 1993 constituted only a little more than 10 percent of its total imports for that year, its own products flooded into the United States and other rich capitalist nations, where average incomes in the tens of thousands of dollars annually allow each person to make purchases equivalent to scores of Chinese consumers. On this basis, analysts in China say that the U.S. government should make a distinction between imbalances with Japan and Europe, which result from the mutual exchange of high-tech items, and the Chinese advantage, which rests mainly on low labor costs.

Regardless of these differences, China contends that it is simply too powerful to be kept out of the global economic system, and that in trade wars it is the United States that stands to lose in the long run from breaking ties to the Chinese market. Exemplifying this relation, the Clinton administration, even as it threatened to impose $1 billion worth of sanctions on China, was careful to exclude toys, since that might hurt its own retailers, and "no tariff was placed on electronic components, because American computer makers feared they would be put at a disadvantage to their Japanese counterparts." So too, only three days after announcing that it would impose up to 100 percent tariffs on a wide range of goods in early 1995, the U.S. government "expanded subsidized wheat sales to Beijing, rather than let European farmers win a bigger share of the Chinese market.... The move points up the complexity of trying to punish a major trading partner even as the Government grapples with protecting the interests of American businesses that are trying to gain a larger foothold there."[49] The wheat deal alone saved China $20 million over what it would have had to pay the Australians, for instance, on the open market. In the global economy the United States, for all its power, increasingly depends on the Chinese.

If trade alone were the essence of the relation of China to the United States and other Western countries, therefore, there is little doubt where the advantage would now lie. The Chinese could continue to play their traditional role of supplier to the West, while absorbing a significant but limited range of goods in return. But with the policy of "opening to the outside world," and especially to massive foreign investment, the situation has become much more complicated. Not only are other countries falling over themselves in the effort to gain a foothold in China, but the Chinese too are every day more dependent on funds from abroad to keep their massive economic expansion from turning back on itself. Year by year, China has opened up more sectors of the national economy to foreign investment, including such key fields as energy. All areas of offshore oil exploration have now been opened to multinational participation. Without help from abroad, the Chinese say they lack the capability to fully develop these resources, which are in turn crucial to continued economic expansion. Even the famous Daqing oil region, which Mao held up as the model for industrial development, can no longer compete in the new global market environment for China without expanding into petrochemicals, but to do so again raises the prospect of growing dependence on foreign financing and technology.

In the U.S.-China trade bargaining, therefore, it was not at all clear that the Chinese held the upper hand. The United States is still the dominant power in the world economic system, and open conflict with it would necessitate limiting not only U.S. sales, but investment in China as well. The Chinese threatened just such restrictions in early 1995 in answer to the high tariffs on $1 billion of imports the United States said it would impose if the negotiations failed. Yet with growing dependence not only on export markets, but especially on global financing, the ability of China to carry out such threats is limited. It finds itself in a weak position when attempting to challenge the leading world economic power which, despite its own growing problems, still dominates international trade and funding institutions.

Even while the negotiations over intellectual property rights were at their most tense, therefore, China was continuing to arrange for new massive inputs of U.S. capital into its economy. Just two weeks before the deadline set by the United States for imposition of new tariffs if agreement was not reached, it was announced that additional energy cooperation agreements between the two countries would soon be signed. With an estimated $82 billion in investment needed to expand its inadequate power generation infrastructure, China is looking to foreign investors for at least a quarter of that total. Thus at the very moment that the intellectual property rights talks reached their most difficult stage, the Chinese announced that the United States would soon sign a cooperation agreement for $4 to $8 billion worth of energy deals. Moreover, even in its export trade, the Chinese economy increasingly depends on capital from abroad. In 1994, of its $121 billion in total exports, $35 billion, or more than one quarter, was generated by firms funded from abroad. Even what is left of the socialist economy is similarly dependent, as "the Communist Party seems intent on preserving a large state sector through invigoration with foreign capital...."[50] China thus finds itself in an increasingly weak position to "bite the hand that funds it," however much it may wish to assert its independent economic position and national sovereignty.

The Chinese understand that this leaves them vulnerable to outside pressure. Thus they see even darker goals behind U.S. trade negotiation policy. As Yu Peiwei, a researcher with the Ministry of Foreign Trade and Economic Cooperation (Moftec), analyzed this situation:

"The real purpose of the US is to pry open China's financial, insurance, telecommunications, transport and other service markets.

"It also wants China to adopt a high standard of intellectual property rights protection and to settle the alleged huge trade surplus with the US."

And areas the US wants most from China are those in which American businesses have the strongest advantage, such as auto and aircraft industries as well as trade services.[51]

Yet automobiles, other transport, and telecommunications, like petro-chemicals, are among the fields where China is attempting to create "pillar industries," massive state-owned conglomerates protected from falling under complete foreign control. For example, it is tightening controls over the importation of auto components to be put together locally because "officials fear such assembly—in which foreign investors benefit from cheaper Chinese labour—could hurt China's own automobile industry."[52]

Yet even these efforts to build "pillars" must be funded in large part by capital from abroad. Thus "China, which has eight sedan manufacturers, seven of them foreign-funded, encourages investment in auto components development and manufacturing so that its auto industry will grow into an economic pillar."[53] But when even the crucial "pillars" themselves rest in large part on foreign soil, this merely leads to a new and contradictory form of dependency. Efforts to pry these sectors open still further therefore threaten the basic strategy of the Chinese to maintain the autonomy of their economy, even as they enter world markets. Typifying this threat, China complained in the trade negotiations that the United States was demanding the right to set up completely foreign-funded enterprises in the intellectual property fields, thereby bypassing any remaining restraints of the joint venture system and excluding Chinese participation in a most crucial high-tech sector. Such demands from Washington for uncontrolled investment are not simply meant to capture the emerging market in China, but to guarantee that profits from future exports will flow only into U.S. and other foreign coffers, thus weakening the autonomous Chinese economy and its potential global role.

Even before the trade deal had been signed, however, China had begun to lose control over significant sectors of its domestic market. In the early years of "opening to the outside world," the primary impact of foreign goods had been in those sectors which the Chinese either would not or could not develop themselves, such as luxury automobiles and clothing, Western liquors, and some high-tech items. Such companies as Mercedes-Benz, BMW, Pierre Cardin, and Benetton are still expanding their sales efforts, and in the next decade, for example, China is expected to become the largest market for imported liquor. Increasingly, however, products from abroad have begun to

displace domestic goods, due not to qualitative differences, but because of sheer multinational economic power.

As a result, the range of foreign-origin items dominating sales in
China is rapidly spreading, posing an entirely new kind of threat to its
own producers.

> With the Chinese market under attack from foreign commercial brand
> giants, makers of well-known domestic goods are quickly circling the
> wagons.
> According to Beijing-based Financial News, Coca-Cola, Pepsi, Nestle
> coffee and Lux soap led their market sectors in 1992 and 1993....
> In the soft drink industry, producers of many famous domestic brands
> such as Shenyang Bawang Temple, Shanghai Zhengguanghe,
> Guangzhou Asia soda, Sichuan Heaven cola and Beijing Arctic now have
> to produce foreign-name drinks with Coca-Cola and Pepsi to keep their
> enterprises afloat.
> Sales of traditional liquor have also fallen. Even maotai, the "emperor
> of Chinese liquor," has been replaced by foreign brands at some big
> banquets.[54]

Nonetheless, however much they may pose a threat of cultural as well
as economic erosion, Western liquor and colas are at least products
which originally came from abroad. The same cannot be said, however,
for items of daily use, like soaps, in which the Chinese up till now have
supplied their own domestic demand.

> Washing powder is another field dominated by foreign brands, includ-
> ing Omo and Ariel....
> The market for domestic washing powder, which had an output of 1.22
> million tons in 1992, is shrinking.
> Former booming brands, such as White Cat, Panda and Flowers have
> been forced to co-operate with foreign enterprises because of poor
> technology and a shortage of capital.
> By the first half of this year, the Shashi Daily-use Chemical Plant in Hubei
> Province, which produces Energy 28, was the only domestic detergent
> producer to remain wholly Chinese-owned.

Now "open to the world," undercapitalized industries in China increasingly cannot compete even in the domestic market, and are
instead forced into foreign dependency in order to survive.

The Chinese are not only losing market share, therefore, but control
over their own production, as a result of dependence on financing from
abroad. This is compounded by an upward creep in the allowable
share of foreign funds.

> Since foreign enterprises usually hold more than 60 per cent stakes in
> joint ventures, they have the decision-making power and the right to
> write off Chinese brands at any time, a detergent factory official said.

Some people fear the Chinese brands could some day disappear altogether.

Soap products are hardly the essence of national cultural identification. But as items of daily use that had been produced within China and carry traditional Chinese names are replaced by foreign-controlled and foreign-named goods, it is just one more sign of the gradual loss of control to outsiders, in ways which are felt even on the personal level. The further result is that China also loses out within the global marketplace.

> In order to compete, Chinese enterprises are trying to develop their own brands, hoping to gain a place in the international market....
> [But] as long as domestic brands seem forced to keep retreating in their own market, their entry into the world market is inconceivable.[55]

Thus dependence by Chinese on foreign investors to gain capital and technology needed to compete in global markets undermines not only domestic control of production, but in the end limits their ability to export into the international arena as well.

This is the context in which China accepted rather harsh conditions to end the trade clash with the United States, not only agreeing to much wider and freer imports of "intellectual" and cultural products, and even allowing totally foreign-owned companies to begin producing in the domestic market for the first time, but submitting to the very kind of interference in its legal system that it had earlier stated would constitute a violation of its national sovereignty. This intervention goes beyond the setting of specific deadlines for a crackdown on illegal producers and steps to prevent the export of pirated goods, but even requires China, "with United States assistance, to create a custom enforcement system modeled on the United States Customs Service" with "expanded search-and destroy powers for Chinese customs officers," and "a series of task forces to collect evidence."

> By sticking to its guns, the Administration has won a series of remarkably specific commitments requiring Chinese authorities to inspect every compact disk factory and software house, and to close down the offenders or force them to license the technology they use.
> It is a far more invasive procedure than China would ever allow an outside power to dictate in other realms—human rights, for example— and all the more remarkable because so many of the factories are enormous sources of revenue for the Chinese Army and the families of leadership.[56]

In return for these deeply interventionist measures, the United States, while denying any linkage, announced that it would renew efforts to help China to gain admission to the World Trade Organization (WTO) as a founding member, though the terms for this sponsorship left many basic issues unresolved. Thus while both sides could claim a certain kind of victory, the only real agreement was over the importance of the Chinese economy, as even Washington accepted that exclusion of China from international agreements was simply too costly for the U.S. economy and the global system to be sustained for a lengthy period of time.

Chinese officials, up to and including President Jiang Zemin, hailed the settlement, but they were somewhat slow to release details to the public, and the post-agreement mood seemed decidedly subdued compared to the brave rhetoric which had led up to it. This would appear to indicate somewhat greater discomfort with the results than was publicly stated. Of course, enforcement of the deal may well be another matter. Nonetheless, perhaps as a sign of the new dispensation, a Chinese court, for the first time since the 1992 bilateral *Memorandum of Understanding on Intellectual Property Right Protection*, and immediately after the signing of the new agreement, awarded a U.S. firm damages for copyright infringement. In this landmark breakthrough for the sanctity of private ownership in the international exchange of ideas, four publishers and distributors in Beijing were ordered to pay Disney Corporation 227,000 yuan or $26,000 for issuing children's books "using cartoons which resembled the well-known ... cartoon characters Mickey Mouse, Snow White, and Cinderella."[57] The offenders were also required to cease further publication of the disputed items, and to apologize to Disney. But regardless of such recent successes, given the close ties of the "pirates" to governmental authorities and leading families at all levels, "many people inside and outside the Administration suspect that new piracy factories may spring up as quickly as old ones are closed."[58]

Despite such doubts about the long-term results, when the showdown came, growing Chinese dependence on exports and foreign financing appeared to outweigh all other considerations. If trade alone was not sufficient to push China into accepting greater U.S. interference in its official policies, the possibility of a loss of confidence on the part of international investors almost surely provided the extra boost. In exchange for keeping the channels of foreign investment and exchange open, the Chinese negotiators accepted terms which, particularly in the area of customs control, reek of the days of gunboat diplomacy, when control over the flow of exports and the collection of tariffs was a standard weapon in the arsenal of imperialist domination, and was often used as an excuse for military action. Of course, nothing of a similar degree was conceded by the Chinese in this case, but the agreement with the United States has a decidedly musty smell, reinforcing the impression that it uses a "big stick" in dealing with

China. Whatever the immediate feelings of relief over having avoided, at least temporarily, an open trade war with the most powerful economy in the world, it would be unlikely that the deep suspicions of U.S. motives and resentments at its strong-arm tactics will soon be forgotten by the Chinese.

Further tensions seem inevitable, in the context of which the trade deal will be seen as only one small skirmish in an ongoing economic war. Already, highly contentious additional issues have been raised, such as accusations of Chinese "dumping" of textiles. As a consequence, China suffered direct losses of several hundred million dollars in fines and other, even larger, indirect retaliatory measures in 1994 alone, while in early 1995 the United States reduced the Chinese textile quota. Even as U.S. trade representative Mickey Kantor arrived in Beijing to sign the new intellectual property rights settlement, he used the occasion to denounce suspension of compliance with a 1992 bilateral agreement to lift barriers on a wide range of products. China, for its part, expressed suspicions about the intentions of the United States in regard to its WTO membership, which was still being denied in late 1995, mainly due to U.S. objections.

At the same time, Washington was again threatening the imposition of the "suspended" $1 billion in tariffs for what it claimed was Chinese noncompliance with the anti-piracy accord signed earlier that year. Publicly giving China just ninety days to enforce the agreement, the administration cited ongoing production at the very facilities it had insisted be closed.

> While the renewed threat of sanctions risks a new breach of relations, American trade officials said ... that China's continued foot-dragging in closing the 29 factories that churn out millions of illegal copies of American films and software had already cost United States corporations more than $800 million this year. In fact, there is evidence that some factories that halted making illegal copies of compact disks had resumed production, this time producing far more expensive CD-ROM's containing pirated copies of just-released computer software.[59]

Thus not only do the issues of pirating and WTO membership fail to get resolved, but attempts to force China to comply with the standards of the global capitalist market constantly serve merely to recreate the same problems, as it were, on a higher plane.

Moreover, the Chinese believe that even international agreements will not protect them from unilateral U.S. acts.

> But, regardless of the outcome of the current dialogue, the landscape of Sino-US relations after China's WTO membership is settled seems clear. To be sure, that landscape cannot be called 'smooth.' The US has made evident its desire to gain as much profit from China as possible, and this

position is not expected to change.
The North American nation has indicated that it can still resort to the
Non-Application Clause at will even if China becomes a full WTO
member—meaning the US could try to hammer out Sino-US trade
policies outside of the international trading framework.
That the US wants to be hard on China for the years to come cannot be
expressed clearer.[60]

The United States moved to impose just such bilateral trade agreements on Japan, outside the structure of the WTO, almost immediately
after concluding intellectual property negotiations with China, no
doubt confirming Chinese uneasiness in this regard. For China it was
a timely reminder that in global affairs, it is ultimately the U.S. government which above all others reserves to itself the right to "play by
its own rules," accepting only those international limitations which
favor it. Despite the apparent clearing of the air over their most
contentious trade conflict in early 1995, therefore, the lessening of
strains proved only very temporary, and fundamental differences
between the Chinese and the United States have been left dangling
without resolution. Tensions remain quite high and are likely to rise
again. In these conflicts, domestic policies will also shape the ability
of China to resist U.S. domination.

But in resolving such contradictions, the masses will also have a
say. During the intellectual property negotiations, one of the defenses
offered by China for the difficulty of enforcing trademark and patent
rights is the relatively low economic level of the country, which creates
enormous demand pressures and supply opportunities for cheap
pirated goods. Despite the rapid growth of a new professional and
technical middle class and modernized businesses requiring advanced
software, the vast majority of the Chinese population, including the
average urban resident, earns barely enough in a year to buy a single
computer program at international market prices. On the more popular level, similar earnings-to-cost gaps exist for CDs, videos, and many
other consumer goods. While the new modernized sector therefore
generates both a demand for foreign products and a segment of the
business and professional community that can afford to buy them at a
global price—a small proportion of the total population, but a large
and growing market—most Chinese still live at an income level that
would exclude such purchases if they were forced to pay full international value.

Even though "opening to the world" has introduced such consumer
products to the masses in China, therefore, it has not provided the
means to buy them. The billion dollars in calculated "losses" to U.S.
producers may as a result be largely on paper only, since at full global

prices many of the sales to Chinese would simply never take place. Of course, exports from China to other more affluent markets abroad is another matter. But the crucial base for pirated products remains the relative poverty of the Chinese in a world of expensive consumer goods, and such contradictions are all but unsolvable within the current market framework. Opportunities for mass pirating are thus likely to continue to grow, as more people are drawn into modern consumerism, and the gap between demand and income widens. In this way, "correct ideas" will still be "socialized"—even if in forms corrupted by the market—whatever the government does.

V. 900-Pound Panda

In what might be taken as an implied threat, Chu Xiangyin, dean of the School of International Trade and Economics at the University of International Business and Economics in Beijing, stated as U.S. and Chinese negotiators met:

> Denial of Gatt access could turn China into a "900-pound gorilla" unbound by the marshalling forces of a world trading system....
> He noted that as decentralization takes root in China, it would be hard for the central government to control localities with international rules if China is out of Gatt.[61]

In this way, Chu indicated once again that China is simply too big to be excluded from the world economic system, and that as domestic policy becomes inevitably intertwined with foreign relations, Chinese admission to worldwide trade associations depends on actions at home, which in turn shape the international economy. On a more basic level, however, issues like the conflict over intellectual property expose the underlying dilemma of fitting China into the global economic system. There is wide disagreement over how strong the country is economically, and even conflicting views over how its economic power should be measured. Underpinning and exacerbating the trade tensions, therefore, is the question of what "rank" China occupies in the world economy.

By global economic standards, China remains a poor third world society, which by traditional World Bank measurements had an annual per capita income of only around $370 per year in 1990, not even one tenth of the international average of $4,200, and ranked ninety-sixth among the countries of the globe. Yet so vast is its scale that even at these low rates China was already, that year, the eighth largest economy in the world. Moreover, by a new set of measurements recently adopted by the International Monetary Fund (IMF) and the World Bank, and based on a global comparison of domestic purchasing power rather than monetary exchange values, the Chinese rose to third in total economic power by the early 1990s, just behind Japan. Confirming this new calculation, the CIA, in 1993, estimated the gross domestic product of China at $2.35 trillion, matching the Japanese economy, and growing many times faster. During the negotiations over intellectual property rights, U.S. trade representative Mickey Kantor insisted that this was their actual global rank. On this basis, per capita GNP in China has climbed to between $1,500 and $2,000 annually. But even if this is an accurate measure of the Chinese economy, it is only equal to between one third and one quarter the level of income in third world countries of comparable size and potential, such as Brazil.

Our personal experience in China suggests, however, that the latter form of calculation exaggerates buying power. We found that goods generally cost, in Chinese yuan, close to what would have been their price in the United States in dollars. The domestic purchasing power of the currency therefore did not seem to be particularly higher than it would have been if measured globally. It is true that, given the simplicity of the prior "socialist" market, in which many purchases were made informally and often quite literally on the street, and without high sales costs, it was possible to meet basic needs relatively cheaply in China. But it is just this system which is now being destroyed by the growth in modern consumerism, and after the January 1994 devaluation, imported products would have risen in price, making the strength of the yuan at home even less, especially given the ever-greater reliance on foreign goods. While the "true" value of Chinese economic wealth may, therefore, lie somewhere between the two forms of international measurement, it remains at a very low level at best.

For their part, official statistics in China indicate a rate of GNP per capita below even the lower World Bank estimates. In 1990, Chinese government figures reported that gross domestic product was only 1,559 yuan, or just $327 per person. By 1994, GDP had risen to 4,380 billion yuan or $518 billion, and 3,650 yuan per capita, equivalent to $432 using the new exchange rate. While there was no doubt a significant increase in income per person in just four years, this still leaves China near the bottom of the international economic system. Moreover, even these figures do not reflect the effects of inflation, which reduced the buying power of the yuan in the domestic economy drastically during this time. Notably, the 35.3 percent rise in wages paid by the state to working people in 1994 constituted only a 7 percent growth in real value, though this was still the largest increase in several years. Even with these gains, the Chinese calculate that average income received by urbanites in 1994 was just 3,179 yuan or $379 per person.

Some 20 million people in the cities still live on less than 150 yuan or under eighteen dollars per month, and even the newly introduced minimum wage is set at only 210 yuan or twenty-five dollars monthly in Beijing.

In rural areas, where 70 to 80 per cent of the people live, incomes in 1994 averaged less than half this minimal level, having reached only 1,220 yuan or $145, despite recent gains. The full meaning of such figures, especially as a basis for international trade, becomes apparent when average expenditures on living needs are given. Thus the typical Chinese farmer in 1993 was estimated to have spent only 70 yuan or eight dollars on clothing and 143 yuan or seventeen dollars on improvements to housing, while fully 600 yuan or seventy-one dollars went for food, most of it domestically grown or bought from local sources. Even in Shanghai, family disposal income—above necessary expenditures—was only 16.1 percent, yet this was still 5.8 percentage points above the national average of funds available for consumer goods, suggesting how limited a basis exists in China, even today, for the purchase of costly foreign items.

These figures must be compared with international standards set by the World Bank, which uses $370 per capita national income as an upper poverty line, and defines the very poorest as those below $275 per year. By this measure, even the urban Chinese population on average is just now barely breaking through the upper limit of impoverishment, and the rural population is still at one-half the cutoff point globally for the desperately poor. By another international standard, percentage of income spent on food, most people in China have only just emerged from deep impoverishment. UN indices define those spending more than 60 percent on foodstuffs as below the poverty line, those in the 50 to 60 percent range as having enough food and clothing, the 40 to 50 percent range indicating a comfortable life, and less than 40 percent as being well-off. Chinese rural families spent 58 percent of income to feed themselves in 1993, down some ten percentage points from 1978, and urban residents devoted 50 percent to this category, a drop of almost 6 percent from 1981.

Thus, by this measure too, the average family in the countryside has barely escaped poverty, while those in the cities are just reaching the borderline between subsistence and basic comfort. There are of course those in China who are doing much better. A survey of 30,000 households in Shanghai in 1994 found an average income of 5,566 yuan or $661 per capita, and 11,630 yuan or $1,381 for each member of high-income families. In Beijing the same year, average family income was said to have risen to 15,000 yuan or $1,760, with one-third of families having 20,000 yuan or $2,353, and 5 per cent soaring to 40,000 yuan or $4,705. But this means that even the very top stratum of total family incomes in Chinese urban areas, where families average 3.19 persons, barely begins to reach the average income for each individual in leading Latin American countries.

By any of these measurements, therefore, China remains overwhelmingly a poor nation compared even to much of the third world, and this too must certainly be considered, together with such factors as total GNP or impact on international trade balances, in evaluating the power of its economy within the global system. An even more recent World Bank measurement, which combines natural resources, capital investment, and productivity, including lifetime earnings, further confirms this assessment. This standard attempts to calculate "national net worth," based on both physical and human capacity, rather than relying on annual economic output alone. By this measure, Japan ranks fifth in the world and the United States twelfth, but China is only number 162, once again near the bottom of the world system, and far down the list even among the 163 poorer countries that share only 16 percent of global wealth. This must be contrasted with the twenty-nine richest nations which account for 80 percent of world net worth.[62]

Thus even as they point with pride to the tremendous explosion in overall economic growth and in mass consumption over the past decade or more, the Chinese continue to stress that their country is still a "developing" one. This attitude was exemplified by one of my graduate students, clearly among the "best and the brightest," already a rising star at his home university and the kind of young professional who will no doubt soon be moving into even higher positions of authority. Yet for his course paper he chose to write a challenge to the calculations of the World Bank and IMF "that China has become one of the top countries in economic strength," and he took issue especially with the new estimates based on domestic buying power. He argued instead that for all its recent growth, the Chinese economy lags far behind not only the world leaders, but even most second-rank countries in a wide range of economic measurements.

For example, according to his study, China now has an annual per capita consumption of electricity of only 750 kilowatt hours, less than seventy other nations, and some 110 million people, or almost 10 percent of the population, have no access to electric power at all. In 1994, national electrical generation grew by over 11 percent, but this was 9 percent below industrial production growth, and 8 percent less than rising electric consumption by households, so even as absolute expansion takes place, the relative supply of Chinese energy is falling. In Changchun, a leading industrial city, there were frequent electrical outages. The coal-fired heating system where we taught, one of the national "key" universities, was so poor that students kept on their army-style greatcoats and thick down jackets in the classroom throughout the sub-Siberian winter. One reason they liked visiting our apartment so much was that, though it too was often semi-freezing, it was still much warmer than their dorms. South of the Changjiang River, heating of public buildings is generally forbidden, though temperatures can be quite low in many places during winter. Thus energy resources are often inadequate for minimal comfort, or even perhaps survival—Chinese point to this as one cause of the many deaths in a Shanghai orphanage that recently came to light.

Water supplies at the university in Changchun were even more sporadic, and the hot tap in our bathroom, which usually did not function at the same time as the cold, ran a murky brown that often left a thick layer of grime on the bottom of the tub. Throughout China, water must be boiled to be potable, even in most four-star hotels. Such problems are nationwide and massive. In announcing a water-saving campaign in mid-1995, Construction Minister Hou Jie pointed out that half the 600 Chinese urban areas lack sufficient supplies, with thirty of the top thirty-two cities experiencing long-term difficulty in meeting even basic requirements. According to his statement, an average of 230 billion yuan or $27.4 billion in industrial output value is affected by such deficiencies each year. In Guangdong alone, water consumption is expected to quadruple between 1990 and 2010, but even existing supplies are becoming so polluted that without immediate action, "the region will be severely hindered in future economic development."[63] In 1994, over 3.37 billion tons of waste were dumped in provincial rivers, most of it inadequately treated.

There are now plans to build a series of massive channels—the biggest such projects since the construction of the Grand Canal in the thirteenth century—to carry water from the West and South to the thirsty cities of the North and East. Yet China already has only one-fourth the average per capita resources of the world as a whole, and given the intention of the government to develop the Chinese interior, such attempts to reorder the natural environment may well end up robbing Peter to pay Paul. An example of such problems is in Western Xinjiang Province, where the Eb Nur Lake, which has shrunk dramatically in recent years, is in danger of drying up entirely. Of the six tributaries that flowed into this body of water, three of the main rivers dried up as the population increased, arable land expanded, and large-scale building of water conservancy projects was carried out.[64] Thus diversion of supplies to meet the growing needs of people and farms, and even the very effort at conservation itself, can exacerbate the problem. If Eb Nur Lake disappears, the climate of the entire region would be endangered.

Nor is water supply the only problem. In Guangdong Province, environmental damage such as acid rain continues to increase "in spite of great efforts to curb it." Release of sulphur dioxide into the air grew 63 percent between 1990 and 1994. As a result, "the frequency of acid rain has risen 50 per cent, or even 90 per cent in certain areas of the Pearl River Delta... the polluting industries from overseas or those that have moved from urban to rural areas are considered the major culprit."[65] By 1995, 20 percent of the country was affected by acid rain, up from just 18 percent a decade earlier. Thus development constantly threatens to overwhelm the environmental base on which it rests, with consequences for not only growth but even basic survival.

It was by pointing to such weaknesses that the student in my class argued that China, despite its massive economic power, should not be rated among the global leaders, nor even as a developed nation. In particular, he stressed, "if a country's per capita output and income is just enough for its people to live simply, how can its comprehensive national strength be strong?" From this standpoint, economic power must be measured not only by its global impact, but by the basic living standards of its people. His attitude suggests that among the emerging young leadership in China there are those who will not be content merely with overall growth in the national economy as a measure of its international strength, unless it brings clear gains in daily life as well. Such an argument appears to reflect the continuing socialist side of the Chinese revolution, for it flies in the face of standard capitalist analysis, which constantly celebrates the rise of "boom" economies in the third world, even when they bring increasing poverty for the masses. From this opposing viewpoint, China stresses that it is still "developing," regardless of gross figures for its total economy.

Yet there is an apparent anomaly in the Chinese assertion that they are still relatively poor, since the government is at the same time clearly concerned to lay claim to major improvements in economic conditions for the masses, as well as to restore the historic role of China as a leading global "player." To some extent, this seeming contradiction arises from the need to be honest about the limits of development until now, and not to exaggerate the gains made, which might raise the expectations of the population beyond realizable goals. But the Chinese position also reflects hard bargaining over the conditions for their entry into the global trade bodies—GATT, and its successor, the WTO.

While intellectual property rights were the immediate issue of contention in the negotiations with the United States on this issue, the deeper conflict lies in how the Chinese economy is to be defined. China insists on admission as a developing country, Washington just as adamantly calls it a developed one. The categorization is highly significant, since under WTO rules the level of trade barriers permitted and the length of time allowed to remove them varies according to this difference in definition. For "developing" countries the standard to be achieved within five years after joining the organization is a tariff level not to exceed 10 percent, while for "developed" nations the goal is 3.5 percent. At present the average rate in China is 19 percent, requiring it to cut its tariffs by almost half even to reach the higher range allowed third world countries, and as of early 1995 it had only pledged to reduce its tariff levels by one third within five years of being admitted to the global trade system. A World Bank study in 1994 found Chinese tariffs "higher, more numerous and more dispersed than those of most other large developing countries," and the new "pillar" industries are meant to add even further layers of protection against foreign ownership and competition.[66] Yet China runs a trade deficit with much of the world. According to Singapore Prime Minister Goh Chok Tong, it is "more open than Japan, South Korea and Taiwan were at a similar stage of development."[67]

But regardless of its exact degree of openness, the underlying issue remains how to measure the economic power of China globally. According to Chinese commentators, "as a developing country, China should be allowed to protect its fledgling industries, subsidize its exports and enjoy tariff reductions and other preferential treatments the Gatt offer developing countries."[68] But the United States has "insisted that China enter as a developed nation, citing the country's potential for export growth."[69] There is thus a basic disagreement over how Chinese economic power is to be measured.

The insistence by China that it is still a relatively poor country is found at the very highest official levels, and is viewed by them as raising basic issues of sovereignty. Wu Yi, minister of foreign trade and economic cooperation, insists on just such a linkage. Welcoming back representatives negotiating the entry by China into GATT, she stated that the delegation, "attaching importance to the country's fundamental interests ... and stressing its position as a developing country,' has demonstrated the spirit of defending national interests."[70] This theme was constantly raised in the negotiations, where efforts by Washington to define China as "developed" were seen as just one more instance of its bullying methods. "China is still a developing country with a per capita income below that of most countries today," Liu Chuntian, a professor at the Intellectual Property Centre of People's University in Beijing, reminded U.S. negotiators. "It's unreasonable for the US to ask

China's legislation to keep in line with a timetable set for developed countries."[71]

The Chinese stress the hypocrisy of the United States, whose multinational enterprises, unlike the administration, seem to have no difficulty recognizing China as a "developing" economy.

> Few American business people can claim, as the US Government has done so, that China is a developed country. Otherwise they would not have pledged over $10 billion in the Chinese market to take advantage of one of the world's cheapest labour forces....
> Just make an excursion into China's vast interior, and one can well reason with those contracting parties which insist on labelling China as a developed nation.[72]

In this view, the Chinese economy is still a weak player in the international market, and needs protection against the global leaders, especially the United States.

A particular complaint is that while the U.S. government treats China as "developed" when it comes to trade, at the same time it insists that despite fifteen years of reform, China still has an "underdeveloped" market system. But "marketization" is itself one of the requirements for GATT admission.

> Another senior Chinese economist said the US demand is simply contradictory: on one hand, the US insists that China enter Gatt as a developed country; on the other, it says China is far from having a market economy in the real sense.[73]

Such contradictions are not only taken as an insult by those who believe China should be rewarded for its rapid marketization, they also raise deep suspicions about the larger goals of U.S. policy. The determination of the United States to treat the Chinese economy as "developed" is thus seen as going beyond trade, to the struggle for world economic dominance.

In this view, it is the Chinese potential to lead not only Asia, but the third world in general, that is the real threat as perceived by the U.S. government, and leads to a policy of "containment" of China to prevent it from growing too strong. This was expressed by Vice-Premier and Foreign Minister Qian Qichen.

> In the most recent period, there has been an international tendency to exaggerate China's strength, alleging that China will become the world's No 1 or No 2 economic power in the coming 10 to 20 years, he said.
> Qian maintained that some believe this because they overestimate China's economic development, while others, with malicious intentions, try to find evidence for a "China threat" theory.[74]

Regardless of U.S. intent, it must be asked why such growth is "threatening" at all. The issue is clearly more than trade.

The fear of China as a potential power, and as a leader of other developing nations, goes back at least to the turn of the century. Writing in 1902 in *Imperialism: A Study*, J.A. Hobson—whose work helped Lenin formulate his own classic thesis on the imperialist stage of capitalism[75]—gave vent to the disquiet in the West at possible competition from Chinese industry. "In our dealings with backward races capable of instruction in Western industrial methods there are three stages," he wrote. The first is normal commerce, the second investment by the European powers.

> But a third stage remains, one which in China at any rate may be reached at no distant period, when the capital and organizing energy may be developed within the country, either by Europeans planted there or by natives. Thus fully equipped for future internal development in all the necessary productive powers, such a nation may turn upon her civilizer, untrammelled by need of further industrial aid, undersell him in his own market, take away his other foreign markets and secure for herself what further developing work remains to be done in other undeveloped parts of the earth....
> It is at least conceivable that China might so turn the tables upon the Western industrial nations, and, either by adopting their capital and organizers or, as is more probable, by substituting her own, might flood their markets with her cheaper manufactures, and refusing their imports in exchange might take her payment in liens upon their capital, reversing the earlier process of investment until she gradually obtained financial control over her quondam patrons and civilizers.[76]

Thus for almost a century, the "threat" of China has haunted Europe and the United States, not only as direct competitor, but as leader of a bloc of poor nations, underselling the West even while excluding imported products in return, and draining it of profits. U.S. fears in this regard are merely the latest version of the Western nightmare of Chinese power turning the imperialist tables, rejecting the "civilizing" pretensions of those who have oppressed it, and leading a revived Asia to global dominance. Of course, this takes its own special forms today, especially given the remnants of a revolutionary socialist legacy in China.

In the eyes of many Chinese, including high officials, in the struggle over intellectual property rights, "the US has ulterior motives well beyond the IPR issue."[77] Thus Yu Peiwei, the Moftec researcher,

> noted that the US has been applying similar policies in trade talks with Japan and the European Union.
> "In the psychological analysis, the US fears that a rapidly growing Chinese economy would enable China to join hands some day with developing countries to pose a threat to the US' dominant status in the world economy."

Therefore, it wants to weaken or contain China's potential economic growth momentum by imposing unduly high demands on China's Gatt access.[78]

Others note that the issue of Chinese economic strength is inseparable from global politics, and that this is where the real conflict with the United States lies.

The per capita income of the Chinese people is so small and the level of China's modernization is so low, that we wonder how some people could insist at the talks that China is a developed, rather than a developing, country and should be treated as such. Is this another example that political prejudice can blind one to reality?[79]

Such "blindness," in the Chinese view, has a long and grim historical basis.

Thus beyond commercial motives, China sees the spectre of more serious political threats, with U.S. anticommunism again raising its head. This is a source of resentment both because it denies to the Chinese the right to determine their own social system, but equally because it ignores the fifteen years of market reforms that have so transformed the socialist economy—and how far some authorities have gone in abjuring the past.

On the political front, there's entrenched hostility against Communism among certain high-ranking officials in the White House and on Capitol Hill alike.

"Disregarding China's market-oriented reforms, they insist that China's economy is still a planned one because the country is led by Communists."

This outmoded, biased attitude is reflected in the current Gatt re-entry negotiations, with US officials attempting to force China into accepting the American political and economic system outright.[80]

From this viewpoint, the United States still sees China, just as it did in decades past, as a threat, not only economically, but politically and ideologically as well. Given the current statements coming from Washington, this view is well-founded. Whatever remains of the Chinese socialist system, however weakened it may be, there are those in the U.S. government who are still determined to eliminate it, both to fully "cleanse" China itself, and to prevent it from offering any alternative to international capitalism as dominated by the United States.

In the trade conflict over intellectual property rights, the Chinese thus see the whole universe of issues separating them from the United States. They believe that what is at stake is not just economic power, but the entire global system. As Wang Jisi, director of American studies of the Chinese Academy of Social Sciences, analyzed the contentions between the two sides:

Concern over its own economic and political well-being is the final reason the United States erected barriers to China's Gatt re-entry....

Both government officials and media in the US have spread their notorious view of the so-called "China threat" over the past year.

Traditionally, increasing military fees of China were the basis for America to publicize its "China-threat" view.

But now, China's positions on issues such as business, politics, arms sales, immigration and environmental protection have become new grounds of American efforts to defame China.

And now the US is spreading its view of the sluggish condition of intellectual property rights in China which has already caused a severe tit-to-tat fight from China.[81]

From this standpoint, the Chinese are presenting a challenge to the United States, not only because of the massive expansion of their economy, but also due to the system of market socialism which they are using to develop their power. Thus even the very nature of the reforms themselves is still considered to be threatening.

Some Americans feel that China's rapid economic growth, coupled with its political structure, is the most significant threat to the long-term interests of the United States.

Such people believe that China's increasingly important role in changing the world's status quo will interfere with the US's interests in the existing world political structure....

With the end of the four-decade Cold War, the United States has retained its most powerful status in global politics, but it is beginning to lose some of its clout.

At the same time, China is becoming more influential world-wide, thanks to its 16-year programme of opening-up and reform.

However, the two countries are neither strategic enemies nor allies, and communication and co-operation between them will be furthered.

Accordingly, struggles over political systems and values will remain serious.[82]

Attributing current tensions to a U.S. fear of losing its own position as the dominant force in the global system, the Chinese believe that relations between the two countries will continue to be troubled, as China regains its position as a world power.

Only in this light can one grasp the full import of statements such as that of Professor Xu Jie of the Chinese University of Political Science and Law: "China's actions to protect intellectual property have helped build a legal system of intellectual property rights protections with Chinese characteristics."[83] Or as Qiu Xichun, a senior official with Moftec, states, "China is marching along its own path in foreign trade reform, which is consistent with international practice and the merits of a socialist market economy."[84] The Chinese, in other words, see pressure from the United States not only as a threat to their economic interests. They also view it as a fundamental challenge to "market socialism with special Chinese characteristics," that is, to their unique path to development. Long Yongtu, assistant minister of Moftec, has warned that

> although re-entry into Gatt is important for China, there are even more important things for the nation.
> He stressed that China will not let Gatt re-entry be used as a lever to cripple its infant industries, which by all measures cannot match those of the developed world. Moreover, the nation cannot risk massive unemployment at the hands of fierce world competition.[85]

Under GATT rules for "developed" countries, pressures of the global economy might quickly force abandonment by the Chinese of any remaining socialistic aspects in their economy. In this view, efforts by the United States to impose its trade policies are an attempt not only to keep China from emerging as a major world power, but to strip it of the ability to practice "market socialism with Chinese characteristics," preventing it from offering an alternative to the U.S.-dominated system, and thus driving it into forms of capitalist exploitation it cannot socially afford. For China, such pressures constitute the most basic challenge to national independence, for they both limit it externally, and threaten it domestically, undermining its social order.

The conflict with the United States over GATT and WTO has thus taken on such a contentious tone because of the enormous stakes on both sides. Since 1992, China has "spared no effort in promoting a new economy, in compliance with the Gatt principle of using the market mechanism to allocate resources."[86] Should it now be required to accept "developed" status in order to join that body, its doors will be flung open even wider to a potentially overwhelming flood of goods from abroad, which will in turn force the Chinese to accept greater foreign investment and control of its economy. This would provide leverage for intervention in the political and social system as well, as the United States seeks to completely stamp out socialism—however much it may have already been weakened through the marketization reforms. On the other hand, if China is allowed to enter the global market as a still-developing nation, its massive economic potential, even at low levels of GNP per capita, is likely to present a serious challenge to current world leaders.

The dilemma for the Chinese is that they are trying to hold on to their own economic resources at the same time that they are inviting massive investment from abroad, in effect asking global capital to finance their rise to power and allow their low-cost products to flood the international markets, while continuing to treat China as if it were just another poor third world country. Recent statements on the Chinese

WTO application suggest that there will be some compromise struck between the "developed" and "developing" positions, though the details of any such agreement are still subject to hard bargaining. But even such a finessing of the issue of trade relations cannot permanently resolve the more basic conflict over the role of China in the global system.

Whatever its exact economic level, there is a fundamental contradiction between the individual relative poverty in which the vast majority of the Chinese people continue to live, and its enormous power in the world economy. This difference lies at the heart of the conflict with the United States and other dominant capitalist powers, for while China points to the still weak status of its population and of its economic infrastructure, U.S. leaders focus on the massiveness of the Chinese challenge in global markets. That there is truth in both assertions does little to ease the tension or point the way to a solution, since it is inherent in the contradictory global effect of "market socialism." Thus there is a basic disconnect between the legacy of the self-reliant and collective struggle against poverty that occurred under the earlier Chinese socialist system—which is still claimed as the basis of social policy, but which had virtually no effect on the international system of trade—and the new role of China as a powerful player in the global capitalist economy, where its marketized industries use low-paid labor to undercut its competitors.

The fundamental contradiction is expressed by a non-U.S. Western diplomat. "If China got a special deal getting into Gatt, all the smaller countries would squawk like hell. If anything, China is so huge, it should definitely not have special terms of entry."[87] But this kind of calculation has no meaning from the standpoint of the mass of Chinese, who only want the right to escape from historic poverty and obtain an income roughly comparable at least to the level of other leading third world nations. Leaders in China even speak modestly of trying to move the country into the lower ranks of the intermediate stratum of nations in terms of GNP per capita, following the pattern of the "four dragons" of the Pacific Rim. A report from the Chinese Academy of Sciences "estimates that the annual GDP growth rate will be 9.3 per cent until 2000, 8 per cent for 2001-2010 and 7 per cent for 2011-2020," and by 2040-2050 will rank first in the world in total output. Yet even then per capita income and other major socioeconomic indices will only be equal to developed nations back in 2000, and it will take over 100 years for China to catch up with the leading countries.[88] According to Zhou Caiyu, director of the Economic Institute of the State Planning Commission, "it is estimated that at a growth rate of 10 per cent, China will need 30 years to reach the level of a medium-developed country with GDP averaging $3,000 per capita."[89]

Thus even assuming that such a fantastic expansion can be continued for so long, which in itself would be unprecedented historically—and that the figures used represent constant dollars, so that the rest of the world remained relatively at the same income level as at the present—the Chinese would still rank at the end of three decades in the lower level of the global "middle class" of states, barely rising into the semiperiphery of the international system as measured in economic terms. Even so, without allowing for population growth, such an increase in GDP per capita would mean almost a tenfold multiplication of the economy of China, and a greater and virtually exponential growth in its nonagricultural sectors, an almost unimaginable reordering of world power. In this regard, it should be noted that Guangdong Province alone, with 68 million people, is approximately as large as the "four dragons" combined, suggesting the potential impact of any multiplying effect on even one part of the Chinese economy, not to speak of the country as a whole.

For even should the more optimistic projections being put forward in China prove unrealizable, as seems likely, anything approaching them would soon vault the Chinese into clear second place behind the United States in economic scale, and perhaps even into the position of global leader. If the new higher measurements now being used by the World Bank and IMF prove more accurate, China would be catapulted into unchallenged international leadership, with two to three times the might of the present U.S. economy. Such a reordering of the world system would inevitably produce heightened conflicts not only in the economic arena, but very likely political and even military clashes as well. Yet any such struggles would inevitably affect the domestic situation in China, limiting its growth. The report issued by the Chinese Academy of Sciences in early 1995 shows what is at stake here. To maintain its projected rapid expansion, the study notes, China must not only "prevent chaos like the cultural revolution (1966-76) and any other turmoil from happening," but "special attention must be paid to fighting corruption, and the widening gap between the rich and the poor, the urban and rural areas, and different regions." It must "at the same time overcome looming shortages of energy, farmland, mineral resources, as well as inadequate bottlenecks in economic and social development." As if this were not enough, catching up with and overtaking developed countries will require "a peaceful international environment," even as the growing power of China challenges the global leaders.[90] Yet such rapid and sustained economic expansion is almost certain to exacerbate these very same domestic and global tensions.

Faced with such difficulties, what seems more likely, therefore, is that Chinese growth will fall short of its most grandiose anticipations, but still be sufficiently massive in its impact to be highly troubling to the current world leaders, the United States above all. To take just one example, China expects to become the largest synthetic fiber producer by the end of the century, surpassing the current leadership of U.S. companies. But if the Chinese economy were to expand tenfold, such gains would require even more long-term growth of this and similar industries, and a corresponding expansion in exports, threatening to flood the world markets. Yet despite such growth, the ability of the people of China to purchase goods from abroad—even with an expanding middle class, now estimated at anywhere from 60 to 300 million, with an increasing amount of disposable income—would still remain at a very low international level, comparable only to that of Brazil in the 1990s.

On the other hand, any failure by China to reach its goals would also be likely to generate a series of problems for the global capitalist system that would be almost as great as success. With the vast amounts of capital now pouring into the country, and the new lifestyle expectations which have been raised among the Chinese people, setbacks would be almost certain to produce economic turmoil and generate political repercussions which would extend far beyond the borders of the country itself. This is especially so given the U.S. dependence on "newly emerging markets" as an outlet for its own goods. Having itself entered into the world market in such a massive way, China has become a crucial, if not overwhelming factor in the global economy, and its future course, no matter what its direction, will have fundamental international significance.

As such, there is almost guaranteed to be a conflict between Chinese national aspirations and autonomy, and the growing centrality of the country in world affairs. This will tempt others, the United States above all, to try to exploit China, while at the same time attempting to contain Chinese power and determine the shape of its society. China will thus be forced to resist both exploitation and containment in order to continue anything approaching its current rapid economic expansion. Yet any failure to meet the new aspirations of its people may well create wider social divisions as well, with the potential to open the door once again to imperialistic meddling in its internal affairs. In meeting these challenges, China will face the contradiction that it is too large, and has become much too powerful, to be anything other than a major player in the world economy, and yet it remains too weak to impose its own will on the global system now dominated by the United States.

VI. The "Chinese Threat" to the U.S. Global Security System

Through the very growth of their economic strength and related political and military power, the Chinese are perceived as threatening other countries and U.S. dominance in Asia and the world. But it is increasingly China itself which is threatened. From the triumph of the revolution up until now, the Chinese have been able to isolate their own society from external domination and interference. This has been a primary basis for the rapid expansion of their economy, as well as the foundation for their foreign policy, as is constantly stated by top leaders (especially in recent years), including President Jiang Zemin: "On more than one occasion, Jiang reiterated that China is concentrating all its energy on economic construction at home; and for this reason is very much in need of a peaceful international environment."[91] When on the Chinese mainland, there is a sense of being as far removed as is still possible in the world today from outside threats and the overweening power of the United States—in notable contrast, for instance, to the constant and visceral presence of Yankee imperialism everywhere in Latin America.

However, as China is drawn more deeply into the worldwide capitalist economy and challenges U.S. global dominance, its autonomy and relatively benign international setting may well be lost. For the moment, the Chinese and the United States may be "neither strategic enemies nor allies," and so "relations between the two countries will be a mixture of cooperation and friction."[92] But this form of mutually dependent tension may deteriorate in the not-so-distant future.

> US policy makers now say China has not yet formed a "direct significant threat" to US security policy though they are very much concerned about China's booming economy and military power which they see as a "potential threat" to America's security system.
> Some Americans suggest the US should implement a "containment policy" in developing relationship with China so as to relieve the so-called potential threat from China to US security.
> In line with the policy, Capitol Hill may take a tougher stand towards China and may be difficult to compromise when conflicts occur in the future....[93]

The Chinese already see campaigns to limit their power and even to break up their national unity in the efforts of some powerful forces in the United States.

In this view, it is not simply the growing economic and military power of China, but its political and ideological system that makes it a perceived "threat." According to Chen Baosen, research fellow at the Institute of American Studies of the Chinese Academy of Social Sciences:

Many US politicians have an inborn bias on communism, socialism and
public ownership which are now dominating China's political system.
They are unhappy to see the booming economy in socialist China.
This is the behind-the-scenes reason for the booming "China threat"
theory in the West. Some Americans even imagine ridiculous military
conflicts, between the two countries.
Human rights concerns as well as the Tibetan and Taiwan issues, which
are China's internal affairs, are often subjects of American slander over
China.[94]

Such doubts about U.S. intentions and motives were further seriously
inflamed by the May, 1995 decision to allow Lee Teng-hui, President
of the Taiwan government, to visit the United States "privately." There,
despite professing that he still adhered to a "one-China" policy, Lee
made a plea for strengthened diplomatic ties between Washington and
Taipei, denounced communism as "dead," and constantly stressed
"democracy," the key term being used today to justify U.S. global
interventionism. That same month there were attempts in Congress to
require the State Department to appoint an ambassador to the "government" of Tibet, that is, the exiled followers of the Dalai Lama. In
addition to these blatant threats to the status of territories which China
has long considered as part of its national entity, there are further
tensions over Chinese claims to the South China Sea and relations with
nations the United States defines as "outlaw" states, such as Iran.

Though Taiwan and Tibet were conquered relatively late in the long
course of imperial consolidation, Chinese claims to both areas are still
older than the formation of the United States, much less its own later
imperialist expansion into Texas, the Southwest and California, Puerto
Rico, and Hawaii. The control exerted by China in its own outlying
territories has waxed and waned over the past two centuries, during
which time internal movements for autonomy or independence have
sporadically arisen, some of which continue to the present day. In this
sense, there are the same legitimate questions about relations to national authority, the survival of historic cultures, and issues of human
rights that arise in all global areas of regional or ethnic division. But
by the same token, such tensions are rife with possibilities for being
inflamed by those whose only real interest is to create trouble for the
Beijing government and to limit the growth in Chinese national power.
It is precisely in this regard that China rejects outside interference and
meddling, especially on the part of those who come with unclean
hands and imperialist intent.

The problem is once again unequal application of supposedly
"universal" standards. "Some countries in the world," as Premier Li
Peng put it, obviously referring to the United States, "always intervene

into others' affairs."[95] Thus China rejects any foreign involvement in its relations with Taiwan and Tibet in the same way that the U.S. government would be outraged by Chinese sponsorship of calls for autonomy or even independence by the "model government" recently set up by indigenous Hawaiians (whose islands lie thirty times farther from the continental United States than Taiwan does from the mainland), or demands for a "right of return" for millions of Mexicans to New Mexico and the rest of their country stolen from them in the 1840s. In relation to its two outlying provinces, China is only following the established practice of the leading global power, which brooks no outside interference in its "own" territories, and explicitly rejects application of UN decolonization policy to Puerto Rico, or any similar attempts at international control. For the Chinese too, the issue is one of sovereignty and the right to resolve their own national issues by themselves, and they see behind all foreign intervention a threat to unification.

China is increasingly promoting the gradual economic "merging" of Taiwan with the mainland through both investment and trade, as well as in discussions on future reunification that are diplomatic negotiations in all but name. There are estimates that more than 100,000 Taiwanese—mainly businesspeople and their families—already live on the mainland. These growing ties reinforce a close historic connection between the island and Fujian Province across the straits, with many existing links, including family relations, as even the majority population of Taiwan is historically of mainland origin. Toward the Taiwanese, the Chinese take a similar "one country, two systems" approach as that which has served them so well in easing the reintegration of Hong Kong. But it is just this gradual merging which upsets some in the United States, as was noted at the time of the Lee visit in an article by Li Jiaquan, director of the Institute of Taiwan Studies of the Chinese Academy of Social Sciences.

> Over the past few years, such relations, which focus on economic, trade and cultural exchanges and contacts, have been growing vigorously, it said.
>
> Under these circumstances, some people in the United States harbouring malicious intent towards China are worried about this trend.
>
> They fear that both sides of the Taiwan Straits will improve relations steadily and will even discuss the issue of peaceful reunification.
>
> They always regard China as a "potential enemy" and do not want China to be reunified, united, and powerful, it said.
>
> In their view, it is only by maintaining a state of division and conflict across the Taiwan Straits, can Taiwan be used to contain China.[96]

Thus, by allowing Lee to visit the United States, "Washington is brazenly supporting his action of attempting to split the motherland by advocating 'two Chinas' or 'one China, one Taiwan.'" To the extent that the U.S. government helps him in the presidential election of 1996, it will also make him more politically beholden, thus reducing the Taiwanese authorities even further to the position of pliant agents. Such policies serve mainly to advance the goal "of splitting China, which aims only to keep Taiwan within the US's sphere of influence."[97] These actions undermine efforts of the Chinese themselves to resolve the issue in a peaceful manner and one mutually beneficial to both sides. The Lee trip was especially galling, therefore, as it came just four months after Jiang Zemin made a major policy address on Taiwan, outlining a set of initiatives offering the island economic, political, and even military autonomy within a reunified national state.

Similarly, in Tibet, China argues that its revolutionary policies have brought liberation from a feudalistic theocracy to the Tibetans, along with modern social development and increasing benefits from integration into the rapidly expanding Chinese economy. In the traditional society of Tibet, wrote one student of the country, the "vast majority of the people ... were serfs" and monasteries "had the right to *take* children to be initiated as monks if the voluntary supply was insufficient."[98] These conditions only slowly gave way under Chinese control during the early part of the century, and especially after the revolution. Deputies to the National Congress from rural Tibetan ethnic areas speak of health care, schools, roads, and decent homes now widely available, which were totally lacking prior to the 1950s, when the Dalai Lama fled into exile. They also claim to have greater opportunities for political participation now. "In old Tibet ... we Monba and Lhoba people lived in harsh conditions and had no rights whatsoever. The parliament of the old Tibetan government met every year, but we were never invited to attend."[99] China has only recently undertaken massive new investments in the autonomous region, opening it up to marketization, as well as steps to preserve the indigenous culture of Tibet, such as renovation of the Potala Palace and of major religious sites—albeit in some cases only as museums, not active social centers. It has also published an encyclopedic compendium of Buddhist scriptures in Tibetan, similar to actions it has taken in regard to other nationalities, and part of a wider program that included a 1995 conference in Beijing of 600 Chinese, Japanese, and Korean leaders of Buddhism.

It is in light of such actions that Raida, chairman of the standing committee of the Tibetan People's Congress, recently "reaffirmed China's 'consistent and clear' stand on the Dalai Lama: China welcomes him back home provided he casts off his independence ideas and splitting activities."[100] Going back at least to the early twentieth century, there have been pro-Chinese sentiments among some of the Tibetans who resisted the authority or policies of the lamas and favored secular society and government. When the Dalai Lama moved to declare independence at the time of the 1911 revolution in China, "the end of direct Chinese influence in Tibet was 'far from obtaining the unanimous approval of the Tibetan population.'"[101] Today there are many strong advocates of closer integration into China, even within the Buddhist leadership, just as there are others who work toward separatist goals and foreign intervention. Meanwhile, even such issues as "finding the reincarnation of the Panchen Lama," over which there was a major dispute in early 1995, involve complex church-state formulas going back to the Qing Dynasty in the eighteenth century. It was 1793 when Chinese authorities first presented Tibetan officials with a golden urn from which to draw lots for the contested final selection of a Dalai Lama—a method employed once again at the insistence of Beijing to resolve the recent choice of a new Panchen Lama. Attempts to impose Western formulas on these relationships, especially for political reasons, are thus likely to flounder in the face of deep historic traditions.

While such historical and contemporary relations do not reduce the importance of all other issues—including cultural autonomy, colonization policy, treatment of dissidents, and Tibetan or Han control of regional and local political positions—neither can such ties be dismissed as irrelevant or purely negative as they frequently are in the United States. Of course, ever closer merger into the Chinese mainstream is viewed as a greater threat by those in Tibet who oppose it. But in this regard, it is almost amusing to hear the same forces in the United States who do not think twice about opening a McDonald's outlet within sight of the Forbidden City or a KFC fried chicken franchise a block or two from an ancient Daoist temple in Suzhou, or who threaten a trade war over the "right" to force the likes of "Forrest Gump" and "True Lies" on Chinese moviegoers, crying crocodile tears over the "poor Tibetans" who are losing their culture to the "evil empire" in Beijing. As one observer noted, the most authentic "American" solution to this problem of Han cultural impact on the indigenous population of the region would be the opening of Tibetan gambling casinos. Thus, like such relations throughout the globe, the ties of Tibet and Taiwan within China are complex historical connections which contain contradictory aspects of nationality, ethnicity, culture, religion, and class. But they cannot be solved by foreign dictates issued arbitrarily from the United States. Attempts to do so will only raise the possibility for major clashes, with serious global repercussions.

Therefore, more is at stake here than just hypocrisy on the part of the United States. It is the right of the Chinese to solve directly with the peoples involved issues of ethnic relations, regional autonomy, and social policy, free from the interference of outside powers each with their own imperialistic interests. To understand this, it must be remembered that both Taiwan and Tibet have long been arenas of control and machination by Western and Japanese imperialists, intent on dominating the Asian mainland and China. Tibet was a fiercely contested region in the early decades of the century, in large part as a result of British imperial ambitions there. This included invasion by an expeditionary force under Colonel Francis Younghusband from 1903 to 1904, which resulted in a treaty that, "For all intents and purposes ... made Tibet a protectorate of the British Empire."[102] The Russians also had pretensions there as part of the "Great Game" for Central Asia, and even the Indian Gurkhas, allied with the growing British power, several times crossed the border beginning in the late eighteenth century. Among the legacies of the imperialist map-drawing in the region resulting from these conflicts was the brief but bitter 1962 war between China and India, which took place along the Tibetan border.

As for Taiwan, it was the first of the overseas colonies of Japanese imperialism, which controlled the island from 1895 to 1945. Thereupon, it rapidly became the base for post-war U.S. "containment" of the Chinese Communists, in alliance with Chiang Kai-shek, whose forces carried out a massacre of tens of thousands of Taiwanese in 1947, including most of the elite of the island, preparing the way for the Guomindang retreat there in 1949. Later, from small offshore islands, the mainland itself was shelled, while the Seventh Fleet patrolled the straits, preventing any effective retaliation.

In China, talk of U.S. concern about the autonomy or even independence of Taiwan and Tibet, or with the human rights situation in these two areas, therefore not only rings hollow, but is seen as a threat to national integrity and an opening wedge to renewed imperialist domination, reawakening the worst horrors of the recent past. The Chinese spent a century freeing themselves from outside control and division, and they will fight before allowing such a "Great Power" role in their internal affairs again. To fears of a revival of historic oppressions are added modern ambitions to restore their former unity and power. As Jiang Zemin stated in regard to Taiwan, "It remains the sacred mission and lofty goal of the entire Chinese people to achieve the reunification of the motherland and promote the all-round revitalization of the Chinese nation."[103]

The question of Taiwanese independence is thus one issue over which the United States should not count on compromise, as the Foreign Ministry made clear in a statement at the time of the Lee visit.

> Some people in the United States calculate that China will swallow the bitter fruit on this question as it needs the United States. This only reveals their ignorance about history and the reality. For over 100 years, the Chinese people struggled unswervingly for independence and sovereignty. To the Chinese people who have already stood up, nothing is more important than state sovereignty and reunification of the motherland. In order to uphold national sovereignty and achieve reunification, the Chinese Government and people are ready to stand against all odds.[104]

This invocation of the words of Mao announcing the liberation of China in 1949 should be taken as a sign of the seriousness of the Chinese. "Throughout history they have despised traitors and fought against splitists to the death."[105]

In light of the experience of Yugoslavia, where a Western eagerness for "national independence" for former provinces helped lead to bloody disaster, some international restraint might be expected in pushing similar policies in the case of China. But perhaps it is just such precedents which encourage those who wish to frustrate the reunification with Taiwan, and to see Chinese power hobbled before it can challenge that of the United States. For China, however, such threats are potentially catastrophic. The reunification issue is the one policy area in which the Chinese government has not renounced use of military force, "not directed against our compatriots in Taiwan, but against the schemes of foreign forces to interfere with China's reunification and bring about the 'independence' of Taiwan."[106] Specifically, Beijing has made clear that a declaration of independence by Taiwan would be met with an armed response. "'We have consistently stood for reunification of the motherland by peaceful means,' Prime Minister Li said. 'But we have not forsworn the use of force.'"[107] Speaking of the visit to the United States by President Lee, there was no mincing of words by the New China News Agency.

> The issue of Taiwan is as explosive as a barrel of gunpowder. It is extremely dangerous to warm it up, no matter whether the warming is done by the United States or by Lee Teng-hui. This wanton wound inflicted upon China will help the Chinese people more clearly realize what kind of country the United States is.[108]

Shortly after this statement, China recalled its ambassador to Washington for "consultations."

Despite efforts at peaceful relations, therefore, tensions can quickly flare up. In the early months of 1995 the Chinese authorities reported several incidents in which Taiwanese armed forces fired on fishing boats from the mainland, killing one. In July of the same year, China tested long-range rockets by firing them north of the island, disrupting international air flights. In December, the United States sent an aircraft carrier squadron through the Taiwan Straits for the first time since diplomatic relations were reestablished in 1979. It did so ostensibly to avoid bad weather—but as the first such event in seventeen years, the ill winds would appear to have been more of a political than atmospheric nature. Shortly after this incident, the Chinese government announced that the issue of reunification with Taiwan would be at the top of the national agenda after 1999, following the reabsorption of Hong Kong and Macao, a sign that there is a limit to how long China is prepared to wait. At about the same time, it advised a visiting U.S. official that it had "completed plans for a limited attack on Taiwan" that could be launched following the March 1996 Taiwanese elections.[109] By early that month, China was firing missiles into the ocean near the main port cities on Taiwan and conducting military maneuvers at sea. Washington responded by moving two naval battle groups into the region, warning it would not stand by if the mainland government launched an attack on the island. A Congressional resolution in mid-March called on the United States to defend Taiwan in case of invasion, while the administration stepped up supplying high-tech weapons to the island military, as it has done for five decades.

As the Chinese keep reminding the United States, it agreed to a one-China policy and the downgrading of ties to Taiwan when diplomatic relations were restored in 1979. Reopening this question challenges the entire basis for U.S.-Chinese relations, and will inevitably spill over to affect their economic exchanges as well. Attempts by the United States to determine what constitutes the territory of China and to intervene in what the Chinese consider their internal affairs are thus seen as a renewal of "big stick" policies and an especially dangerous form of imperialist hegemony as practiced by the "last remaining superpower."

Given the eagerness of some in the United States to prevent the development of a united and stable China, it is easy to imagine the schemes which might arise should the Chinese mainland see serious internal disorder and looming fragmentation along ideological, economic, political, or even military lines. In such circumstances, it is not hard to conceive of the United States trying to extend a "two-Chinas" policy to the entire country, including the mainland itself—perhaps a Southern capitalistic stronghold counterposed to a still socialist and Communist Party-dominated Northern state. Such speculation has already begun in certain Western circles:

Imagine that the Chinese empire run from Beijing were to disintegrate—
Guangdong, Fujian, Taiwan and Hong Kong could form the Republic of
Southern China. This new country would have a population of 120
million and a combined GDP of roughly US$31m, which would put it
on a par with Brazil.[110]

This may be a quite unreal scenario, but certainly the pattern of
industrial development and the differential growth rates of productivity and prosperity seem likely to create increasing stresses on the unity
of the state. Inconceivable as such a prospect may seem today, there is
ample precedent for such intervention, given the U.S. experience as
the primary creator of the North/South divisions of the "two" Koreas
and Vietnams. It would no doubt be aided in such ventures by the
British, who have already tried to employ Hong Kong as a "Trojan
Horse" in China, and who are the best since the Romans at the policy
of *divide et impera*, leaving a worldwide legacy of racial, national, and
religious conflicts on which the sun has never set. Of course, the
Chinese are not so easily divided, but given their long history of
oscillation between centripetal and centrifugal forces, the potential for
imperialist meddling could well arise.

There is therefore a growing probability of increased efforts to
"contain" China, both politically and militarily, and even the possibility of foreign intervention cannot be excluded, should there be signs
of Chinese disintegration in the future. In the post-revolutionary period, it is virtually impossible to think of China succumbing to external
military control, at least as long as it remains united. But as United
States actions toward Taiwan and Tibet already make clear, and as a
growing right-wing "America first" attitude spreads, combined with
a renewed expansion in the Pentagon budget, the U.S. government is
well prepared to exploit any weakening of Chinese unity. Having
fought with each of the closest Asian neighbors of China—Japan,
Korea, and Vietnam—within a little over fifty years, any sign of
regional divisions on the mainland may tempt U.S. interventionism
once again, as it has so often in the recent past.

Fears among Chinese about such threats are therefore hardly just
paranoid musings. They are a reasonable reaction to many open
statements in the United States, such as these comments by Michael
Lind, a senior editor of *Harper's*:

An "Asia first" foreign policy would entail maintaining an economic and
military balance between Japan and China, ending America's military
agreement with Japan, increased cooperation with Russia on Asian
affairs, forcing open Japan's and China's markets to U.S. goods, and
dismantling NATO.
In the very long run, China may be the greatest threat to our interests. A

China with only a quarter of America's per capita income would surpass us as the world's largest economy and, perhaps, as the preeminent military power. It has already replaced the Soviet Union as the major military supplier for anti-American regimes, and is insisting on great-power hegemony over the South China Sea.

Seeing Japan's success in exploiting the open U.S. market while placing barriers on foreign investment at home, China is building up a huge bilateral trade surplus. Americans who hope that capitalist development will inspire a democratic and peaceable China will almost certainly be disappointed: after all, it took military defeat and occupation to bring democracy to *capitalist* Germany and Japan.[111]

Though Lind warns against overestimating Chinese power, especially vis-a-vis that of Japan, the thrust of his argument is unmistakable: "Asia" represents a "threat" to the U.S. global security system and economy, and China in particular must be contained starting now, using not only the Japanese but the Russians, with at least a hint that the "pacification" and "democratization" of Chinese society may necessitate foreign military intervention. As his piece strongly implies, U.S. policy should thus entail encircling China even more completely than it does now.

Similar sentiments were voiced by Stephen Sestanovich, vice-president for Russian and Eurasian affairs at the Carnegie Endowment, who complained that

Vast amounts of geopolitical pundit-time go into thinking about how to deal with the looming emergence of China as a military and economic colossus. Russian-American relations, strangely, are almost never treated as part of the equation.

This is a mistake. Isn't it obvious that, if we ever had to organize a broad coalition to contain China, Russia's orientation would be crucial? For that matter, aren't we less likely ever to need to organize such a coalition if China sees that the other major powers enjoy good relations that would make it easy for them to unite?[112]

Even more blatant statements come directly from high officials.

In the United States, the expression "containment" is applied increasingly to China. The Administration's position is that it wants to engage China, rather than contain it, but that if necessary in the future it can switch to a containment policy. "We're not naive," Winston Lord, the Assistant Secretary of State for East Asian and Pacific Affairs, told a congressional committee in June. "We cannot predict what kind of power China will be in the 21st century. God forbid, we may have to turn with others to a policy of containment. I would hope not."[113]

Such statements make clear that "containment" is already on the U.S. agenda for China, which is rapidly replacing the former Soviet Union as the focus of global bipolarity, a new "threat" to substitute for the "ended" cold war.

In this vein, recent pressure in the United States for recognition of Vietnam has been based in part on the argument that it too may be able to help serve as a counterbalance to Chinese resurgence. Such views are stated quite openly.

> The United States should normalize relations with Vietnam as a means to counter Chinese domination in the region, Sen. John McCain, who spent six years in a Hanoi POW camp, said yesterday.
> "We need a strong Vietnam in the region as part of a counterweight to what is a disturbing pattern of behavior on the part of the Chinese," the Arizona Republican told NBC's "Meet the Press."[114]

Leading U.S. officials are therefore well on their way to stirring up once more an historic enmity that has already found expression in one recent war. This growing move toward the encirclement of China may even be extended into South Asia. Following a visit by Defense Secretary William J. Perry to the Indian subcontinent in June 1995, he noted that "India wants to retain its nuclear capability to deter the Chinese military, which is superior to India both in nuclear and conventional capability."[115]

> To some Indian military experts, Mr. Perry's words suggested that the limited military contacts between India and the United States could give way, as China's military might grows, to something much broader, possibly even to the United States' encouraging Indian military growth as a counterbalance to China.[116]

This is already being implemented through practical measures. As part of U.S. strategic planning, stretching from the Middle East through all of Asia, a "Fifth Fleet would be established for the first time since World War II" in the Indian Ocean and Persian Gulf. At the same time, "Washington and New Delhi recently agreed to increase their defence co-operation."[117] With half of the Korean peninsula already under "armed guard" by tens of thousands of U.S. troops, and even larger forces in Japan, including military bases that occupy 20 percent of Okinawa, and with the Seventh Fleet patrolling its offshore waters, China is even now militarily "contained." To the Chinese, it is therefore the United States itself that represents the growing threat, surrounding them on all sides with an ever tighter web of military alliances, and undermining their national security—from this viewpoint, it is not China, but U.S. imperial might and its worldwide claim to hegemony that needs "containing."

In this regard, the possible reassertion of a Chinese role as regional or even global power must be kept in historical and geopolitical perspective. It should be recalled that there is nothing new in the

United States "forcing open China's markets" and threatening it militarily. It has been doing so for more than a century and a half, from its own first unequal treaty dictated to China in 1843, taking advantage of the Opium War, to the Korean and Vietnam Wars, which reached to and threatened to cross the Chinese border. Yet despite this history, important voices in the U.S. government and media are being raised to prepare the public for the idea that it is China which "threatens" the United States, and to promote intervention in the old regions of Western and Japanese colonial rule and influence that surround the Chinese mainland, especially Taiwan, Tibet, and Korea. From a historical point of view, it is thus very clear who is a threat to whom, and which country is projecting its power far beyond its own borders to constantly intervene in the affairs of others.

It is only from this perspective that issues such as the build-up of the People's Liberation Army must be understood. The Chinese do have national and even regional interests which they may well be preparing to defend militarily if necessary. These include, most notably, assertion of control or at least dominance over the South China Sea. In the West, some suspect that the Chinese have even larger aspirations. This is often expressed in the concept of a "Greater China," in which the mainland, having reabsorbed Taiwan, Hong Kong, and Macao, would again become the center of a much wider region, with the many "overseas" communities extending its influence and financial linkages throughout most of Southeast Asia as well. However, even the regional power of the Chinese is quite limited. Thus despite a rapid buildup in its military—accelerated in the aftermath of Tiananmen in 1989, with defense spending more than doubling—China is a relatively minor player in the global arms race, especially in relation to the vast and overwhelming superpower force of the United States.

Estimates differ, but the Chinese put their expenditures on the armed forces in 1993 at 43 billion yuan, or only some $7 billion at the old exchange rate, and even lower at the newer level.[118] U.S. sources suggest greater spending, but still in the range of $15 billion in 1991—based on CIA figures—to $22 billion in 1993. Even these much higher estimates must be compared with the $40 billion which Japan invested in 1993 in its military, which remains limited because it enjoys an "umbrella" of strategic protection from the United States. The Chinese that year were also well behind other major powers such as France at $36 billion; England, $35 billion; Germany, $31; and Russia, $29. By contrast, the Pentagon spent $324 billion in 1991, and even after post-cold war cutbacks was still spending $277 billion in 1993, almost thirteen times that of China, even at the higher estimates for that country—forty times as much if Chinese figures are accepted—and

$39 billion more than all the next nine countries, including China, combined.[119] The U.S. defense budget declined only marginally to $263 billion in 1995, and will rise again in 1996. By Chinese calculations, therefore, Pentagon spending every year is equivalent to more than half the entire gross domestic product of China, which was only $518 billion in 1994. The contrast is even more striking if it is calculated on a per capita basis. In the United States, the government spends almost $1,000 annually per person on defense, in China the comparable figure is from $6 to $20, depending on which figures are used. To compete on a dollar for dollar basis of expenditures on its armed forces, China would have to spend at least one half of the per capita income of each of its people. As Chinese officials have pointed out, they are in no position to build up such a military force and at the same time finance the economic goals they have undertaken, and it would require an extraordinary explosion of their economy to allow them to launch such an expansion of their armed forces in the future.

Faced with such limits and choices, and under the pressure of marketization with its prioritizing of profits, as well as the requirement that the People's Liberation Army be in large part self-financing, many arms manufacturers in China have converted much of their production to consumer goods, since "civilian products bring the highest return for Chinese military factories."[120] So too, the National Nuclear Corporation saw a decline in weapons-related output in 1994, while production of nonmilitary and even non-nuclear goods soared, so that as of early 1995, civilian products accounted for 80 percent of its total activity. To the extent that its own output of arms declines, China is becoming more dependent on foreign suppliers—primarily the United States and Europe—for weapons. In 1994 it was the second largest purchaser globally of armaments from abroad. But this reliance on foreign suppliers, many of whom are potential economic or military rivals—or even increasingly, as in the case of the United States, concerned with containing China—greatly reduces China's ability to act independently as a major power.

Partly as a result of the heavy conversion from military to consumer goods by arms manufacturers, as of now the People's Liberation Army remains at a "technologically unsophisticated level," as was found by a U.S. delegation led by former Defense Secretary Robert McNamara which visited China in 1994.

> Chinese warships, for example, have little or no effective air defense, and their targeting radars cannot reach over the horizon. China has no hope of financing aircraft-carrier development for at least a decade. Its submarines are noisy and vulnerable and are equipped with poorly functioning torpedoes.

The Chinese Air Force has yet to produce a modern, supersonic aircraft with all-weather air-to-air combat abilities. And China's air defense system could not stop penetration by the French Mirage 2000 attack planes recently purchased by Taiwan, whose pilots get more flight training hours in a month than Chinese pilots get in a year, experts say. "We are aware that our weaponry of all services is far behind the present equipment of the United States," Adm. Liu Huaqing, China's top military officer, told the McNamara group. "We hope to modernize, but the problem is that we have no resources; and if we compete with economic needs, we will be in competition with the economy, and that is not in China's interest."[121]

In this respect, Chinese military strength is like its economic power, big enough to be a "threat" on a world scale, but internally weak and flawed. There can thus be no question of China challenging the United States in global militarization. It is only, at most, an issue of its military causing regional problems, especially for the U.S. global security system and its Asian allied and client states. Even the ability of the mainland forces to retake Taiwan militarily has remained problematic.

VII. Spheres of Influence

The process of economic expansion through marketization, which forces China to compete globally, does generate increasing pressure for it to reclaim its own historic sphere of influence, and even to attempt to gain access to other parts of the world. As the growth of the Chinese economy begins to strain its resource base, its need to obtain raw materials from abroad inevitably escalates as well. "Although China ranks third in the world for volume of mineral reserves, it is expected to face a severe shortage of mineral resources early in the next century." Many of its raw materials lie in remote or not easily accessible regions. But in addition, "Reckless mining and waste of mineral resources are also serious problems in China. The situation has been worsening recently."[122] About one half of the 80,000 township coal mines operate without legal permits. As a result of uncontrolled mining and other abuses, in the chaotic and corrupt environment of "get rich quick" schemes, even many of those reserves which China does possess are being wasted or inefficiently exploited, increasing the already accelerating pressure to look outside the country for raw materials.

But this in turn requires further dependence on foreign capital and ties to governments and companies abroad. "Chinese geologists plan to travel beyond national boundaries to explore and exploit mineral resources through multilateral co-operation."[123] A report quoted Song Ruixiang, minister for geology and mineral resources: "'Such closer teamwork will help narrow the widening gap between demand and supply.'... He said the nation's continuous economic growth, projected at 8-9 per cent annually, faces serious shortages of crude oil, sylvite and copper, and an inadequate supply of iron, manganese, lead, zinc and aluminium." Across the globe, China is moving into the raw materials business. "Chinese geologists are currently helping Iran with a chemical survey and prospective mining of gold, and taking part in the re-exploration and re-development of used oil fields in Peru to boost their yield."[124]

But while much of this activity involves normal commercial exploration and production, the Chinese response to its raw material shortfall includes, as well, the desire to control contingent areas, notably the South China Sea, which has potentially vast oil fields, minerals, and rich fishing grounds. China claims the region based on historic control, going back to the thirteenth century, especially in the Nansha or Spratly Islands lying between—and claimed by—Vietnam and the Philippines, as well as by Brunei, Malaysia, and Taiwan. Thus "400 Chinese scholars recently completed 10 years of research on the Spratly Islands and 'proved historically' that China 'discovered and developed'" them, and that they are "'a sacred and inviolable part of Chinese territory.'"[125] China has begun exploration for oil in the area, and though it has called for regional cooperation in exploiting these resources, there have been naval incidents with its southern neighbors, as well as between such unlikely opponents as Vietnam and Taiwan—the latter still maintains troops on Itu Aba, the largest of the islands under dispute—with the opposing landing of garrisons and conflicts over fishing. In early 1995, China and the Philippines similarly sparred briefly but sharply at Meiji or Mischief Island.

The Chinese have been promoting the peaceful resolution of all such territorial disputes, as they try to gain acceptance within the Southeast Asian economic and political blocs. This included a friendly tour through the region by President Jiang in the fall of 1994. The Chinese have also been undertaking extensive military contacts with other countries, including in Southeast Asia, as well as with the United States and other Western nations, relations which they view as being "of great significance in safeguarding peace and stability in the Asia-Pacific region and the world as a whole."[126] But tensions in the South China Sea remain high, and some analysts even believe that the People's Liberation Army is being specifically tailored for operations in that region.

> As Chinese diplomats talk of peaceful coexistence with their Southeast Asian neighbors, China's military leaders are refurbishing a portion of their large and antiquated military to enforce claims of sovereignty over the South China Sea and its resources, Chinese and Western experts say.

In this effort, Chinese military leaders have nurtured specific industries to develop advanced weapons technology and are tailoring their naval and air forces for the region, the experts say, even as the country's overall level of military production is declining.[127]

Still China insists that there is no basis for armed clashes there, and that all issues can be settled regionally without outside "hegemonic" intervention from the United States. This policy was clearly stated by Shen Guofang of the Foreign Ministry.

> On the possible US military presence in the South China Sea after it resumes normal relations with Viet Nam, Shen said normal Vietnamese-US ties will be welcomed by China because they are conducive to regional security.
> However, China always opposes nations setting up military bases and stationing troops on foreign soil, he said.
> "All countries should act with a view to preserving peace and prosperity in the region at a time when the whole of Asia is devoted to economic growth."[128]

However, the United States is already expressing its own "national security" concerns, especially with the looming Chinese control over sea lanes through which pass 70 percent of oil for Japan and others in the Pacific Rim. The U.S. role in the region has only recently been reduced and could be revived again.

> The Chinese threat to the Spratlys was contained for decades by the presence of the United States Navy. But after the Americans left their base in Subic Bay in the Philippines in 1992, the security umbrella offered to the islands by the United States has mostly disappeared.
> Southeast Asian leaders have long worried that China would someday use the Spratlys as a springboard to assert control over the entire South China Sea—turning it, as Asian diplomats often say, into a "Chinese lake."[129]

China has recently insisted that it will keep the issue of free sea passage separate from whatever tensions may develop over regional territorial claims.

But U.S. strategists are nevertheless raising alarms over future developments.

> "The danger of what we have on the question of China's military is that people are beginning to make the case that China is benign," said James R. Lilley, a former Ambassador to Beijing and longtime Central Intelligence Agency officer in Asia.
> "China says it has no military objectives, that on the South China Sea it wants to cooperate to find a diplomatic solution while exploiting the resources, that there are no military solutions and that China is focusing on the economy," he said.
> Arguing that by all appearances, China's military buildup is tightly

focused on the South China Sea area, Mr. Lilley added: "I'm afraid the evidence tells us otherwise. And it is quite clear that that is their objective in 10 to 20 years."[130]

Though other analysts in the United States take a less dire view of the situation, it is clear that China cannot assert its claims to the region without raising resistance within the U.S. government and its global security apparatus, where long-term strategy always includes preparing for military contingencies.

Whatever the legitimacy or complexity of each issue taken individually, such as Taiwan or the South China Sea, they are merely the reassertion of Chinese power within the "normal" sphere of influence it has maintained historically. This may well pose a serious problem for some of its neighbors, notably Vietnam, with its long history of resistance to the imposition of domination from China. But it has no meaningful effect on U.S. "national security," except insofar as the latter appropriates the entire globe within its imperialist "boundaries," and abrogates to itself the role of universal mediator and global gendarme, and thus considers the rise of any regional power not under its direct control as a threat. What China challenges, in other words, is not the United States *per se*, but its imperial system of international dominance. But this means that even the "natural" rise of the Chinese to centrality within East and Southeast Asia and its reassertion of a dominant role over regions historically under its sway is fraught with explosive tension that could easily result, in the near future, in military confrontation with the United States. Thus regionally China might try to claim an outdated and unacceptable sphere of influence. But its actions would still pale beside those of U.S. imperialism, which takes as its "sphere" the entire globe.

To the extent that China is driven onto the world scene as a competitor with the United States, the potential for clashes is even more likely. Specifically, Chinese petroleum imports, which have come mainly from Southeast Asia, have begun to shift to the Persian Gulf, including closer ties with Kuwait and Iran.

> Economists have estimated that China will become a net oil importer within the next few years.
> In an apparent sign that it intends to increase oil imports from the Middle East, China has planned to upgrade its refineries so that oil from that region can be processed in the country.
> The official revealed that China was also ready to bid for large petrochemical projects in the Middle East.[131]

If there is an action guaranteed to raise tensions even to the point of armed conflict, it is any perceived threat by the United States to "its" Middle Eastern oil. Notably, in 1994 Sino-Iranian trade was only a few hundred million dollars a year, compared to the billions of dollars worth of petroleum U.S. firms were buying from Iran for resale before President Clinton imposed an embargo. But China may be moving to pick up some of the oil formerly handled by these companies, and its sales of arms and atomic reactors to the Iranians raise the potential for closer strategic ties, and thus of clashes with the United States, which has already made such deals a major point of contention. If such dire scenarios may seem farfetched today, it should be recalled that unilateral military action is always just below the surface of Pax Americana, ready to be used if other means do not suffice.

This is the deeper implication of the *Yinhe* incident of 1994, in which U.S. ships stopped and boarded a Chinese freighter off the coast of Iran, on the grounds that it carried ingredients for chemical weapons. Such actions by the United States cannot be understood only as attempts to enforce its "new world order," in which nations that it designates as "outlaws" must be isolated and kept from gaining any autonomous power. The *Yinhe* incident was in addition a "shot across the bow" of China, reminding it to keep its proper "place" within the global system, with a not-so-subtle implication that should it get out of line, its own lifelines, such as growing dependency on foreign oil, are subject to easy disruption. This "lesson" surely has special import for Chinese claims to the South China Sea, where whatever China's local power, U.S. naval might could easily prevail. The Chinese have asserted that they have territorial waters there extending over a wide area. But in the summer of 1995, the Clinton administration "committed itself to using American military force, if necessary, to keep international shipping lanes open in the South China Sea."[132] Further tensions may follow, and China may protest as an outrage the actions taken against it—as it did in the case of the *Yinhe* interdiction. But as that incident so well showed, in any global conflict the Chinese would be virtually helpless against U.S. military power.

Over all the clashes of the United States with China hangs the ghost of Japan past. U.S. fears that the Chinese will play a role similar to that of the Japanese, only stronger and even more challenging, find expression in government and media circles.

> It is a fight to make sure that the United States does not make the same mistakes with China that it made for decades with Japan....
> Throughout most of Japan's post-war rise, Washington found every reason possible not to make trade—and America's own economic health—the No. 1 issue with a close ally. There was a cold war on, and the Japanese islands were America's unsinkable battleship in the Pacific. By the time anyone realized the enormity of the American mistake, it was already too late.

> In some respects, China today is about where Japan was in the late 1960's, a powerhouse of growth, a huge exporter, and the leading candidate to overtake the United States someday as the world's largest economy.[133]

This view is increasingly shared by the Japanese as well. In a series of annual polls, people in Japan have been asked which country they believe will be the leading economic power in the world in the next century. As recently as 1989, 45 percent said the Japanese would be dominant, against only 40 percent who indicated the U.S. economy, and 3 percent for the Chinese. But by 1994, the results were: the United States 31 percent, with Japan and China at 25 percent each.[134] Clearly many Japanese see the Chinese as the rising Asian force, and even a contender as the new dominant global economic power.

This is a view increasingly shared in China itself among some leading elements. Accordingly, in recent decades,

> Local economies no longer followed Japan like "flying geese" as they had in the 60s, said the vice-director of the Institute of Asia-Pacific Studies at the Chinese Academy of Social Sciences.
> Now the region's economy was advancing like a train with two engines—Japan towing and China pushing.[135]

No doubt there are Chinese who look forward to reversing even this relation.

But history suggests that such a development will meet with great opposition, with the potential for generating serious international turmoil. In this sense, the situation of China today may more closely resemble that of Japan in the 1920s and 1930s than in the 1960s. In that earlier period, the Japanese also had growing strength within the Asian and world economies, and required increasing raw materials from outside, especially oil and minerals from Southeast Asia. They too asserted that Asian countries had suffered too long under Western domination, and that only the rise of a regional great power could restore a proper global balance. In these respects, China now resembles prewar Japan, with its ambitions to become a world force, its growing need for external resources, and its frustrations and containment at the hands of the West.

Despite such similarities, however, there are even more fundamental differences. The Chinese have never shown any inclination to imitate the Western imperialists through modern forms of foreign conquest, and their response to threats from abroad has been a turning inward and profound social revolution, not outward expansionism. China also lacks both the militaristic history and samurai-type caste of the kind which for so long dominated Japan. It remains technologically and economically limited, and is faced with the already highly developed Japanese military and its U.S. security blanket. Thus despite being similarly situated to Japan in the pre-war era, China has a profoundly different history and global perspective. There is little prospect that it would ever take the kind of path pursued by Japan in the past.

As Chinese leaders themselves constantly point out, neither historically nor in modern times has China shown the slightest inclination toward a globalist expansionism, and it has neither the rationale nor the power to undertake such an effort now. Rather, it is the Chinese who have been the object of imperialist attacks by others. Thus U.S. talk of a military "threat" from China is seen as a perfect example of "blaming the victim"—or in a more contemporary Chinese phrase, the case of "a thief yelling stop thief." As Vice-Premier Qian Qichen pledged in a speech at a 1995 trade conference on "China and Its Neighbors: Economic Relations in a Region of Rapid Growth":

> China will never threaten or invade other countries, a stance which has been proved by history.
> "In the past century or more, the Chinese people suffered tremendously from aggressions by foreign powers. And historically, China has never engaged in expansion or aggression into other countries," he said in response to allegations that China would pose a threat after it becomes economically developed....
> "China is opposed to hegemonism of any form and will never seek to be a hegemonist itself," Qian said.

And in an effort to separate Chinese foreign relations from any revival of Cold War tensions or the recent "hegemonism" China associates with its northern neighbor, he continued:

> "It is not preordained that China's military power will turn into a threat, or that it will behave like the former Soviet Union," the prime minister said.[136]

Of course, historically the Chinese were also "hegemonist," and as recently as 1978 their armed forces once again crossed into Vietnam, which had in turn intervened in Cambodia. Nonetheless, there can be no question that it is China itself which has been the victim of imperialist attack and colonialist policies in the past century and a half on the part of the United States, Japan, and others claiming "great power" status, while it has shown no similar tendency toward a policy of outward expansionism—even when, as during the Korean War, its military forces were already on foreign soil. Today its leaders vow that it "will never seek hegemonism or become a superpower, and it does not, and will not station a single soldier in any other country."[137]

The Chinese fear of being "contained" therefore stems not from frustrated desires for its own expansion, but as a response to threats—

economic, political, and even military—from the United States. This
was made evident in early 1995 when China strongly objected to talk
in the Clinton administration of a "theater star-wars" antimissile
system, to be deployed around U.S. forces and allies in Asia. Noting
that they have only 300 long-range atomic warheads, compared to
15,000 or so in the Pentagon arsenal, the Chinese government stressed
that such a program would "increase the danger of nuclear war" and
"trigger an arms race in outer space." But their greatest fear is that is
would open them to "blackmail." Thus "China's opposition to antimissile systems stems from fears in the military leadership that an
American antimissile system, if deployed in Asia to protect Japan or
South Korea, could render China's small force of nuclear-tipped strategic missiles completely ineffective." Rejecting once again the idea
that the Chinese are somehow threatening the United States, rather
than the other way around, one official stressed:

> "I think the so-called China threat originated from a faraway place," he
> said. "We are tired of all these allegations. For the last 100 years, we have
> been hearing the same story."
> He complained that since Communist China was founded, it has been
> portrayed as a threat to peace.
> "When China was poor, we were a threat, and when China is rich, we
> are a threat," he said. "But history is history. We have been the victim of
> aggression and occupation. We are tired of all these allegations. Enough
> is enough."
> The official apologized for getting "a little emotional" and then added,
> "We do not pose a threat, but we are entitled to defend ourselves."[138]

President Jiang Zemin expressed the same thought when he stated that
"China will not change its independent foreign policy of peace even if
it becomes rich and prosperous in the future."[139] Regardless of such
pronouncements, U.S. containment seems destined to take forms that
are increasingly threatening in the future.

The behavior of the Chinese therefore does not resemble that of the
Japanese before World War II, and they represent no similar expansionist militaristic threat, even regionally.

> China is not bent on international conquest. Beijing may wish to domi-
> nate the region, but it does not wish to raise the Chinese flag over Jakarta
> or Tokyo.[140]

What does remain constant in the situation of China and prewar Japan
is the refusal of U.S. imperialism to allow the rise of any power which
will challenge its own dominant role in the East Asian region and its
self-defined global needs. This was made very clear at the time of the
March 1996 flare-up over Taiwan.

Defense Secretary William J. Perry said in Washington that the Pentagon's sending of two carrier battle groups to the Western Pacific this month was meant to remind Beijing that America was the dominant power in the region. "Beijing should know, and this will remind them, that while they are a great military power, the premier—the strongest—military power in the Western Pacific is the United States," Mr. Perry said at a ceremony on Capitol Hill.[141]

Even if Chinese ambitions remain very modest, therefore, and well within the "natural" limits of the reassertion of their historic role in Asia, they are likely to face resistance from the United States, with the possibility of a growing frustration and mounting indignation within China itself. "A senior Chinese foreign policy expert told a recent visitor that when Chinese leaders get together these days, the country they express the most anger toward and dislike for is the United States," a "resentment and perplexity ... indicative of the underlying suspicions about how the United States really views China."[142] Or as David Shambaugh of the University of London noted, "the emerging Chinese hard-line view" is that

> the United States is trying to divide China territorially, subvert it politically, contain it strategically and frustrate it economically....
> "They're prepared to hunker down and resist the assault, and they frequently compare it with the 1950's, when Mao called the United States its principal enemy."[143]

Whatever the protestations of China about its own limited goals, it is nevertheless likely to see tensions with the United States increase, and even as it bids again to become a major power, it is being driven back toward its past forms of self-reliance.

VIII. Global Contradictions of Chinese "Market Socialism"

The contradiction for China lies even deeper than the immediate issue of whether it can reclaim its historic role, and meet what it considers its reasonable needs for raw material resources, without clashing with the United States. Those who proclaim the coming "China century" must face the reality of how the English and American centuries which preceded it were realized. In this regard, students in Changchun and economists such as Lin Yifu, and no doubt others both within and outside of government, seem to share a similarly naive vision of how China can rise to world power, following the supposed "model" of the rapid climb of the "new" United States to become the largest economy in the world.

British and U.S. global dominance were not, however, built or protected through the benign working of "marketization" and economic growth alone. They were the succeeding centers of a vast global system in which the wealth of the entire world was mobilized and appropriated for the benefit of the imperialist core. This international power always rested on military might and has never been willing to surrender its dominating role except at the point of a gun. Even those, like Japan, who have recently risen to challenge the United States economically, have done so beneath its imperialist and militaristic umbrella, which guaranteed that most of the globe, and much of Asia, remained open to capitalism. If China wishes to be the successor as the third great global power, even in economic terms, it will not be sufficient merely to become the largest national economy in the world. It will have to replace the United States as the leading imperialist center, presiding over the entire globe. But this is a role for which the Chinese have no historical preparation, which is contrary to their deepest inwardly focused cultural traditions, and for which they lack the economic strength, military power, and ideological drive.

The practitioners and theorists of "market socialism" who dream of a "China century" may therefore be in danger of repeating an earlier and fatal conceptual flaw. For the Chinese empire, even at its most powerful and "central," was never more, indeed never seriously aspired to be more, than a regional Asian bloc. As such it may long have been the largest economy and most highly developed society on the globe, including at the time of its first modern contacts with the West. But despite its vast trade with other regions, it remained, in the concepts of Immanuel Wallerstein, a "world-empire"—an historic unit of the global system exercising great power over extensive territory, but not one capable of centrally organizing the entire range of international exchange.[144]

Under this theory, its very imperial structure, by combining both economic and political power in the same hands, restrained its ability to "go global," a restraint which would also operate in the case of "market socialism with Chinese characteristics." It thus remained for capitalism, centered in the West, and separating the control of the "world-economy" from any one political/military state, to achieve this higher level of international organization. This contradiction between Chinese domestic strength and regional dominance on the one hand, and the global power of the leading capitalist countries on the other, produced the confusion so evident in China at the time of the first Western challenge, and led to its inability to understand the threat of modern imperialism. It left the Chinese vulnerable, not only to those who had more military might, but especially to those who had knowledge of the whole globe, and the ability to organize imperialist economies on a worldwide basis. In all the talk of China as potentially the greatest economic power in the next century, therefore, lies at least implicitly the same conceptual error. For the Chinese can once again become both the dominant center in Asia and even the most massive economy in the world, without overcoming U.S. imperialism and its partners.

The dilemma is represented in a statement by Zhou Shijian, vice-president of the International Trade Research Institute. "Strategically, China and the United States have no fundamental conflicts," Zhou said, adding that a healthy Sino-US government relationship and economic links are of mutual benefit.[145] Such a Pollyannish attitude ignores that the very rise of the Chinese economy to global power represents a "fundamental strategic conflict" for the United States, and that despite "economic links of mutual benefit," it is almost certain to employ the full range of its power, including political and military, to "contain" China.

There are no doubt more hard-headed elements among the Chinese leadership who understand this, especially in the Communist Party and Peoples Liberation Army. But even top leaders, like President Jiang Zemin, often put forth the line that, in effect, everything would be all right if the United States would just "behave fairly." It is not ultimately the subjective attitude of the Chinese that will control these relations, however, but the objectively greater strength of the United States. China may call for a new era of good feeling and fair behavior between the two countries, but this will have little or no effect on the U.S. determination to retain its own global dominance. As long as this contradiction persists, it leaves the Chinese once again vulnerable to containment, exploitation, and even outside attack, without the capacity to project its power in ways that can protect it from the imperialist threat. China, in other words, may once again be able to build the largest economy in the world, yet fail to translate that strength into sufficient political and military capacity to protect its economic position, or even suffer loss of control over its wealth to the imperialist centers of global capitalism, thereby undermining its national sovereignty.

In this sense, "market socialism" replicates on the international level the contradictions which plague it in its domestic relations as well. Focused on the goal to "get rich quick" at virtually any cost, there is a tendency to believe that economic expansion alone will solve all problems, and that world dependence on the Chinese market will force the resolution of international conflicts in a form favorable to China. But those who hold this view may be blinded to the deep and growing weaknesses which undermine the Chinese system of marketization both internally and externally. In the globalized economy of the present, it is not the "wealth of nations" that counts, so much as the "stealth" of transnational corporations and international financial centers. These have the worldwide ability to insinuate themselves into the body of even the most powerful economies, and to gain control without ever "firing a shot," though they are ultimately backed up by military power if needed.

As the recent example of Mexico reveals, this international dominance has the deepest and most explosive implications for internal class relationships as well. There is therefore the closest interrelation between the struggle of classes and the maintenance of national sovereignty. Even as the Chinese economy grows, it is being weakened from within. The growth of an openly *comprador* class, those who serve as the domestic agents of foreign economic forces, and whose interests lie in facilitating the capitalist takeover of China and enriching themselves as the go-betweens, threatens to reopen the door to outside domination as in the era before the revolutionary triumph. This threat has set off a crucial struggle among contending factions, so that

> China is abuzz with debate over whether foreign investors will be allowed to hold a majority stake in local enterprises.
> Those in favour argue that China, still a developing country, will not be able to raise enough money itself for its ambitious economic growth goal.
> Those against the idea, however, say that the dominance of foreign capital would squeeze out domestic industries and markets.[146]

But the process is already so advanced that critical control is being lost at the center of the new marketization regions, threatening national autonomy.

> At present, the majority stakes of most of the country's 220,000 Sino-foreign joint ventures are held by Chinese partners.
> "But foreign investors are indeed holding majority stakes in more and more joint ventures in China," says a trade official who spoke on condition of anonymity.
> In Shanghai, the country's economic hub, 82 of the 107 big industrial projects approved last year are controlled by foreign investors.
> In the breakdown, foreign investors held a more than 70 per cent stake in 38 such projects, and a 100 per cent stake in 13.

From Shanghai, such control is rapidly spreading to inland areas.

The compradorist element in facilitating this control is equally evident.

> Among those who support foreign investors holding a majority stake are some domestic industrial departments that hope to use foreign capital to restructure ailing enterprises in the face of a tight monetary policy.
> "We have nothing to lose if the enterprises can duck bankruptcy with foreign investors coming to the rescue," the trade official said. But he

cautioned that it's improper to allow foreign investors to hold a majority stake in all industries.[147]

The critical term here is "we." For in the anarchy of capitalism, it is not the individual entrepreneurs who will lose out by selling out. They may indeed flourish. But the loss to China of its national autonomy may follow. Nor is the threat only economic, for those compradors who have "nothing to lose" in selling Chinese state property to private foreign interests might equally find that in future conflicts their loyalty lies more with their transnational bosses and imperialist handlers than with China as a whole.

Even to the extent that such factors are understood, market socialism will most likely lack the ability to keep such contradictory forces under control in the present mad rush for growth. This issue of the permissible degree of foreign ownership of Chinese enterprises is apparently now being debated at the highest official levels. But though temporary stability between opposing government factions on this question may be achieved, there is an ever more fundamental split developing between the demands of marketization and global dependence on the one hand, and the need for national economic autonomy, resting on internal stability and world peace, on the other. Just as the growth of class polarization is rapidly proving to be the Achilles heel of the uncontrolled profiteering within the domestic economy, so growing reliance on the global market without the power to defend its interests against the U.S.-dominated imperialist system will likely prove the decisive weakness in Chinese foreign relations. If such contradictions deepen in China, it faces the prospect of renewed domestic turmoil within, and growing containment and control from without. As Chinese history shows only too well, these two aspects are closely related, each "feeding" on the other.

With China increasingly dependent on external economic relations, its vulnerability can thus no longer be measured only domestically. As the resources of the Chinese mainland, both financial and material, prove to be insufficient to support the unbroken expansion on which market socialism and domestic stability depend, it is ever more captive to worldwide forces beyond its own control. Thus even if China itself lacks any expansionist goals, economic necessity will require it to seek an ever-growing share of global resources, and to develop the network of international relations necessary to maintain their accessibility.

Such efforts, however, are likely to meet increasing resistance from the United States and other core countries, which may well take further steps to make sure that there is no fundamental challenge to the existing world distribution of power. Ongoing threats by the U.S. government to revoke most favored nation status for China, ostensibly because of human rights issues, and the looming potential imposition of economic restructuring demands by the IMF or other international lending organizations as Chinese debt dependence grows, show how fragile may be the current "cooperation and tension" balance. Thus the "China century" will likely prove an illusory goal, no matter how powerful economically, or dominant within Asia, the nation becomes, because of growing resistance from other global powers. Attempts to break out of such restraints are equally problematic in the foreseeable future, because of continued Chinese domestic economic weakness and growing dependence on foreign funds, and because such efforts are unlikely to succeed without an open clash with U.S. imperialist power. In an era when even the United States has suffered a loss of its ability to dominate either the world economy or its political/military structure, the idea that China will have sufficient clout to replace it at the "center" is increasingly problematic.

There is, however, an alternative scenario, one which lies much closer to the heart of the official foreign policy of the present Chinese leadership. This is the possibility of building a new global structure of nonimperialistic relations as the basis of the international system. Since the era of Mao and Zhou Enlai, China has consistently called for just such a reordering of the world, an appeal recently given new impetus by the fortieth anniversary of the Asian-African anti-imperialist conference in Bandung, Indonesia. Returning to themes presented there, Chinese leaders never miss the opportunity to raise the "Five Principles of Peaceful Coexistence," which include respect for state sovereignty and noninterference in the internal affairs of other nations, regional settlement of disputes by those directly involved, and negotiated resolution of all potential conflicts. They have also stressed that they are eager to move toward complete nuclear disarmament, and have called for an immediate ban on all testing and on the first use of atomic weapons, but only if all the other major powers agree to act simultaneously. Despite their own permanent membership on the UN Security Council, they have called for a body more representative of the world. In these areas, China has shown global leadership which stands in sharp contrast to the norms of U.S. imperialism.

More immediately, the Chinese have striven mightily over the past few years to overcome earlier tensions with their Asian neighbors, and to emphasize the spread of regional economic integration and sharing of resources. In particular, China has championed the right of small nations to equality with the powerful and opposed the use of the UN as a cover for imperialist interventionism. It also calls for economic development to be recognized as a global goal on a par with the

Western themes of democracy and other human rights, and for world-wide equalization of wealth to reduce the North/South polarity.

China no doubt sincerely wishes to see these values become the dominant norms of the international system, as they allow for maximum economic growth within an environment of domestic stability and global peace. For the Chinese, these goals are inextricably linked. But though up until now they have been able to isolate their own society from external domination and interference, and have been relatively successful in the development of bilateral and regional relations based on these principles, they have had little or no role in shaping the larger global environment. Their major source of diplomatic power, the UN Security Council veto, has lain unused as the United States has exercised a largely free hand in constructing its own concept of a "new world order" behind the facade of "international" approval.

> At the United Nations, the Chinese are usually isolated and self-absorbed, and their actions are a clue to their priorities. Internationalists they are not, unlike the Soviets. On the Security Council, a diplomat said, "China is just not a part of the party." Silent on most issues, the Chinese weigh in only when they see themselves or their principles threatened.[148]

At the time of the Persian Gulf crisis in 1990-1991, for example, a Beijing-oriented newspaper in Hong Kong, *Wen Wei Po*, described the conflict as "a war for the interests of the U.S.A., a war contending for hegemony over petroleum, and a war between world hegemonism and regional hegemonism."[149] But after first voting with the West to impose UN sanctions on Iraq, China abstained on the crucial decision to use force. Despite fears that "Chinese criticism of the allied forces would weaken the sense of international alliance and could increase the perception in the third world that Western countries are ganging up against a smaller nation," China adopted a posture of "relative neutrality." Presumably, the restraint which the Chinese have shown in such matters reflects their desire not to "rock the boat" and antagonize the imperialist financial centers on which they are increasingly dependent for funds, conflicts which could also stir up political repercussions or even militaristic threats. Thus despite some efforts by China to limit UN intervention against third world countries, including allying itself in that body with India, Iran, Mexico, and others, it has not seriously attempted to rally a bloc to counter the leading powers. This failure, however, has meant that the global system has remained largely unaltered, dominated by the imperialist "values" of the United States, Britain, and France, and thus available in the future to "contain" the Chinese as well.

The contradiction here again gets to the heart of market socialism. For it is only on the basis of a profoundly different system of political economy that a nonimperialistic and truly "new" world order could be built. But for China to take the lead in constructing such a set of international relations, it would be necessary as well to assume that the "special Chinese characteristics" of its "marketization reforms" are actually universal and capable of becoming the prevailing norms for the entire globe. But "China has pledged many times not to export its ideology nor search for hegemonism."[150] While this restraint is no doubt good for "business," and may show an admirable determination not to intervene in the internal affairs of others, it also means that the "special Chinese characteristics" of its system will remain just that, a basis for national mobilization, but not for global reorientation. In this sense too, China has abandoned any pretense to its revolutionary past as a leader in the struggle for a truly new world order.

Still more fundamentally, Chinese market socialism is itself becoming increasingly merged with, dependent on, and therefore indistinguishable from global capitalism. As China abandons its socialist semi-autonomy and becomes a "player" within the international capitalist system, its needs increasingly clash with those of the already existent powers, but its policies, far from offering a viable alternative, instead become more and more inseparable from the prevailing global norms. In a particularly striking expression of this, some Chinese are now looking to creation of their own transnationals as a way of escaping from the rising costs at home—just like any globetrotting capitalist. Thus according to Kang Rongpin of the Chinese Academy of Social Sciences, "China's entry into the World Trade Organization would stimulate its overseas investment and the development of Chinese-based multinationals (MNCs)."[151]

Such investments would help enterprises in China "adapt to international practices and sharpen their competitiveness" as part of their "survival strategy." But "adaptation" to such global standards can only mean adopting the goals and methods of the dominant capitalist multinationals. For Chinese companies this means joining the worldwide scramble to find low-paid labor to exploit, as their own workers begin to demand a share of the rapidly expanding economy. Thus foreign expansion is not just a result of new opportunities opened by greater global involvement.

> In addition, swiftly growing per capita income here—especially in the coastal areas—has started to erode China's cheap-labour advantage. "This might be an impetus for China's investment in South and Southeast Asia," Kang noted.[152]

Such Chinese multinationals would clearly be expected to merge fully into the global system, with close ties to transnational capitalists worldwide. Thus a Moftec official "noted that setting up enterprises overseas is a good way to use foreign capital, as Chinese projects overseas often involve foreign partners and investment from international institutions." The goal, as stated by Xie Gang of the Shanghai Academy of Sciences, is to turn the country from a net recipient of funds from abroad into one which is mainly a global investor.

> Even as it attracts a myriad of foreign capital, China is preparing to snowball its direct investment overseas by 2000.
> At the turn of the century, growth of capital outflow will outpace that of inflow for the first time, says a senior Chinese economist.[153]

According to Xie, drawing on the theoretical model of British economist John Dunning, such a transition is a crucial step in the "optimal" development of any country. So too, Sun Guangxiang, director-general of the aid department of Moftec, has stated that "it is imperative that reform in the way China assists foreign countries be carried out to promote direct co-operation links between Chinese businesses and those of the recipient countries."[154] Even assistance to other nations, which China has previously granted on very generous terms, would thereby be converted henceforward into an opening wedge for multinational economic exploitation.

Thus even were its "marketization with special Chinese characteristics" able to become the world standard—and there is little to suggest that China has either the desire or power to spread its methodology or ideology globally—it would still not constitute a fundamental break with the present scramble for world power and resources, nor with the exploiting of other peoples. As a result, there is little to suggest that the Chinese can change the current international environment by the policies it is now pursuing. Instead it faces continuing difficulties as it challenges the dominant global role of the United States, with its European and Japanese allies, who will almost certainly not allow an undermining of their international power without attempting to block China. Thus not only Chinese regional ambitions, but even the continued growth of its economic strength within a world dominated by global capitalism, will face the most profound contradictions.

The United States, of course, is also far from omnipotent in the reach of its power, especially today. Despite still being the largest national economy, backed by its superpower military, U.S. society is increasingly hollow within, as it proves both unwilling and unable to protect its own working people from the effects of globalization, and as its class, race, ethnic, and gender relations polarize. This has in turn made people in the United States increasingly reluctant to support the costs of imperialism and to demand attention to the "home front" instead. The Chinese are therefore correct when they insist that economic development in a peaceful international environment is the growing demand of the entire world, and that multipolar centers of power are replacing U.S. hegemonism. So too, while the United States has, within little over half a century, fought a major war with every one of the closest Asian neighbors of China—thereby indicating its willingness to intervene as needed in the region to protect its interests—the U.S. public has in the process lost its taste for land wars, above all on the mainland of Asia.

In this sense, as Mao stated, U.S. imperialism is becoming a "paper tiger," which though strategically wounded is nevertheless still tactically strong and dangerous. It may be more and more unwilling to act, but it is still capable of lashing out in a sudden and brutal attack against those who get "out of line." Yet in facing this power, China itself increasingly lacks the ability to offer its own strategic alternative, and thus finds itself ever weaker in its tactics as well. As a result, the contradictions of "market socialism with Chinese characteristics" are rapidly deepening, not only within the domestic society, but in relation to the outside world as well, and on their resolution will depend the direction that China takes in the near future. Either it will be dragged further down into the maelstrom of the global capitalist system, under a weakened but still dominant U.S. imperialism, or it will move back toward the revolutionary transformation of its own society, based on the renewal of its now abandoned class struggle, offering protection from the ravages of capitalism, and hope for the world.

MAO AND DENG: "ONE-AND-A-HALF-" OR "TWO-LINE" STRUGGLE?

I. The "70 Percent Positive, 30 Percent Negative" Solution

Among the more striking experiences of teaching in Changchun was that the students, in endless hours of classroom discussion and debate, almost never mentioned the names of the two leading party and government officials, President Jiang Zemin and Premier Li Peng. This by no means meant that official actions were not discussed—quite the contrary. But it was as if, as individuals, the top governmental authorities hardly existed as personalities, only as the embodiment of the state itself. There was a well-worn formula for referring to them and their policies, especially when the students wanted to distance themselves to some extent from the official line. Thus, if I raised—or more commonly stumbled on—a somewhat touchy topic, it would often be met first with silence. Then someone, usually one of the leading students, would state the official policy, but only, as it were, *pro forma*, using phrases such as "Our government says that...." or "The position of our leaders is...." After these rather cautious openings, there would often be a quite free and even critical discussion, but without referring to the name of any specific leader involved. In part, this was no doubt an unwillingness to be perceived as criticizing the top leadership. But it also seemed to reflect the lack of personal charisma and even popular authority on the part of the current leaders, as well as, in the case of Li Peng especially, residual resentment at his role in crushing the 1989 Tiananmen movement. Whatever the exact meaning of this reticence, it left official policy in a strangely disembodied state, an abstract authority without a human face.

This depersonalization of the top leadership of the Chinese government stood in sharp contrast to the constant references to Mao Zedong and Deng Xiaoping. There was almost certainly a relationship between neglect of the actual governmental leaders, and focus on the two primary architects of present-day Chinese society. This was evidenced most directly in the continuing role of Deng, who still held the paramount power despite his having withdrawn from all official positions and his rapidly declining health. However weak he might be physically, it was clear that he still provided the "center" of all government positions, even if no longer of its daily activities, and that his hand-picked party and state agents, Jiang and Li, derived their authority primarily from his anointment and by association with his policy of "market socialism with special Chinese characteristics." Thus there was little to say about the personalities or actions of the actual leading officials of the government or Communist Party, since theirs were merely derivative powers from Deng Xiaoping.

The "senior leader" himself—as he was referred to in the Chinese press—appeared to be held in a kind of awe, based primarily on great respect for the perceived successes of his policies, which most of the students appeared to support with honest, though clearly varying degrees of enthusiasm. Toward Deng, however, there never appeared to be any sense of personal warmth. Rather, he seemed to be regarded almost like some kind of natural force, representing the momentous changes in China, and architect of its rapid rise to economic wealth and world power. The lack of popular connection to him personally reflected an aloofness on his part felt even by those who most enthusiastically shared his vision of Chinese society. Deng himself has almost certainly cultivated this aloof image intentionally, as a way of putting his policies, not his personality, to the fore, providing a clear contrast to the adulation with which Mao was constantly surrounded, as well as allowing him, in effect, to "lay low" after his own history of twice being purged during the period of the Cultural Revolution.

But with the full import of his policies only now beginning to emerge, and the growing uneasiness which they are generating, this personal reserve also means that his legacy too has a certain disembodied character, which may yet prove to be a weakness after the death of Deng. In an apparent—though perhaps too belated—attempt to correct this problem, his daughter Deng Rong (Maomao) has written a biography, showing him as a good "family man" as well as a great leader, in an effort to "humanize" him. A movie of his life is also planned, numerous books and articles have been written about his contributions, and posters and badges with his visage have even shown up, in an effort to give a personal face to his policies. Some even see in these acts an effort to create a "cult of Deng." But such top-down campaigns seem unlikely to inspire any great new warmth toward him from the masses in China.

It remains for Mao, therefore, to continue to fill the role of the national leader still "in the hearts" of the Chinese people, though this affection has historically been shared, especially with Zhou Enlai. Commonly, the same students who stated their rejection of some of the policies of Mao in one breath, in the next would express a profound and warm appreciation of his contributions to China and of the personal values that he represented. This was evident even among those whose families had suffered under him, and who spoke with unrestrained bitterness, in particular, about the Cultural Revolution. These attitudes were most obvious in December 1993 as the 100th Anniversary of the birth of Mao approached.

Such continuing expressions of positive feelings toward the Great Helmsman himself, despite personal histories of hardships during the period of his leadership, sometimes took quite striking forms, as was highlighted by the Chinese press. One such case was a painter of the commemorative postage stamps which were issued as part of the hundredth anniversary celebration, but whose own family history seemed starkly at odds with that role.

> How can an artist whose father was killed during the "cultural revolution" (1966-76) enjoy painting Mao's picture?
> Wei Chuyu, 47, painted two of a set of four stamps commemorating the 100th anniversary of Mao's birth.
> Wei's father, Wei Siwen, a former secretary of the Party committee of the Institute of Industry in Beijing, was a devoted communist who joined the revolution in 1925....
> Because his father's loyalty to communism had been questioned, Wei Chuyu, who had just graduated from Zhejiang Academy of Fine Arts, was not trusted either.
> He was sent to the countryside and then to a factory.

Finally able to leave the factory in 1970, after his father received a posthumous rehabilitation, Wei became a soldier.

> While in the army, Wei took up painting again. In the 1970s most of his paintings were huge portraits of the Chairman.
> As an artist, Wei wasn't satisfied with just painting from Mao's photographs. He wanted to inject into the portraits the spirit and ideals that Mao had been fighting for.[1]

Such an admiring attitude exemplifies the position which Mao still holds in China some twenty years after his death, despite almost two decades in which his policies have been subjected to criticism and his historical role officially "revised." But more is involved than just enduring admiration for the Chairman. The revival of a more positive interpretation of the Maoist period began in earnest after the crushing of the Tiananmen movement. While by no means representing a full endorsement of everything which happened under his leadership, it draws its strength not only from an open admiration of Mao, but also from a powerful and largely underground stream of criticism of the post-Maoist leadership, providing a legitimate cover for the expression of values increasingly absent in the marketized China of today.

For months before the hundredth anniversary, there was a growing crescendo of praise for Mao, with more and more events, exhibits, historical reviews, and television dramatizations of his life, as well as governmental and academic conferences evaluating his contributions. A veritable "Mao craze" emerged, with the issuing of tape recordings of his speeches, videos, books, articles, t-shirts, and buttons (at times dismissed in the United States as mere kitsch); those from the Cultural Revolution are especially valued. Over 5 million copies of a single tape, "Red Sun—Odes for Mao Zedong" were sold in late 1992 and 1993. Television, in particular, appeared to be the venue through which, intentionally or otherwise, a kind of surreptitious criticism of the current government and state of Chinese society crept in, through programs that, day after day, seemed more and more starkly to contrast the spirit of self-sacrifice and "serving the people" of the Maoist era with the rampant corruption and "get rich quick" atmosphere that pervades China today.

As the anniversary date approached, the warmly human image and positive values associated with Mao in the widely presented reviews of his life, with their implicit criticism of the current leadership, could not be left unchallenged. It was President Jiang himself who, in a major and public commemorative address before 10,000 in the Great Hall of the People, reminded the Chinese of the official verdict on Chairman Mao: that despite his many contributions, his later policies were seriously flawed and had been harmful to China. This position is often expressed as a numerical formula—a device popularized by Mao himself—with his role semi-officially declared to have been "70 percent positive, 30 percent negative." This "solution" to the problem of how to evaluate the Chairman claims to incorporate his legacy, while promoting public criticism as well. Yet it is doubtful if the attempt by Jiang at "damage control" was particularly convincing to the Chinese masses, who reserve their own private verdicts, comparing the current leadership and the reign of personal enrichment and corruption over which they preside, with the legacy of simple living and incorruptibility of the Maoist era.

The continuing focus of attention on Mao and Deng, though the one had been dead for almost two decades and the other was increasingly enfeebled and reclusive, was all the more striking because of the constant public exposure given to the actual party and governmental leaders, who were the ubiquitous feature, almost without exception, of daily newspaper and especially television reports, and who are notable for their vitality and activism in running the country. It is easy to dismiss this kind of lingering concern with the two paramount leaders of the Communist period as an example of "cultism," or even to portray them as the "new emperors"—a fashionable approach in the West. But there may be a deeper and more contemporaneous reason for the disregard of the personal roles of the current leadership in favor of Mao and Deng. This is the recognition that there are still two fundamental forces contending in China, alternate visions for the social order that are represented by the conflicting ideologies and policies of these historically dominant leaders.

In this sense, whatever cultist or even imperial patterns of thought may be involved are essentially irrelevant, for the roles of Mao and Deng are seen as embodiments of forces larger than themselves, with importance beyond the differences in their individual personages. The Chinese thereby exhibit, by the attention they focus on these past leaders, that the issue of how their society should be ordered not only still has immediacy, but that—despite the current dominance of Dengist policies—the mass of the population remains open to the possibility of a continuing struggle between its two fundamental tendencies. The relation of the ideologies and policies of Mao and Deng thus forms the crux of the contemporary debate over the direction of the future for China, and though these two figures can no longer participate personally, their presence continues to be felt as the representation of these social poles.

Given the continued strength of personal feelings toward Mao on the part of the Chinese masses, even among the professional elite, the practitioners of "market reform" face a sharp dilemma in relation to his legacy of unrelenting opposition to the "capitalist roaders," and the implicit critique which his revolutionary values and actions offer to the quality of the current leaders. On the one hand, they must assume the mantle as his rightful heirs, in order to legitimize their own rule, and yet at the same time they must disarm his criticism of their own policies which lie at the very heart of marketization. This balancing act is made even more difficult in light of the history of purges of Deng and his associates during the Maoist era.

Mao, as leader of the Communist revolution, symbolizes their most fundamental claim to legitimacy. Yet at the same time he remains the one person who ever succeeded in throwing them from power.[2]

The attempted resolution to this contradiction by the current leaders— employing a formula devised around the time Deng returned to power—has been to lavishly praise Mao for his earlier revolutionary leadership, while denouncing his more radical activities following the triumph, especially during the Great Leap Forward and, above all, the Cultural Revolution.

In the same way, those now in power have tried to picture Deng Xiaoping as both the heir of Mao and, at the same time, the one who "corrected the mistakes" of "Maoism." This formula served as the basis for the hundredth anniversary speech of Jiang Zemin, in which he

recalled Mao's historic contributions and vowed to realize the country's modernization goal envisioned by senior Chinese leader Deng Xiaoping. In his hour-long speech, Jiang hailed the late chairman as "a great Marxist, a proletarian revolutionary, strategist and theoretician, and a great patriot and national hero."

Jiang said Mao's chief contribution that brought about fundamental changes in the nation's history was his integration of Marxism and Leninism with China's specific conditions.

He said Mao Zedong thought would remain a "theoretical treasure-house for the Chinese Communists, a spiritual pillar of the Chinese nation and a guide for building China into a socialist and modernized country."

Jiang said Mao's mistakes in his final years were secondary to his accomplishments.

After Mao's death, Jiang said, Deng and the central Party authorities developed the theory of building socialism with Chinese characteristics....

Jiang quoted Deng as saying that China is finishing what Mao put forward but failed to accomplish and also correcting the great leader's mistakes.[3]

In this way, the reformers have adopted toward Mao what might be called a "one-and-a-half-line" struggle, claiming that they are following his path, even while they put themselves forward as more "correct" than the Great Helmsman himself. In particular, this formula attempts to criticize the legacy of Mao, while keeping within bounds any remnant ideological conflicts.

This official policy appears to have been relatively successful in providing one part of the theoretical underpinning for the era of market reforms, and there can be little doubt that it reflects the views of many Chinese in varying degrees. But its long-term usefulness as an ideological support for the policy of marketization depends on its ability to accurately capture the essential character of "Mao Zedong Thought" and, even more fundamentally, to demonstrate an objective unity, however strained, between "market socialism with Chinese characteristics" and this still vital legacy. In other words, if the essence of the vision of society put forward by Mao is in fundamental opposition to the current ideology of the Chinese leadership, then his thinking cannot ultimately serve to legitimate them, but will almost certainly reemerge as the basis for a critical "revision" of their policies. In that event, the ideological debates of the past will be revived, not only with great import for China itself, but for theory and practice of market socialism as a whole, and in particular its viability in the current era of globalized capitalism. It is thus necessary to reexamine the essential aspects of Mao Zedong Thought, and, especially, the character of the policies he pursued in his later years.

There are three primary accomplishments of the revolution led by Mao that form the "positive 70 percent" with which the market socialist leaders in China still associate themselves. The first was to end the imperialist domination of the Chinese mainland, and to allow its people to "stand up," reclaiming their position as one of the greatest nations in the world. This forms an explicit aspect of the market socialist ideology, though now given its own specifically nationalistic twist. Thus in calling on the Chinese people to study the third volume of the *Selected Works of Deng Xiaoping*, Jiang Zemin

> noted that the theory of building socialism with Chinese characteristics is a scientific theory in which socialism is integrated with patriotism.
> He described patriotism combined with socialism as the "great ideological driving force" that binds the Chinese nation together and promotes China's development.[4]

It is especially through this "science" of nationalistic socialism that the market reformers claim to be heirs of Mao, whatever else their differences with him in other respects.

The second critical aspect of the revolutionary legacy of Mao is the transformation of the social relations of China, and in particular the freeing of the Chinese countryside from the millennial domination of feudal landlords. However much they may have differed from Mao in the specifics of rural policy, like him, the reformers clearly favored releasing the productive potential of the peasants from the burden of the idle and exploitative Mandarin class. Only in this way could the feudalistic relations of China be decisively broken and the underpinnings of a modern economy begin to be constructed. Thus there was ample basis for Deng Xiaoping and other future proponents of marketization to follow the leadership of Mao in his most crucial practical and theoretical contribution leading up to the revolutionary triumph in 1949, the decision to root the struggle for Chinese socialism in the peasant masses. Only on this basis did it prove possible to liberate rural China, and then to extend Communist Party rule to the urban areas, from which they had earlier been driven out by the alliance of Chiang Kai-shek and the imperialists. Social transformation, therefore, was the necessary foundation for creating a "new" Chinese nation, but equally for freeing it once again from foreign domination.

The third "positive" element in the leadership of Mao with which the reformers can associate their own policies is the beginning of the process of economic development, from the depths of poverty of the pre-liberation era. While there was again sharp disagreement over how this should be accomplished, there was never any fundamental conflict between Mao and those leading the marketization forces that the goal in China should be the rapid expansion of the economy, putting an end to the millennial impoverishment of the broad Chinese masses. This included the beginning of industrialization, which would provide the peasantry with needed goods, while laying the basis for modern urban growth. So too, though the reform forces later began their transformation of the economy in the countryside, again recognizing the fundamental role of the peasantry, their goal was increasingly focused on rapid industrial growth as well. In his program of "four modernizations"—in agriculture, industry, science and technology, and national defense—Deng was following the broad direction of the policies earlier adopted by Mao, which broke the stranglehold of the past over China, favoring new ideas and initiatives over ancient concepts, in the service of both rural and urban development and a strong nation-state.

The reformers have thus worked within the broad context of the goals set by Mao, and to this extent can claim to be merely extending his own aims. Nevertheless, in each of the three "positive" areas of the revolution led by Mao, there were profound differences in theory and policy with the aims of his market reform opponents. His insistence on self-reliance for China stands in the sharpest contrast to the dependence of the reforms on foreign investment and technology. So too, the transformation of Chinese social relations, for Mao, rested above all on the development of collective ownership and labor, and egalitarianism in class relations, against which Deng and his associates have advocated the releasing of individualistic initiatives and the forces of the market, encouraging some to "get rich first." In the development of the economy, Mao supported "putting politics in command," that is, the belief that only with the organized initiatives of the masses, guided by ideological as well as practical concerns, could there be solid growth while still ensuring the construction of a socialist society. Deng, on the other hand, called for "making science and technology the No. 1 productive force,"[5] placing the emphasis on technical means to promote rapid expansion, without allowing ideology or politics to "disrupt" economic processes. In each of these areas, therefore, there was a basic "two-line" struggle of opposing theories and policies. Yet in spite of these sharp differences, it has still been possible to picture them as merely alternative means to achieving the same overall goals for China, shared by both Mao and the market reformers.

The achievements of the Chinese revolution in these three areas—freeing the country from imperialist domination, profound social transformation, and the beginning of modern economic development—were vast and, given the role of China in the global system, were of world-historic significance. They would certainly be more than enough to establish Mao as the great modern liberator of the Chinese people, accounting for both the feelings expressed toward him by the masses, and the efforts by the reformers to associate their policies with his legacy. If these three achievements constituted the essence of the practice of Mao Zedong Thought, then it would be possible for the advocates of marketization to declare that they are followers of his ideological program, "finishing"—in the words of Jiang Zemin—what he "put forward but failed to accomplish," even if they used profoundly different means to do so, while dissenting only from those later actions that constitute his "mistakes." But this interpretation rests on the assumption that the policies adopted by Mao in the 1950s and 1960s were aberrations, which deviated from the basis of his earlier "correct" ideas. The "negative 30 percent," in other words, must be shown to lack fundamental connection to the "positive 70 percent" in the overall contribution of Mao, so that the one can be counterposed to the other.

II. Once Again: "It's Terrible" or "It's Fine"

The difficulty with this interpretation is that it ignores the critical continuity which unites the concepts and actions of Mao in his early years with their extension in the postliberation period, and the significance of these later activities as central to his conception of building socialism. Thus when he first reported on the movement among peasants in Hunan in 1927, an investigation which led to his own emergence in the leading role over that struggle, Mao had to confront the negative attitude toward these revolutionary activities, which often involved violence against the landlords, widely denounced as "terror."

From the middle social strata upwards to the Kuomintang right-wing-ers, there was not a single person who did not sum up the whole business in the phrase, "It's terrible!" Under the impact of the views of the "It's terrible!" school then flooding the city, even quite revolutionary-minded people became down-hearted as they pictured the events in the countryside in their mind's eye; and they were unable to deny the word "terrible." Even quite progressive people said, "Though terrible, it is inevitable in a revolution." In short, nobody could altogether deny the word "terrible."

For Mao, however, there was nothing "terrible" about the mass struggle:

This is a marvelous feat never before achieved, not just in forty, but in thousands of years. It's fine. It is not "terrible" at all. It is anything but "terrible." ... No revolutionary comrade should echo this nonsense.[6]

Presumably, few in China today would question that Mao was right in 1927.

However, more than thirty-five years later, on the eve of the Cultural Revolution, Mao took the same attitude in his battles against the Soviet "revisionists." In 1961 the Russian leadership had declared a socialist "state of the whole people ... the first ... in the world with no class struggle to contend with and, hence, with no class domination and no suppression."[7] The parallel connecting the language and form of Mao's expressions of opposition to the Soviet "line" and what he believed was its "social-imperialism" to that of his earliest work was quite apparent to one of his later biographers.

"The imperialists and colonialists tremble before the great revolutionary tempests ... they say: 'It is terrible, terrible.' But the revolutionaries acclaim it and say: 'It is good, it is excellent.'" Mao has reproduced here exactly the style and almost the words of his first expose, *Report on an Investigation of the Peasant Movement in Hunan*, when he revolted against the wrong line practiced then in the Chinese Party.[8]

This attack was soon extended by Mao from the Soviets to those in China itself who he believed were adopting a similar revisionism in "taking the capitalist road." Thus, far from departing from his earlier policies, the campaigns of the 1960s were for Mao a direct continuation of the revolutionary attitudes and mass mobilizations that launched the struggles among the peasantry that led to liberation. But just as in the mountains of Hunan, he again was confronted with denunciations of popular "terror," including by those who are otherwise "quite progressive" or even "quite revolutionary-minded people."

The essence of the "it's terrible" versus "it's fine, it's excellent" viewpoints is the issue of class struggle—and under what conditions, and by what means it is supportable. For Mao, it is always correct for the masses to rebel against oppression and exploitation, and they are justified in using those methods which allow them to overcome their previous powerlessness and suffering, even if these involve forms of violence that are inevitably viewed as "terror." This was not just a practical matter, for Mao believed that in theory as well, the act of rebellion was at the center of the struggle for socialism:

> In the last analysis, all the truths of Marxism can be summed up in one sentence: "To rebel is justified." ... According to this principle, stand up and resist, struggle, build socialism.[9]

From this standpoint, one could not be a practitioner of Marxism or Leninism, much less of Mao Zedong Thought, if one attempted to limit or halt the popular rebellion of the masses. Of course, Mao was not an anarchist, and "to rebel" simply for its own sake was not the point. Rather, it was always rebellion in support of the class struggle that was justified in his view.

Essential as such concepts were for Mao, they did not by themselves constitute anything new in the development of Marxism or revolutionary theory. Marx had put class struggle at the center of his entire concept of history, as well as making it the basis for the socialist revolution of the proletariat. He too had celebrated the rebellions of workers and peasants everywhere. What Mao added—if not as an entirely new concept, at least in the central importance which he gave it in his own "thought"—was that this process must continue in the period of the transition to socialism itself, and must be conducted within the ranks of the revolutionary forces themselves, including the state and party, in order to prevent them from slipping back to capitalism.

> Socialist society covers a considerably long historical period. In the historical period of socialism, there are still classes, class contradictions and class struggle, there is the struggle between the socialist road and the capitalist road, and there is the danger of capitalist restoration. We must recognize the protracted and complex nature of this struggle.[10]

If the Chinese people forget this, if they do not continue the class struggle,

> "then it would not be long, perhaps only several years or a decade, or several decades at most, before a counter-revolutionary restoration on a national scale would inevitably occur, the Marxist-Leninist party would undoubtedly become a revisionist party, a fascist party, and the whole of China would change its colour. Comrades, please think it over. What a dangerous situation this would be!"[11]

Regardless of the eventual outcome in China, there can be no disputing that for Mao the continuing class struggle, and the "right to rebel," remained central to his ideology and practice in the era of the transition to socialist society—so much so that he suggested that not one, but several cultural revolutions would be needed, on a recurring basis, for socialism to overcome capitalism.

In this fundamental sense, campaigns such as the Great Leap Forward and the Cultural Revolution cannot be seen as aberrations or merely the follies of an old man. They were the logical continuations of the youthful revolutionary leadership of Mao. This does not, by itself, make them "correct"—they may, of course, as the current leaders of China and many others contend, have been "mistakes." But that they were central to the "thought" of Mao himself is undeniable. Criticism of them cannot properly be based, therefore, in claims that they were opposed to the central ideological conceptions of Mao. They can only be rejected on the basis that the campaigns were mistakenly conceived or put into practice, or that those against whom the "rebellion" was directed were not truly class enemies.

Here indeed is the crux of the matter. For though the words of Mao will have, for many today, an archaic ring, this should not obscure the essential role in his "thought" of the concepts of class struggle and mass rebellion in the socialist era, nor the accuracy of his prediction of what was likely to happen to China in "several years or a decade, or several decades at most," if these fundamentals were suppressed in the building of socialism. His grim vision of the future has now been proven all too correct, as Deng and other post-Mao Chinese leaders have taken long steps down the "capitalist road," even if the question is as yet unresolved whether this will lead to a full restoration of capitalism, and whether China will "change color," that is, from revolutionary "red" to reactionary "white."

From this dialectical or holistic way of viewing Mao, it becomes relatively unimportant whether one "likes" or does not "like" the specific actions of his later years, or considers them to be "terrible" or "excellent." These activities are, of course, open to critical analysis like any others. But they must be understood in the light of his overall "line," that is, his unyielding opposition to the imperialists and capitalists, and their potential compradorist allies, in seeking control of China, and the danger of their restoration to power in the post-liberation period. From this standpoint the later campaigns led by Mao can be viewed favorably, in a sense, even by those who oppose them. Thus, "Li Rui, author of several popular works on Mao and noted for his sharp criticisms of Mao's errors, says Mao was such a complex person that 'even his mistakes constituted a valuable legacy to us.'"[12] Such an evaluation reflects the complexity of the feelings of many Chinese toward Mao—and can help explain why even someone whose father was killed in the Cultural Revolution can still aspire to paint his portraits.

To many of those raised in the West, and especially the United States, with its "good" versus "evil" conceptions of reality, this may seem incomprehensible. Yet it should be remembered that leaders of U.S. struggles for the unity of the country, the liberation of oppressed classes, and broader mass participation may also be forgiven the costs of their actions, even by those who suffer in the process. After all, Lincoln is widely revered as the most popular of the presidents—except perhaps among Deep South whites—though he led the bloodiest conflict in which the country has ever engaged. He is held in such high regard despite the vast losses of life and property in the Civil War that, proportionately, exceeded those in China during the Cultural Revolution, and in spite of the "terror" which his forces inflicted, for example, in the March Through Georgia of William Tecumseh Sherman. Lincoln is often followed in public respect by Jefferson, the great revolutionary thinker among the presidents, whose own calls for periodic rebellions to "renew" society in the United States are hauntingly similar to the view of Mao that it would take many cultural revolutions in order to see the building of Chinese socialism. Not surprisingly, the much more recent leadership of Mao is similarly viewed by the Chinese in terms of his whole lifework, and not on single acts or methods. Thus the official attempt to divide Mao into "good" preliberation leader and "bad" post-triumph radical, not unlike the similar efforts in recent decades to oppose the "young" and "old" Marx, rests on separating what is unified. It can only be accomplished by a one-sided exaggeration of certain aspects, whose importance is inflated without a fundamental grasp of the dialectical whole.

III. The "Thought of Deng Xiaoping"

This metaphysical quality, however, runs through the entire ideology and practice of "market socialism with Chinese characteristics." For it was one of the great strengths of Deng Xiaoping, compared most notably with leaders in the former socialist countries like Gorbachev, that he put forward a very comprehensive ideological system to underpin his practical programs. The publication in 1993 of the third volume of his *Selected Works* provides the opportunity to summarize the latest formulations of his theory, explicating the full-blown "market socialist" system. For Deng, "only socialism could save China and only socialism could develop China."[13] "China cannot go back to capitalism," he asserted. "It must build socialism."[14] As this is interpreted by Li Yining, professor at Beijing University,

> According to Deng, "The essence of socialism is to liberate and boost the productive forces, to eliminate exploitation and polarization, and to achieve common prosperity eventually."

Deng says that "the most fundamental task during the present phase of socialism is to develop the productive forces." This thesis helps us to resolve all other problems, Li said.

"The criteria for judging the rights and wrongs of economic development and the reform and opening-up policies should depend on whether they are conducive to the strengthening of comprehensive national strength and whether they are conducive to the improvement of the living standards of the people," according to Deng.[15]

In this ideology, "development" is the "fundamental task," and though "to eliminate exploitation and polarization, and to achieve common prosperity eventually" are also included as part of the "definition" of socialism, it is the growth of "productive forces" that will "help us to resolve all other problems."

Here is the essence of the "thought of Deng Xiaoping," a one-sided theory of "developmentalism" to which all other goals are to be sacrificed, and through which all other difficulties, even including exploitative or polarizing tendencies, can be resolved, if growth is just fast enough. Thus the speed of economic expansion itself becomes crucial according to Deng.

"Don't hinder the development pace. Wherever conditions permit, you should develop as fast as possible.... Low speed is equal to coming to a standstill or even retrogressing." ...

Development is of overriding importance.... It's like a boat sailing against the current which must keep forging ahead or [it] will fall behind.[16]

Rapid growth therefore not only constitutes the essential "definition" of socialism, it is the goal which "overrides" pursuit of any other social values. This, in turn, is the foundation to "save China" and its national sovereignty.

But this developmentalism, by the same token, also becomes the crucial basis for criticizing the "later Mao," as expressed in a 1994 report by the State Statistics Bureau.

Between 1949 and 1978, China's economy developed slowly, as did the living standards of the people.

Economic progress was hampered during the 1950s and 1960s by political upheavals, particularly the "Great Leap Forward" and the "cultural revolution" (1966-1976). In 1976, when the "cultural revolution" finished, the national economy was on the verge of complete collapse, the bureau explained.

The annual per capita income of Chinese urban residents was 132 yuan ($15.3) in 1952. After 26 years of development, however, the figure had only reached 316 yuan ($36.7) by 1978.[17]

Though the latter amount seems unaccountably low given the level of GNP per capita for China in international statistics, it does reflect the official position, haunted by the spectres of the Great Leap Forward and Cultural Revolution. The "political upheavals" of the last Mao years thus hold for the reformers a special historic horror, because they held back "development."

But with developmentalism as the irreducible core of the ideological system, all other elements are virtually dictated, and this leads to internal contradictions that are exacerbated, not resolved, as the economy accelerates—above all the very exploitation and polarization that are the inevitable products of marketization itself, and that "rapid growth" is supposed to "override." Thus even as the economic system is transformed at breakneck speed, causing massive instability in the lives of hundreds of millions, success of this rapid expansion requires that there be no disruptive acts by those affected.

> To guarantee the success of the modernization drive, Deng said that social stability is an overwhelming issue. Without stability, economic construction is out of the question and without relatively fast economic growth, there won't be long-term social stability in the real sense.[18]

But this is not simply a practical matter of avoiding social disruptions. It also provides the theoretical underpinning to oppose all those who "deviate."

> Deng stressed, "Nowadays, we are influenced by both 'right' and 'left' deviations. But the 'left' ones are deep-rooted.
> "'Right' deviations can bury socialism, and so can 'left' ones," Deng said.
> "We in China should guard against 'right' deviations, but our main guard should be directed against 'left' ones. There do exist rightist phenomena, such as political turmoils. There are also 'leftist' phenomena, such as the assertion that reform and opening to the outside world are equivalent to introducing and developing capitalism, and the view that the main danger of peaceful evolution toward capitalism comes from the economic sphere."[19]

A direct line therefore runs from "development" to opposition to "bourgeois liberalization," a "right" deviation.

Thus in contrast to those who believe economic growth will lead to political easing, as the "free market" creates demands for democratization—a theory especially popular in some circles in the West, and among some Chinese as well—in the conceptions of Deng it is "developmentalism" itself that requires the crackdown on liberal dissent.

> "With bourgeois liberalization, our society will be in disorder, and no construction can be undertaken. And this is a key issue of principle to us," Deng stressed.[20]

This circular argument—in which "development" and a stable society are inextricably linked, each a prerequisite for the other—leads directly to Tiananmen Square in June 1989. That movement, from the standpoint of Deng, represented primarily a "right deviation," since it threatened to let loose "bourgeois liberalization" and created "political turmoil" in opposing corruption and demanding broad democratization. But more was involved there than merely maintaining Communist Party control. It was the very theory of "developmentalism" itself and its demand for a stable society that was at stake in 1989.

Nevertheless, despite the bloody events at Tiananmen, for Deng it is the "leftists" who pose the greater threat, because they raise the spectre of the "capitalist road," and the claim that it can arise from "the economic sphere." Nothing threatens so profoundly the fundamental concept of "market socialism."

> "The superiority of socialism should, in the final analysis, be reflected in the fact that productive forces under socialism develop faster and higher than under capitalism, and the people's material and cultural lives improve steadily on the basis of the productive forces.
> "Socialism must eliminate poverty. Poverty should by no means be construed as socialism. The most fundamental task of the stage of socialism is to develop productive forces."[21]

But this "superiority," as Deng expresses it, can only be achieved by turning to some of the forms of capitalism itself, creating a fundamental internal contradiction. Thus,

> "by bringing into play the innate features of socialism while adopting some capitalist methods we are aiming at accelerating the development of the productive forces," he said.[22]

Nothing expresses the contradictory nature of market socialism so profoundly as that it depends for its crucial "acceleration" on using capitalist methods. Thus capital becomes the engine that increases the speed of development.

To escape the obvious conflict of "using capitalism to build socialism," Deng has thus had to insist that both the "market" and "planning" are neutral. In other words, neither is intrinsically either "capitalist" or "socialist." Thus they can be "mixed" without altering the nature of the social system.

> The planned and market economy are socialist if they serve socialism; they are capitalist if they serve capitalism, he said....
> "Don't think a smattering of the market economy means taking the capitalist road. Not at all. Both planning and market means must be in place," he said.[23]

But though both aspects may be needed, Deng himself is hardly "neutral" on this matter, for "practice has proven that to apply the planned economy only slows the development of productive forces." Thus in the last five years especially, the "market" has grown from a "smattering" to become an almost irresistible force, overwhelming everything in its path, including a full-scale assault on central planning. Moreover, the Chinese economy is not sufficient to sustain this "development" by itself. The more rapid the growth of its economic power, the more desperate the effort to avoid "low speed," the more dependent China has become on foreign and openly capitalist investments. In this way the internal "socialist" market and the external "capitalism" being employed to stimulate and accelerate it have become inextricably linked, to the point that they are ever more indistinguishable.

Yet as late as 1992, during his tour of the South, Deng was insisting that everything done in the name of "reform" was by definition "socialist."

> At the very beginning of the establishment of the special economic zones, Deng recalled, opinions differed and some worried that [they] would give rise to capitalism. "Shenzhen's construction achievements give a ringing answer to those with worries of one kind or another. The special economic zones are socialist rather than capitalist," he said.[24]

At this time Shenzhen was probably the fastest growing city in the world, fueled by billions of dollars of foreign investment capital, notably from Hong Kong, exploiting a rapidly growing influx of low-paid Chinese, and especially migrant women. As one student of China notes, "special economic zones" are everywhere "privileged spaces for the global motions of capital through which governments around the world put themselves on the pathways of transnational capital while sustaining the fiction of national sovereignty and development."[25]

Yet on the contrary, Deng argues, after describing the growth of Shenzhen as "socialist":

> There is no cause for alarm when a greater number of foreign-funded enterprises are established. The advantages are on our side, we have large and medium-sized State-owned enterprises, we have rural enterprises, and most importantly, the political power is in our hands.[26]

Here "left" and "right" deviations merge. For Deng, the charge that China is taking the "capitalist road" is "disproved," not only by the continuation of sectors under state ownership, but by defending the realm of politics from any taint of "bourgeois liberalization." Capitalism, in other words, can be contained by "economic" means alone, but only if society is politically stable and quiescent, so that "the power" is still "in our hands."

That for Deng "leftism" remains the greater threat is nevertheless demonstrated by the brutal suppression of the workers who took part in the Tiananmen movement—even more than that directed at the students, on whom most Western attention has focused. This neglected aspect of the June 1989 events was brought out by Robin Munro in an article published on the first anniversary of the events, "Who Died in Beijing, and Why."

> A massacre did take place—but not in Tiananmen Square, and not predominantly of students. The great majority of those who died (perhaps as many as a thousand in all) were workers, or *laobaixing* ("common folk," or "old hundred names"), and they died mainly on the approach roads in western Beijing. Several dozen people died in the immediate environs of the square and a few in the square itself. But to speak of that as the real massacre distorts the citywide nature of the carnage and diminishes the real political drama that unfolded in Tiananmen Square.[27]

"Bourgeois liberalization" may undermine state and party power, but a proletarian uprising would bring the whole system of "developmentalism" crashing down. In all of this "socialist" theory, there is thus virtually no talk of class. Where it does occur, it is only to condemn the ideology of the "left."

> What is the driving force for development of the economy after the founding of socialism? For quite a long time, some people continued to regard class struggle as the dynamic force for economic development. To make the issue clear, Deng pointed out that "reform is also liberation of productive forces," "reform is a revolution" and "reform is China's second revolution." The reform of system and structures were the driving force for economic growth under the socialist conditions....[28]

Thus despite official claims that the Chinese proletariat is the leading force under market socialism, the line still being publicly proclaimed in early 1995, the "reformist revolution" sees the class struggle not "as the dynamic force for economic development," but only as an obstacle, a source of social instability. The revolutionary masses are reduced to a passive state, replaced by the reign of "system and structures."

This top-down attitude and the broad implications flowing from it are made clear in a report by the Department for the Study of National Conditions of the Chinese Academy of Sciences.

> In order to catch up with developed countries, China must overcome difficulties and meet challenges, such as political and social stability required for sustained economic growth. It must prevent chaos like the cultural revolution (1966-1976) and any other turmoil from happening, the report said.
> "Special attention must be paid to fighting corruption and the widening gap between the rich and the poor, the urban and rural areas, and different regions," it warns.[29]

So too, according to the report, China must "at the same time overcome looming shortages of energy, farmland, mineral resources, as well as inadequate bottlenecks in economic and social development." Infrastructural weaknesses must also be addressed. But though these concerns with social polarization and lack of the basis for sustainable economic growth are the very issues that were the focus of the late policies of Mao, there is no role here for the organized masses to play. Rather, they are to be the recipients only of governmental actions initiated from above. That such a program can provide the engine for extremely rapid "development" cannot be denied. It has been well demonstrated by China for fifteen years. But this kind of top-down developmentalism cannot in any respect be considered the continuation of the theory or practice of Mao, as it is opposed to his most profoundly held conceptions of what is required both to build and to maintain a mass-based socialist society.

This in itself would matter very little at present, if it were just a question of the ideological "purity" of Deng and the other practitioners of market socialism. Class, however, lies at the heart of the contradictions now threatening the "reformist revolution." The theories and practice of Mao in opposition to the capitalist road are thus once again becoming even more relevant. For the crucial flaw in the one-sided concentration of Deng Xiaoping on development without the corrective of class struggle and collective mass action is that it fails to take into account internal contradictions which arise in the very pursuit of market socialism, and from the economic sphere itself. Thus it is impossible to "use capitalism to build socialism" without at the same time generating class forces whose primary interests lie in even further capitalization. The capitalist road is not, therefore, merely a figment in the imagination of the "ultraleft." It inevitably attracts more and more followers within the leading ranks not only of the economic system, but of the state and party, as well as at all other levels of society. Far from being resolved by "development," the emergence of these class forces can only be exacerbated if rapid growth is the overriding criterion of success.

No doubt there are sincere attempts on the part of some in official positions to limit these contradictions, for example by efforts to direct investment from the richer areas of the country to the poorer. Thus in March 1995, Finance Minister Liu Zhongli announced a new initiative through which the government will "institute a revenue-transfer system in a bid to narrow the gaps in economic development between developed and underdeveloped regions.... He said as a trial, the central government will start to appropriate part of its increased revenues as subsidies to eight provinces and autonomous regions in central and western China."[30] Such transfers of public funds may bring about a certain evening out of the development process between different areas. But even these plans at geographical balance depend heavily on attracting new private investment into the poorer areas of the country. Thus in addition to government construction projects and other forms of revenue transfer, redistribution rests largely on further promoting marketization itself.

But the "market," in the last analysis, has its own momentum, and as its dominance grows, even greater polarization will result, as decisions are made based only on the profit motive and the goal of individual enrichment, and not on overall social need. With all collective action by the masses suppressed as causing an unallowable instability, there is no popular check on this process of ever more total marketization. Yet without an active struggle against the generation of "new" class elements, all efforts at building socialism, and most of all a market socialist system, turn into their opposites, as should be evident in the demise of the Soviet Union and Eastern Europe. For it is not only in development, but in the deepening of revolutionary socialism, that "low speed is equal to coming to a standstill or even retrogressing ... like a boat sailing against the current which must keep forging ahead or it will fall behind."

It is thus from within, not primarily from without, that "using capitalism to build socialism" evolves with virtual inevitability into "using socialism to build capitalism." This is the class nature of the "market socialist" system, an inherent tendency that will only develop more fully, unless it is subject to the corrective action of the workers and peasants and the collective acts of the broad masses of the society. The advocates of marketization reform can, and do, deny this in theory all they want, insisting that they are not on the capitalist road. But their practice reveals the opposite, as becomes increasingly more clear every day. This in turn undermines the ideological basis of the reforms. Thus as the Chinese confront what is happening to their society, and contradictions continue to intensify, it is all but inevitable that a new theoretical and historical revision will also soon emerge.

IV. "Revision of the Revision"

Any such further revising of the record of modern Chinese society will almost certainly have two aspects. The first will be a more critical evaluation of Deng Xiaoping himself, which has been repressed under his leadership. But with the removal of Deng from the scene, a "revision of the revision" of Mao is also virtually certain to take place. This will have to include, in particular, looking once again at the actions of his later years in opposition to the "capitalist roaders." As the contradictions of market socialism deepen, anecdotal evidence is already emerging that many Chinese are once again revising their opinions of

Mao, as the accuracy of much of what he predicted becomes true before their very eyes.

The Great Leap Forward of 1957 to 1960, for example, a drive to consolidate communal agriculture and promote collective activity in the countryside, including infrastructure development and primitive industrialization, has commonly been treated in the West and in China alike as among the most disastrous errors committed by Mao. In making this evaluation, primary emphasis is put on the "foolish" attempts to industrialize the rural areas, notably the ill-fated "backyard" production of steel, the disruptive effects of rapid construction of the communes, and the diversion of resources from agriculture during massive popular mobilizations. But it is the suffering in the period of the Great Leap Forward that is the main basis for the assertion that the entire effort was a disaster which collapsed under the weight of its own inherent "follies." It is now commonly accepted that this campaign, after initial rapid gains in production, suffered major reverses and tremendous losses, resulting in malnutrition and outright famine in large parts of the population. Chinese statistics put the loss of life during this period at at least a staggering 10 million, with estimates in the West of the number of deaths ranging from 15 to 30 million. Though such figures must be treated with caution—statistical measures from the period are problematic, and have been a major battleground on both sides of the political and ideological struggles of the postliberation period—whatever the exact number may be, there is no doubt that there was massive and widespread loss of life, especially among the old, young and sick, weakened by the lack of food. Such a catastrophe, on the scale which is now commonly attributed to the Great Leap Forward, would exceed the losses of the entire war with Japan, which was stretched out over more than a decade, and which included its own years of famine that killed many millions. Yet only six years later, in 1966, vast numbers of people in China were willing to rally once more behind Mao in the Great Proletarian Cultural Revolution, a campaign that extended the policies and dwarfed the scale of the Great Leap Forward. How can such phenomena be accounted for, if we reject the view—not uncommon in the United States—of a blind obedience to "totalitarianism," or an equally slanderous and chauvinistic image of the Chinese as too poor, backward, or uninformed to know any better?

The answer must be found largely in the positive practical accomplishments of the Great Leap Forward, despite the losses which accompanied it. That campaign was not just a period of ultraleft collectivization. The communes and mass mobilizations of that era opened new possibilities for the Chinese peasantry that had been unimaginable under the preliberation regime. By working collectively on massive local projects, the very face of rural China was transformed, with the opening up of new lands, the construction of irrigation systems, and the building of communal facilities, including schools and health clinics. Even the "backyard steel furnaces" played an important role in laying the basis for rural industrialization. Though their actual products were often useless, they nevertheless decisively broke the barrier which from time immemorial had kept the peasants isolated in their rural poverty, unable to participate in either the production or consumption of the urban centers. Most of all, they dissolved the mental fears which plagued so many of the peasantry when confronted with the modern world. These changes in outlook were further promoted by the exchange of personnel between city and country, with many workers and even intellectuals joining in the rural campaigns, while some peasants visited urban areas and universities. Millions learned new skills, and rural enterprises of all kinds grew. In part as a result of such experiences, as well as official encouragement to be self-sufficient in all matters, the authority of local leaders and state and party bureaucrats was often challenged in ways that were previously unthinkable. Thus unlike earlier episodes in Chinese history marked by famine and social turmoil, the Great Leap Forward brought positive gains even amidst the losses. Though Mao, as initiator and leader of the campaign, bore the ultimate responsibility for its costs and the failure to respond adequately to the growing food crisis, he was also credited with its lasting accomplishments. Without such transformations in both material infrastructure and the attitudes of the masses of the rural population, the later ability of the market reformers to promote their policies, including the "individual responsibility" farms with which they launched their economic program, would most likely have been much more limited. So too, the rural enterprises which are today at the heart of the effort to develop the countryside and to prevent even more peasants from flooding into the cities, might well have been delayed or never so widely promoted.

Though the aftermath of the Great Leap Forward is often described in terms such as "economic depression," the campaign nevertheless laid the basis for future advance. Even more significantly, it transformed the nature of peasant communities, breaking down once and for all their millennial isolation, social neglect, and economic stagnation, a result that was brought about primarily through the adoption of a high level of collective organization.

> In retrospect, the main institutional legacy of the Great Leap Forward was the modified rural commune with its mission of bringing industry, education, health, and culture to the countryside. The three-tiered

commune turned out to be a flexible instrument for organizing farmland capital construction, facilitating technical change, introducing some social welfare protection to rural people, and instituting rural industrialization. Many of the small and medium-size industries that sprang up in the countryside after 1962 originated in the backyard factories of the Leap.

It is this debt to collectivization that the "market reformers" and some Western analysts refuse to acknowledge in attacking the Great Leap Forward.

> The commune organization persisted for two decades before succumbing to the reforms of the Deng Xiaoping era. The primary indictment of it when it was finally dismantled was that it was the vehicle through which the state intervened directly and improperly in the affairs of agriculture, thus depriving farmers of the incentive and authority needed to develop their local economies.... However, an argument could be made that the accomplishments of these semi-collective, semi-governmental institutions in developing the rural productive infrastructure made possible the unprecedented spurt of agricultural growth that attended their dissolution; and, further, that such infrastructural development could have been realized only by relatively large and collective institutions.[31]

But maintaining the collective as opposed to the individualistic road to rural development required a constant struggle. The "indictment" later directed against the communes was there all along, and there were always those pushing to weaken collectivism. As early as 1959, in the midst of the Great Leap Forward, "the system of 'production responsibility'—output quotas based on individual households (pao-ch'an tao-hu), which had been acclaimed in the spring—was now denounced as 'reactionary.'"[32] Thus even at this early date, the seeds were sprouting for the individualistic contract system of the post-Mao "market reforms." In a recent summary of *The Selected Works of Deng Xiaoping*, it is apparent how deeply rooted this debate over strategy goes:

> Deng also noted that in promoting the productive forces, not all of Mao's methods and approaches were correct. For instance, he launched the Great Leap Forward and backed the establishment of the people's communes, both of which ran counter to the law governing economic development.[33]

The struggle over the direction of the rural economy, between the communal and individualistic forms of organization, was always present in China, and has never ended. Any major easing, or even reversal, of the drive for peasant collectivization in the late 1950s would almost certainly have opened the door to "family farming" and the class differentiation of the countryside—as it did under the reforms of the 1980s—promoting the advance of those better off, but leaving the mass of poorer peasants behind, to fend again for themselves.

Thus the Great Leap Forward offered many long-term benefits to the peasantry, despite major mistakes and the ultraleft "Communist Wind" which eventually helped undermine it—intentionally carried to the extreme in some cases by opponents of the campaign.[34] Even the worst losses of that period resulted from a complex mix of political and economic decisions emanating from the center, at times based on exaggerated and unrealizable expectations for increased output; the arbitrary authority of newly empowered and often inexperienced cadre at the lower levels, which made the implementation of new policies and the accurate gathering of information difficult; severe drought conditions in some areas and major flooding in others, often cutting grain production by close to half; and the sudden withdrawal of Soviet technicians leaving many construction projects and industrial plants to their own resources. In the face of this combination of human actions and natural disasters—the latter now commonly ignored altogether or at best downplayed in many analyses—the very discipline of the Great Leap Forward, at least in some instances, may have helped to prevent even more massive disruptions, social breakdown, and loss of life, and allowed for recovery once natural conditions improved and policy adjustments were made. As one person who lost a brother at that time remarked to us, there was no generalized "Somalia-type" collapse. Thus though the Great Leap Forward resembled similar periods in Chinese history in the losses of life which accompanied it, the transformations it brought in the economy and in class relations left a legacy of accomplishments unlike earlier such episodes in China or other poor countries.

This can be seen in the figures for production during these years. Between 1952 and 1960, Chinese economic growth averaged 6.0 percent, dropping to 4.7 percent between 1960 and 1965, then rising again to 5.7 percent from 1965 to 1972—the years of the Cultural Revolution—while GNP per capita similarly increased by 3.6, 2.9, and 3.3 percent during the same respective periods.[35] The first eight years, from 1952 to 1960, which included the Great Leap Forward, thus showed the largest average increase. Overall, national income rose an average of 5.6 percent from 1952 to 1976.[36] Industrial output expanded an average 11.2 percent annually from 1952 to 1978, a very high rate for such a poor country, sustained over a quarter century.[37] Grain production per capita, on the other hand, dropped drastically during the Great Leap Forward and had just recovered its 1956 level by the time Mao died in 1976. Still, overall agricultural output, which measures a diversified range of crops and animals, rebounded more quickly and began a slow but steadier upward trend lasting from 1960 through 1976.[38]

Thus while the legacy of the Great Leap Forward was a mixed one, combining elements of both accomplishment and setback, China during these years nevertheless achieved a strong positive growth in the overall economy. Even more significantly, the base was laid for further gains, especially in industry. Though any such "average" data must always be approached cautiously, the record does not support the claims of post-Mao leaders and analysts that this was a period marked primarily by slow expansion or even stagnation, nor the idea that growth in these decades occurred mainly during the years when the power of Mao was in decline. Rather, the most rapid overall rates of increase came precisely in the times of most radical transformation and "turmoil," though these often left behind new difficulties once the first wave of forward movement had passed. While the expansion of the Chinese economy in these years may lack the dramatic quality of the "miracles" in Taiwan or Japan during this period, or in China in more recent years, they are a very substantial and respectable increase for any large third world country. This is especially so given that the growth was sustained over such a long period of time, accompanied by a major effort at radically transforming class relations and economic redistribution, and under conditions of U.S.-imposed global isolation, compounded by a rupture with the Soviet Union as well.

Summarizing the years under the leadership of Mao, one analyst concludes that, despite serious lingering rural poverty,

> For most of the Maoist era, the Chinese socialist development strategy had grass-roots support and successfully harnessed the energies of the entire Chinese population. Morale was generally high, especially in the years immediately following liberation (1949), and this no doubt contributed to China's social and economic development. But there is no accounting system yet devised that can tell us whether the very large economic gains from China's overall socialist development between 1949 and 1976 were offset by the equally large human costs that resulted from the periodic political and economic upheavals. It is, of course, impossible to say what the economic costs and benefits might have been had the Chinese adopted another development strategy during this time period. For this reason, success can only be compared to what existed prior to 1949.[39]

But this is not the single comparison available, and even less is it the only significant measure for the Chinese themselves.

It is perhaps more useful in this regard to compare China with other similar third world countries, in order to grasp what was gained and lost by following Mao. If, for example, we take India—the other subcontinental Asian country, second largest in global population, whose independence in 1947 preceded the Chinese liberation by two years—the comparison is especially instructive. The Indian political and economic system, commonly described as the "largest democracy in the world" has, of course, been spared the "horrors" of "Maoism." No Great Leaps Forward or Cultural Revolutions have devastated its population, no massive famines have cost tens of millions of lives there as the result of ideological extremism or foolish efforts to turn peasants into steel makers. Yet by 1980-1981, shortly after the death of Mao, and too soon to have allowed for any significant "recovery" from the effects of his leadership, China had an annual GNP per capita of $290, 20 percent higher than the $240 in India, according to World Bank figures.

A much greater and even more significant difference, however, is found in such social measurements as life expectancy and other similar standards of well-being. Pre-independence India and preliberation China were both near the bottom of the international system. Indian life-expectancy in 1931 was around twenty-seven years, while a survey of rural China in 1929-1931 yields calculations of a life-span of 23.7 for females and 24.6 for males, probably a similar overall rate if urban areas are added. The Chinese then entered a period of Japanese occupation and civil war, more devastating than anything experienced in India during the same time. According to Yu Quanyu, vice-president of the China Society for Human Rights Studies, the pre-1949 Chinese life-span was thirty-five years, compared to just around thirty-two years in India in 1941, still roughly comparable. Yet Indian life expectancy four years after independence, in 1951, was still only 32.1, while a similar postliberation period, as of 1953, found China with a life-span of 40.3. As demographer Judith Banister states in *China's Changing Population*, a thorough and precise study which is at the same time very cautious in its specific estimates,

> It is clear ... that the PRC attained very rapid mortality decline during the 1950's. It is probable that the pre-1949 crude death rate and infant mortality rate were approximately halved by 1957. This is a monumental achievement for such a huge population. China was similar to most other developing countries during the 1950's in that it achieved significant mortality control through cheap public health measures, but the reduction of mortality in the PRC was steeper and more far-reaching than in most other countries, in part because China started with a worse mortality situation.[40]

This resulted, partially, from the end of colonialism and civil war, and from better storage and distribution systems for food. But falling mortality was also due to the mass mobilizations against poor public health conditions and a wide variety of diseases, carried out immediately after the 1949 Liberation. In addition, the redistribution of agricultural land and the gradual nationalization of business and commercial assets during the 1950's greatly diminished the extremes of wealth and poverty in China. Though the average per capita wealth and income were not much increased by 1957, China's national income was more evenly distributed than ever before. Therefore, the poorest part of the population had a better chance to provide for their own basic subsistence needs than before the 1950's. This change alone surely had a major impact on the mortality of China's poorest people.[41]

Thus egalitarianism by itself, even without sharply rising GNP per capita, brought great benefits.

These gains were disastrously reversed in the years of the Great Leap Forward. Banister concludes that the official figure of 15 million "excess deaths" between 1957 and 1961 are probably only half the actual number, with life expectancy plunging to 24.6 in 1960. Yet her own computer reconstructions show a remarkable "Great Leap Forward" to 53.0 as early as 1962, a full 3.5 years of longevity immediately after that campaign ended compared to the 49.5 life-span in the year it began. Banister stresses that mortality was often underreported, and that data for any specific year may be based on extrapolations, rather than actual demographic surveys. Moreover, many of the weakest members of society had already died from 1957 to 1961, giving a kind of artificial boost to the figures immediately afterward. Nevertheless, 1962 became the new "base" level and the upward trend continued, even during the Cultural Revolution. Though estimates of deaths during that struggle range from tens to hundreds of thousands—some even speak of millions—and there may have been other significant losses due to widespread social breakdowns and medical disruptions, still Banister notes,

> Starting around 1969 or 1970, the first beneficial effects of the massive deployment of barefoot doctors in the rural areas [specially trained personnel, often drawn from the peasantry themselves, to go into even the most remote villages] should have been evident in conditions affecting rural mortality. The rapid spread of the cooperative medical system must have regularized access to simple primary medical care for most of China's people. Once this medical system was functioning by around 1971 or 1972, a rise in life expectancy and decline in death rate would be expected. It is therefore reasonable to suppose that China's death rate, which probably stayed at or above 10 per thousand population throughout the 1960's, dipped and stayed below about 10 from the early 1970's on.[42]

But the "barefoot doctors" were a direct realization of the values of the Cultural Revolution, which promoted attention to the needs of the vast majority of the population, especially the peasantry, over those of the urban elite, and which challenged the goals of a technocratic, and usually Western-derived professionalism, emphasizing in its place the kinds of knowledge available and useful to all. This legacy remains in the 1990s, despite the recent cutbacks in medical care for the rural poor.

> In visits over the last two years to hospitals and village doctors in seven provinces, the first impression is of rustic examination rooms where the doctors are semi-educated peasants wearing frayed and stained white jackets. Yet the more enduring impression is that these unscrubbed, sandal-clad doctors have a broad range of useful skills—treating infections, diagnosing pneumonia, assisting in births and pulling teeth—that in rural areas are more useful than anything at the cutting edge of Western medicine....[43]

These rural programs had their counterparts for the city population as well.

Thus the losses of life in the Cultural Revolution were counterbalanced and most likely outweighed by the enormous gains in health to the masses of Chinese people. According to the estimates of Banister, by 1973-1975, when the first reliable surveys in China were carried out, life-expectancy had reached 63.62 for males and 66.31 for females. The longer lives of women relative to those of men are especially notable, "a switch from the 1930 pattern."[44] These figures contrast with the still very low Indian life-span of 49.4 in the early 1970s—so that even during the worst years of "turmoil," the Chinese advantage in life expectancy grew much wider. Banister summarizes regarding the 1973-1975 period, when the worst clashes of the Cultural Revolution had subsided, but before any major policy changes would have had the effect of undoing damage from that campaign.

> The developed countries, of course, had achieved a significantly higher expectation of life than China, as had several Asian and Latin American countries. Sri Lanka and Chile had about the same life expectancies as the PRC as of the early 1970's. But it is clear that a large proportion of the world's developing countries had estimated expectations of life at birth lower than China's during the 1970's. This enormous group of nations included almost all of Africa, the Middle East, and South Asia, as well as many countries in Latin America. It is noteworthy that China had achieved much greater success in mortality control than India and Indonesia, the other populous developing countries of Asia.[45]

Thus even in the midst of the Cultural Revolution, the Chinese maintained and actually expanded their advantage over other major Asian population centers. This gap in life expectancy reflected the growing economic egalitarianism in China compared to other third world nations. As late as the mid-1990s, the poverty rate was still 50 percent for the Indian and Pakistani populations combined, while in Indonesia, "38 per cent of the population are not adequately fed and clothed."[46]

Other sources suggest even greater disparities between China and India. Using UN statistical data, George Thomas Kurian finds that in 1980-1981, Chinese males could expect to live 60.70 years, and females 64.40. This level is slightly below that of Mexico, but significantly higher than for Brazil, despite the some eightfold greater GNP per capita in these leading Latin American countries. Life expectancy for Indian males at this time was a dismal 46.40 years and for females 44.70, some 15 to 20 years lower per person than for the Chinese. This placed India in the same general rank as some of the poorest countries of Latin America and Sub-Saharan Africa.[47] Of special note is the longer life of women in China, where they lived, on average, almost half again as long as their peers in India, despite historically dismal treatment of females in both traditional societies in those areas favoring male longevity. So too, while the Chinese infant mortality rate had dropped to a still relatively high 56.0 per 1,000 live births in 1980-1981, the comparable Indian figure was more than double, a soaring 122.0. Whatever the exact size of the gap between the two countries, given the population in India in the late 1970s and early 1980s of around 700 million, such a vast difference in life expectancy and infant mortality meant the loss of well over 10 billion life-years among its people, compared to those living in China. These poor Indian life conditions, moreover, were chronic, not resulting from one or two short campaigns.

Nor was length of lives alone higher, and infant mortality lower, in China. When another measurement of social well-being, rate of literacy, is added in, to yield a widely used "physical quality of life index," the Chinese in 1981 had seventy-six out of a possible hundred points, while the Indian rank was a miserable forty-four.[48] Thus despite thirteen supposedly "lost" years during the Great Leap Forward and Cultural Revolution—spanning nearly one half of the twenty-seven years between the triumph of the Chinese revolution and his death—Mao left the Chinese far better off than the Indians or the populations of other major Asian and third world societies, in leading criteria measuring development and overall well-being.

It can and no doubt will be argued that China could have "had its cake and eaten it too," that is, realized the gains of the Mao era without the "extremes" of "Maoism." To some extent this is undoubtedly the case. The improvements made after Liberation were by no means the product only of his leadership, and they continued in the years when his power was in eclipse, though in altered forms and sometimes at a less rapid pace. Nevertheless, the rise in life expectancy and literacy in China from 1949 to 1978 were in large measure a result of precisely the methods and values of the "late Mao" so widely denounced by his opponents: mass mobilizations and collective social actions, egalitarianism and redistribution of income, and anti-elitism in favor of the needs of the broad masses of the population. Despite limited overall growth as measured in GNP per capita—the main accusation by the reformers against the economic legacy of the Mao era—these approaches brought enormous benefits to hundreds of millions, and in ways that were sustainable over a long period of time.

It is thus important to stress what happened immediately after Mao died. According to calculations by Banister, the peak in Chinese life expectancy in the three decades after 1953, at 65.1 years, was in 1978—two years following the death of the Chairman, and a year after Deng Xiaoping regained power and began to assert his dominance over policy matters. Thereafter, life-span actually fell slightly, to 64.6 in 1984. But this fall was entirely attributable to a decline in female longevity, which dropped almost two full years, from 66.0 to 64.1, while male life expectancy continued to rise during this time from 64.1 to 64.9, once again restoring the preliberation pattern. The real story, however, lies in infant mortality, with the rate for males declining from 36.8 to 33.9 per 1,000 live births, even as that for females soared from 37.7 to 67.2—that is, from virtual equality to almost double the level for boys. Even though Banister stresses that "there is ... no independent proof that female infanticide caused a statistically significant number of female infant deaths,"[49] the increased emphasis on population control, combined with a renewed premium on male heirs under the policies of marketization and individual family responsibility in farming, almost certainly accounts for the growing unnatural number of "missing" girls. As a result, overall infant mortality rose again from 37.2 to 50.1, reaching levels not seen for some ten years. Thus after three decades of improvement in the survival rates of children and longer life expectancy under Mao—despite the interruption of the Great Leap Forward—these positive trends began to be reversed almost immediately after his death, and in ways that reestablished some of the worst discriminatory abuses of preliberation China.

In more recent years, life expectancy appears to have increased once again, and today adult Chinese women live longer than men. The human rights official cited above states that the Chinese life-span was seventy-one years as of 1992. But this would still represent a gain of only six years of life expectancy in the sixteen years since Mao died in 1976, compared to the eight-year life-span increase in the much shorter period of twelve years from just before the Cultural Revolution to his death. Nevertheless, in the 1980s and early 1990s, China compared very favorably even with the United States. Thus,

In Shanghai, 10.9 infants out of 1,000 die before their first birthday, while in New York City infant mortality is 13.3 per 1,000 live births.

And life expectancy at birth in Shanghai is now 75.5 years, compared to a life expectancy in New York City of about 73 years for whites and 70 years for nonwhites as of 1980, the last year for which data are available.[50]

A few years may separate these Shanghai and New York statistics, and figures for the United States as a whole are better than for China.

But New York and Shanghai are their country's largest and most crowded cities. How can Shanghai, a dilapidated third-world metropolis in a country with a per capita income of $350, give its infants such good odds?

The answer has nothing to do with modern equipment or with money, for Shanghai spends just $38 a person on medical care, compared to more than $2,100 in the United States. It appears that only about 5 percent of the Chinese gross national product is devoted to health expenditure, compared to 11 percent of America's.

"There's no question that in a time when people are despondent about what's happening in China, the health-care system really is a shining light from the Maoist era that continues to shine to this day," Gail E. Henderson, an expert on Chinese health care at the University of North Carolina School of Medicine, said in an interview. "It's a model for the developing world."[51]

So startling are the figures for China that, according to Dr. B.P. Kean, the World Health Organization representative there,

If you just go through the figures—life expectancy, infant mortality, first three causes of death—without knowing which country it is, it would be very difficult to pick the country as China and almost impossible to pick it as a developing country. The top causes of mortality in the cities are the same as in developed countries: cardiovascular disease, cerebrovascular disease and cancer.[52]

While still way ahead of most other third world countries, there has been recent slippage, as a result of marketization reforms.

China has made enormous strides in medical care in the four decades since the Communist Revolution, and in some ways the health profile of the population resembles that of a developed country more than that of a country with a per-capita income of $300 per year. The World Bank lists life expectancy among Chinese at 70 years, compared with 76 in the United States and 58 in India. But there are some indications that the gains in health care have slowed in the last dozen years, at the same time that China has opened to the world and doubled its per-capita income. By some counts, for example, infant mortality has shown little improvement in recent years. At last count, 31 Chinese infants out of 1,000 die before the age of 1, compared with 10 in the United States and 97 in India, according to World Bank statistics.

The main reason for the slowdown in health-care improvements in recent years appears to be the collapse of the commune system, which used to provide rudimentary health care, usually free of charge, throughout rural China. After the communes were dismantled in the early 1980's, some "barefoot doctors" returned to their farm work or started businesses, and many villages were left without adequate health care, or else had to pay for it. It also became more difficult to mobilize people for large preventative medicine projects.[53]

Moreover, medical care, like every other aspect of Chinese society, is becoming ever more polarized by class and region, so that national averages almost certainly cover up growing disparities in health as well, especially urban/rural ones.

Of course, there is more to life than longevity, and there were political and other social ramifications to the struggles under Mao not reducible to such measurements. But neither can the losses of life suffered during his campaigns be treated in isolation from the overall effect of the mass-based policies which he pursued, and which allowed hundreds of millions to live longer. In confronting such contradictions, the deaths suffered during the struggles led by Mao after Liberation are relatively easy to identify and denounce, while the gains, which for decades—and still today—gave some 1 billion people longer life and more healthy families, are often largely ignored.

> Plague, tuberculosis and other diseases still exist at the margins of Chinese society, but by channeling funds toward prevention of disease and basic care, the Government has saved tens of millions of lives....[54]

It is politically "safe" and perhaps even fashionable these days in U.S. academia or mainstream media, and even on much of the left, to celebrate the "death of Maoism." But the "silent terror" of poverty and poor health that kills tens of millions every year throughout most of the third world is a more diffuse and less "sexy" target for attack. To fight the forces that keep these conditions in place, and that are still very much alive and ever more powerful today, requires a dedication to values and methods which are closer to those struggled for by Mao than to the dominant global forms of "developmentalism." This becomes more apparent every day in China, where marketization reforms threaten to revive the worst aspects of "third worldism"—dependency and impoverishment, and the increasing barbarity of social relations they generate—just as in any other country.

Thus the "unnatural" gap in the number of girls which first appeared after the death of Mao not only persists today, but if anything seems to be growing more extreme. According to recent population figures, "several million little girls" are missing.

> Newly released data from China's 1990 census support previous suspicions that 5 percent of all infant girls born in China are unaccounted for. It is not clear what has happened to them.

Are they killed at birth, drowned in a bucket of water by the midwife, on instructions from parents who want a son rather than a daughter? Or are they given up for adoption? Or perhaps they are raised secretly to evade the one-child policy? Some evidence suggests that a combination of these factors accounts for the missing girls, although officials usually insist that very few are killed.[55]

Even if outright infanticide is not widely practiced, however, "one of the great mysteries of China is what happens to about half a million infant girls who are born alive each year but then vanish." The ratio of boys born per 100 girls, which had dropped from 104.9 in 1953 to 103.8 in 1964, on the eve of the Cultural Revolution, rose to 107.5 by 1982, and a soaring 111.3 in 1990. But the ratios drop as the children grow older, suggesting that many girls are "hidden away" for several years, and then brought out again as toddlers, presenting local officials with a fait accompli. Though outright killing of infant girls is said to be much more rare, "with as large a population base as China's, even a tiny proportion of infanticides would equal a large number of killings."[56] Moreover, the millions of "lost" girls obviously suffer severely disrupted childhoods and discrimination in many cases, even if they are allowed to survive and rejoin society.

A growing number of these infants, having been abandoned, join the swelling numbers of children in "orphanages," though they may have living parents. Others end up on the international "baby market" where they are adopted by those from the United States and other foreign countries, for fees ranging from $10,000 to $20,000—equal to two or three times the entire life earnings of the poor peasant and urban migrant families from which they commonly come—though it is not the Chinese parents who receive these payments. Many of the abandoned babies have physical problems. These, of course, are generally excluded from the foreign adoption market. At one orphanage, where a single mother from the United States received her baby, only those "in good health" were offered to her: "Of the 35, 12 were 'suitable for export,' according to the Chinese facilitator."[57] Such "exports" are growing at an accelerating pace, from just 16 in 1989 and 206 in 1992, to 330 in 1993, 787 in 1994, and a soaring 2,130 in 1995. This made China the largest supplier for the U.S. baby market—followed by Russia—with every indication that the curve is still climbing steeply.

But, unlike other international adoptions, 99 percent of Chinese adoptions have been of girls....
These days, U.S. parents with newborn Chinese babies are a common sight in the streets of Guangzhou. The U.S. Consul there has been granting visas for as many as 50 infants per day.[58]

This would imply as many as 15,000 young Chinese girls potentially being "exported" yearly from Guangzhou alone, the center of reforms. In this way the worst aspects of feudal life in China are being revived, now linked to "opening to the world" under market conditions. Thus the losses being suffered as a result of the reversal of the policies of Mao fall most heavily on the poor, and on women and children, with a great cost in lives and the shattering of family relations. They also lead inevitably to a return to shameful patterns of the past, when foreigners felt free to carry off anything they wanted from the Chinese, who were too impoverished and powerless even to protect their families.

It is in light of these conditions that the record of the years under Mao, and the changes since, must be "re-revised." It is not enough to speak of how "the very large economic gains from China's overall socialist development between 1949 and 1976 were offset by the equally large human costs that resulted from the periodic political and economic upheavals," and to compare this period only with preliberation China. The record of the Maoist era is certainly mixed—as the author of the above summary himself makes clear.[59] But it would be closer to the truth to state that the significant expansion of the economy under Mao was equalled or even surpassed by impressive advances, not only in longevity, but in the quality of human life—stability of employment, housing, health, education, and the security of women and children in particular—which for hundreds of millions of Chinese had previously been beyond any possibility of attainment. This is especially apparent when compared to their peers in other large Asian societies, and even to more economically advanced nations world-wide, much less to preliberation conditions.

These gains came at the cost of intense periods of social turmoil and at times extremely high loss of lives within the span of a few years—but they resulted in social transformations that saved billions of years of life for the broad masses of the Chinese population, and achieved levels of security and well-being only fully apparent compared to the growing chaos of social conditions under market reforms. Yet too often Western authors, even those who recount the high life expectancy and other measurements of social well-being under Mao, fail to adequately grasp that these advances came precisely as a result of the policies promoted in the years of "turmoil," which they elsewhere heavily criticize. There is a connection between the class struggles of the Great Leap Forward and the Cultural Revolution—despite their heavy costs—and the vast and lasting accomplishment of raising almost one quarter of the entire population of the globe, most still living in deep poverty, to conditions of life well above typical third world conditions, and even to levels rarely found outside the very richest countries. These gains did not just "happen," nor were they the result of gradual reforms. They were achieved through the revolutionary struggle of the masses, who at a high price—as always—won for themselves the right to be treated as full and equal members of society, and to receive the services normally reserved for the elite and the well-off. Thus any summary which only emphasizes the costs of the Maoist era without at the same time referring to the "human advances" experienced by the great mass of the people of China in those years leaves a distorted picture—especially in lives lost or gained. It also renders virtually inexplicable why the Chinese returned over and over again to the leadership of Mao, despite the upheavals of his later campaigns.

V. "Foolish Old Mao"

In an exemplary tale by Mao about the value of patient struggle, the progeny of "The Foolish Old Man Who Removed the Mountains" gradually join him in his "illusion" that he can move the two "immovable objects" which lie outside his door—which Mao equated with imperialism and feudalism. Thus the major barriers blocking the forward path of China before the revolution were overcome, once the masses came to believe in the possibility of removing them. Now many Chinese are beginning to recognize a new validity in "Foolish Old Mao" with his "delusions" of the struggles against "revisionism" and "restoration of capitalism," as the view spreads that unless these obstacles too are overcome, China will find itself moving backward once again, despite its apparent development. Though today the language in which such concepts are expressed usually employs less ideological or even political terms than in earlier times, the return of capitalistic methods and their dire social consequences are generating the basis for reinterpretations of the postliberation Maoist era.

As realization of the value of the work of the "late Mao" begins to grow, the Cultural Revolution is thus once again also being subjected to new forms of analysis. For example, in 1992, Han Dongping produced a detailed study of that epoch, through an examination of his home county and village in Shandong Province.[60] No "cultist" of Mao, Han talks openly of "famine" during the Great Leap Forward, and recounts the hatred of a schoolmate who had lost a brother at that time, while his own better-connected family survived. Yet, using remarkably detailed records of production and social services, as well as of incidents among the villagers, supplemented by his own personal recollections as a teenager and interviews with older Chinese who were active at that time, Han finds that the Cultural Revolution was an era of liberation for peasants from the arbitrary authoritarianism of local officials, and from an attitude of submissiveness by the masses to those in positions of power, a millennial yoke of obedience which had continued under early Communist Party rule.

A major reason that the Cultural Revolution gained such widespread support was the abusive practices on the part of many state and party cadre in the later years of the 1960s, compounded by a renewal of top-down policies by those opposed to Mao. Thus "there was a major period of bureaucratic resurgence in the confused aftermath of the Great Leap Forward."[61] With the new and expanded campaign of the Cultural Revolution, therefore, came an emphasis on "learning from the masses," and not simply dictating to them or leading them "from above." This led to a reversal of the flow of power between peasants and officials, with a direct effect on productive relations. More striking yet, as a result of such changes Han shows that on average, output of grain increased during these years, raising incomes, largely due to the freedom to experiment with new forms of agriculture and encouragement of the spirit and practice of collectivism. The rise in productivity was directly related to political changes: "The democratic orientation and practice of the cultural revolution increased villagers' enthusiasm for production too."[62] Far from the official view of this period as one primarily of "turmoil" and "terror," the productive drive of the Cultural Revolution benefited many peasant family incomes—though it did often end in factional conflict and even open violence that eventually dissolved the movement and undermined its more positive aspects.

There were tremendous advances in other areas also, notably education. The number of Jimo County schools multiplied thirty or forty times over and more than 99 percent of children were enrolled at the primary level—contrary to the idea of schooling as having been nothing but a casualty during this era.

> It took the unprecedented enthusiasm and political consciousness created by the cultural revolution to achieve this unprecedented result in education.
>
> This increase in education was made possible partly because farmers had acquired the decision making power in education. Some people questioned the rationale of the educational practice during the cultural revolution that let the villagers have a say in the running of local schools. They believed that it was irrational to let the "ignorant," sometimes illiterate farmers tell the teachers what to do with schools. In essence, the practice of letting farmers have a say in running school during the cultural revolution, was similar to the public school system in the U.S. which gives local people considerable power to decide how much money they want to spend on their children's education and what kind of education they want their children to have.

Before the cultural revolution, villagers did not have any control over education.

The change in educational content was especially important, as elitist knowledge was replaced with forms of learning that were of value to the peasants themselves and relevant to their lives.

It is true that the students of the village school did not learn as many new words and scientific principles as the graduates of the former elite schools did. The students of the village school devoted more time to practical knowledge than the former elite school.... In terms of bookish knowledge, graduates of the village school were inferior to graduates of the former elite middle school. But in terms of practical knowledge we were inferior to none. Most of my old classmates from the village school played a very important role later in the village life. Several of them became heads of production teams, construction teams, and technicians in village factories.

Access to education changed class relations as well:

the fact that more than half of villager's kids who finished junior high school could go to senior high school was revolutionary. It helped reduce the gap in the living standards between the social elite and common villagers.

Thus educational advances had a significant egalitarian impact, not only in social relations, but even in relative incomes. As a result of such changes in production and education,

The gap between the living standards of government employees and villagers in Jimo County ... actually were diminishing. The overall trend in grain consumption and income per capita among the rural population were on the rise, while the relative trend of grain consumption and income among non-agricultural population was on the decline.

The gains were qualitative as well as quantitative, creating time for leisure and culture: "Because of increased mechanization of agriculture, farming became easier and less tiring." At the same time, cultural activities were also becoming mass-oriented.

The most profound effects, however, were in the political realm. Han demonstrates that even the "Little Red Book" of *Quotations from Chairman Mao Tse-tung*, now almost universally derided as the ultimate expression of "cultism," was, in the hands of the peasantry, a weapon against those who still oppressed them in the 1960s, especially at the level of local village officials.

It is my contention that the cultural revolution was different from ordinary peasant rebellion because the common villagers were struggling for their own power, the power to air their opinions and the power to be heard. In this sense it was justifiable to say that the cultural revolution was unprecedented in Chinese history. It gave common villagers some sense of power that they never had before, and it changed the common farmers' mentality. Many factors contributed to this great achievement, one of which was the study of Mao's works.

The study of Mao's works, which was intensified during the cultural revolution, was one of the most important factors that distinguished the cultural revolution from ordinary popular rebellion and contributed most to the common villagers' acquisition of a sense of power. Mao's red books became available to everyone during the cultural revolution. The directives from Mao and the Central Party committee were read and explained to the villagers. Mass meetings became particularly common during the cultural revolution. This was in itself something revolutionary, because throughout Chinese history, the ruling philosophy was *min ke shi you zhi, bu ke shi zhi zhi* (Common people should be led without their being aware of where they are led).

Han addresses directly the issue of "cultism" and how for the peasants, reference to the works of Mao create a base for mass counter-authority to those who had so long oppressed them.

To the outside world, this was Mao's personality cult carried to the extreme. Yes, it was a form of personality cult. But this personality cult was a natural result of the study of Mao's work among the Chinese people. Common villagers found that Mao's works contained answers to their problems. And what most outside critics did not realize was that in the process of studying Mao's works, Mao's words had become a de facto constitution in Chinese politics. More importantly this constitution was available to common villagers....

The study of Mao's works during the cultural revolution distinguished that event from ordinary popular rebellion because the rebels, the common people, justified their attacks on their targets with Mao's works as theoretical base....

What the critics failed to see was that the submission to Mao's works as authority provided common villagers protection against other capricious authorities and gave common villagers a sense of power they never had before.

The liberation experienced was often of the most personal kind, dissolving, in a few months, millennia of patriarchal dominance.

Everybody was equal on the basis of Mao Zedong's works. My father, for example, who had never allowed me to speak with him on an equal basis before, had to tolerate my arguing with him about our political differences, thanks to the political climate of the time. The absolute authority he held over me was broken for no other reason than that Mao said that everybody inside the revolutionary rank was equal. What we argued may not have been of significance now, but the fact that I could argue on an equal basis with my father and my teacher was nothing short of personal liberation for me.

The same was true with the different groups of red guards in the whole county or whole village. One can dismiss the fighting and arguments among the different red guards groups as much ado over nothing or over trifle things only. But one can never deny that these arguments and fighting per se was part of a process of personal awakening and personal liberation for common villagers who had never been active in politics ... a kind of political maturing for the common villagers.

Like the backyard furnaces of the Great Leap Forward, "useless" debates in the villages changed the mentality of peasants. Thus even those aspects generally considered most negative in the Cultural Revolution had a positive side for the peasant masses.

Summarizing the overall effects of the campaign, Han shows that the gains were profound, but incomplete, leaving behind the legacy of "a baptism of democracy for the rural population."

> We are not in a position to discuss whether direct democracy had been set up or not at the end of the cultural revolution because democracy is itself a vague concept. But we can say that the cultural revolution had started the search for democracy in rural China.... It is true, the cultural revolution did not provide the Chinese villagers with a full democracy yet. But all the writing of big character posters and debate between the leaders and common villagers were democratic practices.... It is not fair to expect perfect democracy to take place in a very short time either. However, if the cultural revolution brought any changes to Chinese society at all, it improved the status of common Chinese villagers more than any other event in modern Chinese history.

Such a conclusion makes all the more painful the most recent experiences of Han in his home county, especially in regard to schooling, where he and his generation had gained so much due to the transformations carried out during the Cultural Revolution.

> The village education system supported by the collective fund before had suffered a great deal. Without financial help from the collective, village schools have had to charge the villagers a high price for the education they offered in order to survive. Many farmers did not want to pay the price. As a result of deterioration in mechanization and irrigation, farmers had to work harder than before in order to keep the same level of production as before. Some families took their school age children out of school to help them in the field.... During my research trips to villages in Henan Province in the last few years, we were often followed by large crowds of children. Out of curiosity, I asked children from the crowds to read the headlines of the newspapers. Nine out of ten children would shake their heads shyly. The other children would explain that they had dropped out [of] school years ago.

There are more children than ever, however, to provide uneducated labor for the new entrepreneurs who only want a cheap work force.

> Another long term damage was the loss of control of family planning in the village. Farmers had not liked the idea of family planning all along,

because they worried about their old age. But with the consolidation of collective economy during the cultural revolution, the idea of family planning became more acceptable to them. Farmers gradually came to think that they could depend on the collective to take care of their old age even if they did not have many children themselves. Persuasion was coupled with discipline, and family planning became the normal practice in many rural areas. But with the dissolution of the collective, farmers began to produce more children again. They defied the government policy of one couple one child.

This virtual collapse of entire areas of social advancement made during the years of "turmoil" was largely the result of the attitude of the reformers, who condemned "the cultural revolution as a whole, all the practices advocated during the cultural revolution were condemned. It was like a contagious disease that could not be stopped easily and reasonably." As a result, even the most enlightened gains of that era were destroyed, sometimes virtually overnight, especially for the peasant masses.

As in other areas of social life today, "modernization" in the form of marketization has produced not only a return to capitalistic forms of exploitation, but to feudalistic ones, as Han explains.

Villagers complain nowadays that the feudal tradition of *guan guan xiang hu* (Official tends to support officials) has come back again. In former days, when farmers worked together, it was relatively easy for them to act together to demand justice from local leaders. Now, farmers function as individuals in the village life. It is hard for them to act collectively and effectively to defend their rights.

During my trip to villages in Henan Province I found many cases of abuse of power and corruption that would have been impossible during the cultural revolution years. The old head of the party branch in Qianfu village pocketed all the money we paid to the villagers for coming to our interviews. When villagers raised questions, he asked his son who knew martial arts to beat them. In Qianko village, the village leader told me confidentially that he benefited by our presence in the village. Even though we brought our own food and drink every day and did not eat anything from the village, the village leader said he would charge 50 yuan a day all the same from the village fund which village leaders collected from the village every year.

Such abuses, Han Dongping concludes, were not eliminated in the earlier campaigns, but they "did become less frequent then. Now the condemnation of the cultural revolution and the dissolution of the collective resurrected all these practices. Chinese rural areas returned to the old days before the cultural revolution in this regard."[63]

Restoration of such conditions means that China is beginning to take on the typical third world pattern, in which a largely urban modernized sector rises like an island in the midst of a sea of rural oppression, which not only lacks the full advantages of modern development, but is reduced to the worst premodern forms of exploitation. Experiences such as those of Han in Henan Province could be lifted almost verbatim from reports of conditions in Chinese villages before the arrival of the Communist forces in the 1930s and 1940s—despite obvious anachronisms compared with the previous regime. In this way, ideological repudiation of the late campaigns of Mao translates directly into renewed oppressions, providing a cover for them.

Of course, one county cannot be equated to the whole of China— though the experiences of Han in Henan show it is hardly unique. In the end, the Cultural Revolution left much of the country in disorder, as factional fighting drained the popular energy and undermined the gains of its earlier years, adding to the loss of life. Though many communes had flourished, others did not, and there was still widespread peasant poverty. But a study of the kind carried out by Han Dongping reminds us of the positive side of the campaign, and helps explain why it was enthusiastically taken up and supported for so long, especially by the rural poor, whose experience is now largely ignored, buried beneath a growing pile of autobiographies of persecuted urban intellectuals and former village authorities. Contrasting experiences such as the ones recounted by Han should remind us that those who are now the main public interpreters of the actions of Mao in his later years also come from the very social strata that were the focus of these campaigns, both within China and in the ranks of Western professionals. Thus a class bias is inevitably involved.

We learned this first-hand through teaching educated young Chinese. The greatest disappointment that I experienced with the students in Changchun, who were largely drawn from professional families, was the disparaging attitude many of them took toward the peasantry, whom they would often dismiss as backward and conservative, and even "ignorant" or "stupid." Yet the very free university education and guaranteed jobs that these privileged young people enjoyed were the direct results of the revolution made by such peasants. This survival of the ancient Mandarin spirit of looking down on the "common" peasantry by the educated elite not only made clear how remarkable was the decision of Mao to base his struggles in the rural areas, but how necessary his later campaigns like the Great Leap Forward and Cultural Revolution had been. Not surprisingly, again drawing on anecdotal reports from Chinese who work in the villages, the verdict of many peasants about the events of those years are often radically different, and considerably more positive, than those that are found among the urban and educated professionals. Such opinions do not negate the "mistakes" in these campaigns. But they do suggest a mass base for revising the official line, which sees the "late Mao" primarily as a source of devastating losses.

These popular "revisions of the revision," like the positive comparison between social conditions in China and other nations, may be lost on those in the United States who are so eager to denounce the "terror, mass mobilizations and personality cult" of the Mao years,[64] or who believe that the Chinese,

> caught between the catastrophe of Mao's revolution and the uncertainty of Deng's ongoing 'counterrevolution' (as some wags call it) ... have responded not with an effort to understand how they have arrived at this state of precarious ambiguity but with a wave of national amnesia.[65]

Some of these denunciations appear to have no bounds in their virulence, giving rise to such statements as that "no other leader in history held as much power over so many people for so long as Mao Zedong, and none inflicted such a catastrophe on his nation."[66] But the ability to escape from the worst conditions of the third world was apparently not irrelevant to the masses of the Chinese people, who turned again and again to the leadership of Mao, despite costly losses and setbacks, and these popular assessments remain relevant in China today. This has nothing to do with "amnesia," but rather with thoughtful and reasoned judgments which attempt to come to terms with complex historical phenomena.

In "Mao Zedong in the Hearts of Modern People," a survey of "100 Ordinary Chinese" by the Academy of Social Sciences, released in time for the Mao 100th Anniversary celebration, it was found that opinions varied with age.

> Older people (over) 50 are the group which love the Chairman very deeply, 80 per cent of them said affirmatively that Mao's achievements outweigh his errors.... Speaking of Mao's errors made in his later years, most of the older people showed their tolerance and forgiveness, even though some had terrible experiences during that period.[67]

The next age group, the "Cultural Revolution" generation, was more ambivalent:

> For those in their middle ages, their attitude to Mao showed very mixed feelings. On the one hand, more than half of them felt that they would not simply use "love" or "hate" to express their mixed feelings. Others said they respect Mao, but hardly use "idol" or "love" to express their views. On the other hand, this group showed their rational and positive side, 67 per cent of those in middle age gave a pretty high value to Mao's status in history.
> One middle-age man, who was of landlord-family origin, and was treated as a counterrevolutionary at the age of 16, then suffered all kinds

of humiliation, said "I have a very mixed feeling of Mao Zedong. As far as my personal experience is concerned, Mao's period gave me such misery. But from a historical point of view, people did have a period of good life after liberation, ending several decades of war and split conditions."

Others in this age group were more critical, blaming Mao for disruption of the economy and "closing our country to the world," but among those quoted, there was a general balancing of negative aspects with positive ones.

Moreover, the real surprise came with those in their late twenties and thirties, the age group we taught in Changchun.

It was beyond our expectation that young people would set such a high value on Mao. The investigation results show the people between 26 and 35 are the group which used words like "adore" and "adore very much" the most, 57 percent of them expressing their attitude this way.

The young people do not appraise Mao most often from the historical or political point of view, like the other two generations do. Out of their special historical and political background, they are overwhelmed with admiration for Mao's personality, morals, temperament, knowledge, courage, insight and his being politically-minded.[68]

These young people feel very removed from the Great Leap Forward and the Cultural Revolution. They "lack the perceptual knowledge of Mao's errors," and "some even suspect the stories about a lot of people suffering persecution. They think a small number of people exaggerated the truth in order to give vent to their personal resentment."[69] Such suspicions of the official line reflect a well-founded belief that the current revisionist version of the record of Mao has its own biased political slant.

These three generations, therefore, can hardly be said to consider the Mao era as one primarily of "terror" and "catastrophe." They have adopted a balanced evaluation, sometimes more positive, at others more negative, but in all cases striving to know about and come to terms with the past. Nor do they reflect a desire for "amnesia" so that they can "escape from history."[70] If there is this kind of widespread "loss of memory," it is found not among those who lived their lives under Mao, but among the youngest Chinese.

To youngsters under 25 years old, their unfamiliarity with Mao forms a sharp contrast with the attitude of older young people. In this group, most college students showed a certain respect or adoration toward Mao, but most of the rest hardly know anything about Mao or the relevant history, and social and political situation, so they are not sure what to say. Forty per cent of investigated youngsters belonged to this group. A lot of them said "not very much," "no time" or "no interest" when they were asked whether they wanted to know more about Mao.[71]

It is not those who had direct experience of the Mao years who are trying to forget, therefore, but those raised in the mind-numbing era of consumerism and "get rich before others" ideology. This apoliticism and "amnesia" may indeed now be spreading even among the older generations. But such disengagement and disorientation reflect not so much being "caught between the catastrophe of Mao's revolution" and the "uncertain" policies of Deng Xiaoping, but the internal contradictions of "market socialism" itself, which undermine any coherent conception of historical development or of ideological integrity. Thus the Chinese need no "wags" to make them aware of the "counterrevolution" of the "capitalist road," which opens ever wider in front of marketization reform. Those losing guaranteed jobs, health care, free education, and security for their old age know without being told by pundits that "the market" is every day less compatible with the ongoing claim that it is still "socialist," or building on the legacy left to China by Mao Zedong.

Such concepts as the "Lost Decade," a formula commonly applied to the Cultural Revolution years, must also be understood as internally contradictory. In the official view, the "losses" of this period are measured especially in terms of production, which was at times disrupted on a vast scale, and of education, which saw the closing of most universities and even of lower level schools at times. That many people suffered a loss of jobs and schooling during this period cannot be denied. But while large numbers of students and professionals lost the opportunity to have a "normal" career, many millions of peasants and workers gained the chance to work in more egalitarian relations not previously open to them and to participate in running the society on a daily basis for long periods of time, sometimes side by side with the cream of the educated elite of China and even with top cadre—up to and including Deng Xiaoping himself. Han Dongping again discusses the effect of this contact.

> It was true that the city educated youth did not stay in the village long in many cases, but the impact of their stay in the village on the rural development outlived their presence. These city young people went through the early stages of the cultural revolution. Having gone through the struggles of the cultural revolution at its initial stages, these young people had a daring spirit that the rural population did not have. Village leaders, who used to boss common villagers, had a hard time dealing with these city educated young people. They quarreled, sometimes fought, with village leaders. Their interaction and sometime conflict with village leaders and villagers in general, was in the long run conducive to the transformation of farmers' mentality.[72]

The effect was similar to that in the United States of the mainly young and educated recruits who joined the Mississippi Freedom Summer in 1964, going into the poorest black communities of that state. Their relations with the local population were also sometimes rocky, but the lasting consequence of contact with these students, who intentionally violated the old "way of life" of the white Mississippians, had a transforming effect, deepened by the directly educational impact of informal "freedom schools."

In China, according to Han, there was a similar legacy.

> The influx of educated city youth and local educated youth in the village changed the composition of the rural population. Through interaction with the educated youth, farmers who had been obedient to arbitrary authorities throughout Chinese history were more ready to speak their minds and to criticize their leaders by means of debate and big character posters.[73]

This bridging of class, of urban and rural, of mental and manual would have been unthinkable in any earlier period of Chinese history, and has probably not been duplicated anywhere else in the world on such a scale or for so long a period of time. Thus for every loss there were also gains, not only the "barefoot doctors" who have saved untold rural millions, but educational opportunities, however informal, for those who had never had them, and new experiences and attitudes which the campaign promoted, ideas of equality and the right to full participation in the society even by the poorest and least advantaged that still continue to influence policy today, after two decades.

What is not usually considered, in addition, is that what was "lost" during the Great Leap Forward and Cultural Revolution was the opportunity for those taking the "capitalist road" to implement their policies at an even earlier stage of development, and the consequences had they been allowed to do so. Where would China be today, in other words, had there been no opposition by Mao to the programs that anticipated the later "reforms" when they first arose in the 1950s, in the years when Chinese society had just emerged from decades of colonialism and war? What would the countryside look like now if individual farming had been more widely introduced at that time, when ancient poverty and class divisions were still the dominant context, and without collective efforts at construction, education, and health? How many hundreds of millions of peasants would be "floating," how vast would be the numbers of urban unemployed, had production under marketized conditions predominated throughout the development of modern China? How much more advanced would class polarization be today? What percentage of the economy would foreign investors already control? These questions too must be answered, when one speaks of the cost of "lost decades." For the "losses" of the Cultural Revolution cannot be measured only in terms of disruptions in production and education, nor even in lost lives and careers. They must also take into account the slowing of progress on the "capitalist road," saving China from decades of "development" of the kind that most other third world countries have experienced.

It is the growing realization of these ever-deepening contradictions of marketization that is driving the revised view of the "late Mao" and of his opposition to the policies of the reformers, most especially the opening up of China to foreign capitalists. This is apparent in an article interviewing Jiang Wen, the most popular Chinese male actor, who had the lead in "A Native of Beijing in New York" and such films as "Red Sorghum."

> If China's hottest movie star seems more than a little jingoistic, it is hardly by accident. Jiang, 32, has a knack for catching China's popular mood, and that mood now includes a heavy dose of nationalism.
>
> Consider a couple of recent television miniseries. In one, Chinese women working in foreign companies are shown slaving away on behalf of outsiders who range from dopey (the boss of a German firm) to lascivious and crooked (an American). Another series depicts foreigners as hopelessly materialistic. Only those foreigners who adopt presumed Chinese virtues—spirituality and preference for the group over the individual—are shown in a favorable light.
>
> The films and TV programs symbolize China's changing attitude toward the outside world. Much like the political figures who believe the West is trying to encircle China, intellectuals now view the world with a mixture of bravado and suspicion—sure that China has resumed its place as one of the world's leading countries, but unsure whether the world is willing to recognize this.[74]

Jiang Wen experienced this personally in the filming of "A Native of Beijing in New York," in ways which eerily paralleled the themes of the television series itself. "After returning to China in triumph, he gave interviews deriding the United States and bemoaning New Yorkers' perceived racism toward the Chinese cast and crew, who expected a welcome but were mercilessly ignored."

Any such renewed nationalistic reaction, however, requires a reexamination of the recent Chinese past as well. Significantly, in his own debut as a director, Jiang Wen chose to adapt a short story "that gives a somewhat nostalgic look at the Cultural Revolution." He picked this clearly "revisionist" theme, despite his own urbaneness and wealthy cosmopolitan lifestyle and his frustration with the ongoing political restraints on films, in part because of his disparagement of the work of other directors, who he believes sell out China for the sake of Western acclaim.

The next minute ... he is wishing for a new Mao Tse-tung to lead the country and calling for a new Cultural Revolution. Instead of making movies about Chinese themes, he says China's other directors like to criticize China so they make headlines in the Western press and thereby promote their movies.[75]

Thus a revised interpretation of the Cultural Revolution becomes inseparably linked once again to the issues of foreign "spiritual pollution" and loss of the historic autonomy of Chinese culture.

The implications of the struggle of "line" between Mao and Deng cannot, therefore, be limited to the domestic society. For opposition to any recapitalization was also an attempt to prevent the reappearance of a compradorist class, so increasingly obvious in China today—not in the cultural realm alone, but in all areas of economics and politics. Such a stratum is not only a threat to the internal structure of the Chinese economy, but equally an "open door" through which renewed imperialist pressures can be exerted on China, undermining even its national sovereignty. Thus the "nationalism" of Deng Xiaoping and his followers, resting as it does on unrestrained development, can ultimately threaten the nation as a whole, if "opening to the outside world" becomes a new route to foreign intervention. Nor does the theory of "market socialism with Chinese characteristics," with its focus on national power, have any effective answer, any means with which to counter, the growing effort, led by the United States, to "contain" China. For though the Chinese can and no doubt will stand up to U.S. containment in many ways, they can increasingly do so only by undermining the very developmentalism and foreign investment that they now pursue, any slowing of which, as Deng has stated, could easily lead to instability.

In contrast, Mao—though in his last years he himself initiated "opening to the outside world" with his "ping-pong diplomacy" with the Nixon administration—made the overall thrust of his theories and policies an attack on the roots of the imperialist system. For all his emphasis on the need for Chinese autonomy from global capitalism, Mao was an internationalist in the fullest sense. His concepts of mass-based class struggle, anti-elitism, and national liberation, his ideas of "serve the people" and "it is right to rebel," themselves became "material forces," as it were, "behind the lines" of the imperialists in countries throughout the world, including within the progressive movements of the United States itself. His vision of a more gradual, egalitarian, and sustainable form of development, which takes into account not only GNP per capita, but the need to avoid the polarization rampant in virtually all third world countries, remains a legacy to people everywhere seeking new routes to a socially just and ecologically sound form of economic progress. The determination of Mao to base such development on the resources of China itself, so that foreign dependency is minimized, continues even now to help point the way toward a profoundly different "new world order" of equal nations, "delinked" as much as possible from the ravages of global capital. Thus China under Mao, though in some basic respects "closed," was less alone, more tied to workers, peasants, and intellectuals everywhere, and in the lead of the world struggle, than it is today, for all its recent claims to being a major power.

This view, as well as the reaction to it heard in some quarters, was summarized in an "open letter" by Chinese academics and professionals living in the United States, condemning the "cure and tell" memoirs of Li Zhisui, who claims to have been "Mao's personal physician." Published in English as *The Private Life of Chairman Mao*, this book differs significantly even from its own Chinese language edition—which, among other changes, left out many of the most sensational details—presumably because its lurid claims to sexual perversity on the part of Mao and its scandal-mongering tone would be dismissed as ridiculous lies by the people of China themselves. In a scathing attack on the accuracy of this work, the "open letter" denies this characterization—or more precisely, caricature—of Mao.

> Mao Zedong is a great Chinese and world historic figure. The Chinese people are proud of the fact that China produced such a towering figure. He is revered and remembered for his lofty political vision to which he dedicated his entire life with admirable courage, bold initiative and selflessness. More important, he showed the Chinese people a bright future: a just and egalitarian society was entirely within reach. Some people revile him today, precisely because there are so many Chinese people who still revere him, miss him and cherish his vision.[76]

This letter in turn drew a similar denunciation of the Li Zhisui book by more than one hundred close associates and other members of the inner circle around Mao, including medical personnel, writing from mainland China. The signatories included Wang Dongxing, who served as bodyguard to Mao on the Long March in the 1930s, helped implement the purge of leaders in the Cultural Revolution, and as head of the most elite security force in Beijing at the time of the death of the Chairman, carried out the arrest of the Gang of Four. This communication too reaffirmed the position taken by the authors of the "Open Letter." In the words of Wang Yuyao, head of the Mao Zedong Study Group of the Research Center on Party Literature of the Chinese Communist Party Central Committee:

> "Mao Zedong not only belonged to China but also to the world. He changed the world's destiny as well as China's. One can't understand

modern China without studying him."
This feeling is shared by many Chinese.[77]

There is thus a widely held belief that Mao is a "gift" of China to the world, embodying the aspirations and hopes of its own people, but in a form which expresses universal values and concepts.

From this standpoint, it becomes apparent that a formula like "70 percent positive, 30 percent negative" does not work as applied to Mao. Not because he was free of mistakes and errors—which he naturally made like everyone else—but because there is no fundamental line which can be drawn between these two aspects, "good" and "bad," or between the various periods of his revolutionary leadership. Nor does this mean, as might seem to be the implication, that everything Mao did has to be accepted as either "all positive" or "all negative." It does, however, indicate that there is a dialectical relation between the earlier and later struggles which he led, which cannot be simply divided from each other. For Mao saw in his postliberation campaigns, and the Cultural Revolution above all, not only the continuation of the earlier revolutionary accomplishments he helped achieve, but their very protection as well. In other words, the "negative 30 percent" of his work was necessary to keep the "positive 70 percent" itself from being reversed, as is now occurring.

It is this dialectic which escapes the present leadership of China—though by what mix of intellectual failure, class bias, or brazen cynicism is unclear—a contradiction which threatens not only the direction that the country will take in the future, but the gains of the past. For the slow drift of "market socialism with special Chinese characteristics" back toward capitalism is gradually undoing each of the three great accomplishments of the revolutionary struggle, those very elements which the "reformers" themselves claim to support, and which form the underpinnings of their own legitimacy. All of these advances are now threatened due to the consequences of taking the "capitalist road." Thus the revival of vast social polarizations not only undoes the revolutionary moves toward egalitarianism, but threatens to recreate divisions at least as profound as those that separated the classes of pre-liberation China. In the countryside, in particular, there is a growing revival of landlordism, with wealthy farmers exploiting their neighbors, while hundreds of millions are driven from the land, to seek their "fortunes" in overcrowded urban areas. The new rural entrepreneurs are in turn increasingly allied with officials on the local level, who have reclaimed the privileges and power of old Mandarins.

Though "development"—the second of the basic goals of the Chinese Revolution—continues at a breakneck speed, this cannot obscure the growing issue of who primarily benefits from this explosive rise in economic power, and whose labor serves as the basis for this vast appropriation. For the beneficiaries are more and more the class of "new rich," who may hide their wealth within the shell of "state property," but operate in every other sense as private owners and appropriators, exploiting the mass of workers. The pursuit over the past fifteen years of the concept of developmentalism enunciated by Deng Xiaoping has itself become a tool for the accumulation of profits, resting more and more on the exploitation of the suppressed working masses, with the result that it is increasingly threatened by the anarchy which is inseparable from "marketization," that is, from the capitalist system itself. Thus, far from decreasing polarization—as Deng claimed would happen under "market socialism"—class differences are every day larger.

To prevent these deepening contradictions from getting out of hand and from becoming even more exacerbated, which would be the inevitable consequence of a serious economic slowdown, the necessity of turning ever more to foreign investors as the underlying basis of the Chinese economy has in turn become inescapable. But this inevitably reopens the door to imperialist control—and not only in the economic sphere. Thus the very liberation of China, the most profound of all the victories won in the course of the revolution, itself becomes increasingly hostage to outside forces. Against these gathering storms, the Chinese under Deng Xiaoping have in their own way turned even more inward, substituting the goal of "national power" based on domestic development and "getting rich" at any price, for that of any leadership role in the struggle for a new global system. Yet without a fundamental reorganization of the international economy, the rapid growth of China over the past decade or more will itself almost certainly be threatened by world capitalism, which has an almost unlimited arsenal of weapons—economic, political, and military— with which to attack such "upstarts."

That market socialism itself will soon require a new "revision" thus seems inevitable. Still, the Chinese people neither can nor will simply go backwards, no matter what happens next. The contradictions now arising must of necessity take forms dictated by the many "successes" of marketization and opening to the outside world, as well as by the changed external context of increasingly globalized capitalism. The new landlords rising in the countryside, the joint venture managers and compradors in the cities, the transnational corporations invading every pore of the Chinese economy, and the state and party officials so eager to do business with them, are not the same enemies as the Mandarins of old, nor the Guomindang and their imperialist backers, and they cannot be defeated by the same means Mao employed in leading the revolution. Nevertheless, the basic elements of his "thought" remain as relevant today as they were then. For there can be no separation of the class struggle and the right to rebel against exploitation, including collective actions against individual enrichment and for the promotion of egalitarianism—which were the essence of the late campaigns of Mao and of his policies, even during the period of the transition to socialism—from the ability to hold on to the earlier gains of the Chinese revolution. In this fundamental sense, the work of Mao cannot be divided into a "positive 70 percent" and "negative 30 percent" formula, as though the two parts were contradictory to each other, and the critique which his thought offers to market socialism therefore cannot be reduced to a "one-and-a-half-line" struggle. The opposition between his theories and practices and those of Deng Xiaoping and the "marketization reformers" is both profound and irreconcilable. The historic contradiction between them always was, and remains today, a "two-line" struggle.

CONCLUSION:
THE MOTIVE FORCE OF HISTORY

"Poverty," as Deng Xiaoping says, "should by no means be construed as socialism." Marx would no doubt agree, though it is doubtful that he would "call in the transnationals" as the "socialist" solution to the problem either. There is nonetheless a fundamental dilemma here which up until now has not been solved by those devoted to the building of socialism, whether in China or elsewhere: how does a poor country rapidly raise itself to a standard of living that is acceptable in the modern era, and still hold to the "socialist road," when the power of globalized capital increases every day? For it has become ever more apparent that the world is in a stage of new and even greater homogenization under capitalism, in which some from the third world manage to advance, while many in the economically most powerful countries see their livelihoods flow overseas and their former "good lives" turn into struggles for survival. One of the ironies of this period, therefore, is that the "prediction" of Marx which has been widely considered his most obvious error, that socialism would first arise in the most advanced capitalist countries of the world, may yet come true, if we assume that by a "socialist" society we mean one with some permanency. For it may require a higher level of global development under the reign of capital, and the deepening contradictions that entails, before the world can find a more general and lasting basis for socialism.

In this respect, the Deng Xiaoping reforms may represent an "inevitable" stage in the rise of China from the depth of historic impoverishment—quite apart from any verdict on the "correctness" or the "errors and mistakes" which either he and his followers, or Mao and his, may have shown. From the standpoint of this longer historic perspective, the "marketization" policies of Deng may indeed be the path to socialism for the Chinese people, but not presumably in the way that he means or that his followers anticipate when he states this. Rather, as Mao says, it will be only through the "negation of the negation"— the reconstruction of socialism by the Chinese people themselves.

For it is surely one of the most bitter contradictions to be faced by China in the period after the death of Deng that its new, world-historic chance at "national power" should come at the very moment when, increasingly, the effect of the global system is to dissolve the nation-state as an effective unit of organization as it faces the growing force of transnational capitalism. In a world where even the United States is losing its ability to dominate the globe, the Chinese potential to rise as a new world power is limited. It is more likely that China will instead find itself increasingly sucked into the maw of globalized capital, in which national boundaries have less and less relevance. Its imminent reabsorption of Hong Kong in 1997 exemplifies this contradiction, for even as the nation grows and gains economic strength, it does so by incorporating within its own borders a powerful center of global capitalism. That many Chinese may, through this form of growth, continue to raise their standard of living is itself one reason why capital will find such an "open door" into the country. But such a long-term effect of being drawn into the global "market," which is now happening every day more quickly, means that China will become just one more playground for the powers of international capitalism.

To the extent that this process occurs, the Chinese will find their situation indistinguishable from that of every other people under globalized capital, whether they still call themselves "socialist" or not. Thus they will be driven into renewed struggle, if not sooner, then later, if not to save what they still have of socialism, then to rebuild a socialist society through a confrontation with the "new" capitalism that rises on its ruins. China, in other words, cannot escape from class struggles. It must either undertake them now to salvage the gains of Chinese socialism before they are totally overwhelmed from within and without, or it will have to join with those exploited throughout the globe in finding new paths to resist capitalist power once it has completely triumphed. Either way, the contradictions of "market socialism" will have to be confronted, a process which is almost certain to shatter the social stability on which the developmentalism of Deng Xiaoping depended, and which he enforced with an iron hand.

It is only in this context that it is useful to speculate on what may come next in China after the death of Deng. There will, of course, be many contending centers of power within the complex interrelated system of party, state, army, and economic units, and reams will be written trying to predict how this is likely to get sorted out, and which figures will emerge to lead the country. While such speculations have their role in the short run, it is necessary to keep our eyes on the larger issues that are at stake. It is the class forces released by marketization under Deng and their collision with the remnants of the socialist institutions and values generated under the leadership of Mao that are virtually certain to provide the underlying momentum for the struggles that will be seen at the top of Chinese society in the post-Deng era. For the near future, those representing the "reforms" seem clearly to have the upper hand, but even among the top leaders, including Jiang Zemin, there appears to be a growing hesitancy to go over the edge entirely to full "marketization."

Fearful of the social instability which such a policy would almost certainly produce, signs are already appearing of a pulling back, at least insofar as increased efforts have been introduced to use the central government to buffer the worst forms of polarization and loss of social securities among the broad Chinese masses. There have also been new crackdowns since early 1995 on corruption, including the dismissal of the mayor of Beijing, and attempts to restrain the "princes," the children of top leaders, whose insider deals have reached scandalous levels. However, though such efforts are being made in the name of "socialism," it is increasingly evident that they have become necessities even in the self-interest of those whose goal is a still more rapid move toward capitalism, for the latter goal too cannot succeed if it generates social turmoil on a major scale. It would be a mistake, therefore, to read into the efforts at amelioration of the "market" any serious turn away from even further advances on the "capitalist road," or from the "opening up" of the Chinese economy to penetration from abroad. Quite the contrary, far from reining in the selling off of China to foreign capital, the present leaders are accelerating this process daily.

There are certainly Chinese who are more fundamentally opposed to these current policies, and it is quite possible that in the period following the death of Deng they will find a means to reassert their power in the party and state. The strength of such a faction and the sway which it might still exert within the leading circles is hard to judge, though the prospects for their assuming a dominant role seem slim at present. Their authority may grow, nevertheless, as the deepening contradictions of market socialism become apparent to ever broader segments of the Chinese population, and as the effects of global capital are felt at the local level. The challenge for any such left opposition will not be to turn "back to Mao" in any rote sense, but rather, following the example set by the Great Helmsman himself, to interpret the lessons of the past and of the experience of prior socialist construction to the "special circumstances of China," for the era of globalized capitalism.

This will be a challenge not unlike that which Mao himself faced in the 1920s, and it will require both new theories and practices, and almost certainly a newer stratum of leaders, able to build on the "successes" of "marketization." For it seems unlikely that the Chinese will, in the near future, want to turn their backs on the economic gains of the Deng Xiaoping era, or return to the era of greater austerity and national isolation. It is therefore difficult to imagine a sudden return to "Maoist" values, with their emphasis on "moral" rather than "material" incentives. Yet the Chinese may well choose to temper their new-found wealth with the spirit of egalitarianism and the commitment to collective mass-based advancement which they realized under Mao, and to close at least part-way the "open door" to foreign investment—for without some such actions, they will face global capital virtually without protection. Whether such a reversal of course can be achieved is problematic, and it would set off its own contradictions, if the full-throttle rush to "development" slowed. Thus either way there is a high probability of major strains in the next years, not only in the Chinese economic system, but in its political and social unity.

There is, of course, also the potential for China to veer off in directions which are not apparent today. Among these would be a major revival of the "democratization" movement which has erupted periodically since Liberation, most notably and recently at Tiananmen in 1989. Early 1995 saw a spate of letters and petitions from dissidents and leading intellectuals calling for a new openness in the political system. The yearning for greater democracy among the Chinese people appears to run quite broad and deep, and will very likely find an outlet in one form or another in the near future, whatever else may happen next. But though "democratization," like "development," has a certain universality, it would be a grave mistake to abstract it from the larger forces now contending in Chinese society. Whether China chooses to be socialist or capitalist, or maintains a precarious "third way" balance in the near future, it needs a greater degree of democratic participation to meet the desire of its people for more control over the decisions affecting their own lives. There will no doubt be growing pressure toward this both from within and without.

But "democratization" will come at too great a price if it proves to be just one more euphemistic cover for the dismantling of all that the people of China have gained in the course of their revolution. Russia today is "democratic," but it is increasingly a vast wasteland of rapacious capital, collapsing social securities, soaring death rates and plunging births, and the "mafiazation" of society that has made criminal activity all but the business norm. Between 1990 and 1994 alone, its male life expectancy dropped from sixty-four to fifty-seven years, an unprecedented plunge that left it behind India, Egypt, or Bolivia, while infant mortality soared 15 percent in both 1993 and 1994. It achieved its new "democracy" accompanied by ongoing regional fragmentation and civil war—not to speak of the use of tanks to crush any effective parliamentary limits on the imposition of the "dictatorship of the bourgeoisie" on its population. Even its economic decisions are largely voided by the greater power of the IMF, which imposes its own policies, overriding those put in place through the electoral process.

Such a "democratization" would be an utter disaster in China, given the still essentially third world economic level prevailing in most of the country. It could well have "world-historic" effects on the course not only of Chinese society, but of global progress for many decades. For China is not the Czech Republic, nor is it likely to move easily or soon toward the kind of multi-party system adopted in Taiwan in the past few years. Given the experience of the Soviets, there is no excuse for naivete regarding the possible effects of a sudden lurch toward its kind of "democracy," the negative effects of which would be born most heavily by the working classes, and especially women, as they have been in Russia and throughout Eastern Europe over the past few years. Thus, however admirable their personal dedication or courage in exposing and opposing some of the worst aspects of the human rights record of the country, the Chinese "Sakharovs" and "Solzhenitsyns," and their Western backers—largely inspired by anticommunism— may rightly be asked to state clearly what else encompasses their vision for China besides "democratization," and to show that they have both the will and the plan to avoid a Russian-style collapse for its people.

That there are class issues involved in such questions was well demonstrated in Changchun at the time of Tiananmen. There the students at some universities went out into the streets, even though their appeal met with only partial support at other schools. But it was at the massive First Auto plant that they met with their greatest rebuff. Calling on the workers to join the demonstration, they were rejected. This left the student activists especially exposed to the repression which followed. There may be many reasons for this division between intellectuals and the working class—the greater economic vulnerability of those in the plants and their family members is an obvious one. But this failure to inspire the workers to join in the cause of the Tiananmen movement left a profound impression on some of the students, a warning that their goals for China were not necessarily those of the proletariat and peasants. At the same time, others complained that they had been misled by Voice of America broadcasts at that time, leading them into mistaken actions which they now regretted, and leaving them quite cynical about the value of the supposedly "free" and "objective" Western media. The conclusion which they drew from this defeat seemed to be that they should not take up the risk of massive struggle and social instability again without a clearer sense of what kinds of aims would have greater appeal to other classes, and thereby gain sufficient strength to have a better chance of success. Such a lesson put a damper on the possibility that the "democracy" spirit of the late 1980s might revive in the near term, or that it would easily reemerge in the same form that it had taken during that period.

Given the millennial struggles and revolutionary history of the Chinese masses, however, it seems even more likely that there will emerge from among their ranks new forms of activism which hark back to the movements of the past century and a half: the great peasant rebellions, massive working class actions in industry and the railroads, and student uprisings of the early twentieth century, a legacy reflected, however faintly and briefly, at Tiananmen in 1989. Into these earlier kinds of struggle will be mixed the "participatory democracy" which at least in theory helped to inspire the Cultural Revolution, and which was, at its best, realized in practice for a few brief years. This democratization from the bottom up, which allowed workers and peasants a direct role in the management of the institutions of the society and insisted that the educated elite too must "learn from the masses," goes beyond anything realized by the bourgeois parliamentary and social-democratic systems of the West. Deeply flawed and incomplete as such efforts in China may have been, they were, in the words of Han Dongping, a "baptism" in self-governance by the masses themselves and a lasting legacy of experimentation in participatory democracy that may inspire further actions much more readily than any Western-based models.

Nevertheless, any renewed struggle to adopt such forms of social organization would also have to find means of broader institutionalization unrealized under Mao. For his "error" in making the Cultural Revolution was not its basic thrust, nor even the sometimes excessive and chaotic struggles which it unleashed—reaction to which became focused on the Gang of Four—but his failure to channel the forces he inspired into regularized institutions of popular expression and power, from the local to the national level, that could have formed a solid foundation for a new level of democratic participation by and for the masses. This "mistake" led to overreliance on the People's Liberation

Army as a unifying factor, preparing the way for the elevation and fall of Lin Biao, and to a restoration of the power of the party without sufficient democratic counterbalance, which included turning once again to purged administrators, most notably Deng Xiaoping. Thus it was not the "error" of going too far, but of not going far enough in transforming the society, that undermined the lasting contribution of the Cultural Revolution, and left it vulnerable to being quickly reversed after the death of Mao. This in turn helped to prepare the way for marketization which, as a reaction to the "Lost Decade," now claims to be introducing the modern "rule of law" and regularized channels for political functions in contrast to "Maoist" anarchy.

But there can be no generalized democratic control by the masses under "market socialism" in its present form, and popular efforts to realize it will most likely be suppressed. To reclaim their role of active participation in running the society, the Chinese people will thus have to rethink the policies of the recent era, and come to terms with the realization that marketization and mass power are ultimately incompatible. Participatory democracy can only be realized if the Chinese once again find a way to engage in class struggle and the "right to rebel" against their oppressors and exploiters at all social levels, with the goal of constantly renewing the socialism won by their revolution. This will require new ideas and methods, fitting the present situation in China and the world, not a simple return to the past.

It is precisely such contradictions and choices which Deng Xiaoping tried to avoid with his assertion that "white cat, black cat, if it catches mice it is a good cat." By this he meant that the means are irrelevant, if they serve positive ends, and that China should concentrate on developing without questioning how. For a while, this ideological program "worked," as the Chinese pursued new possibilities for wealth, and no one can begrudge them their desire for a better and more comfortable life. But it does make a difference which "color cat" catches the "mouse" of development. "Red cats" often "play with their prey," putting other values before that of pure "material consumption." In the process, sometimes the mouse even gets away, leaving the cat hungry. "White cats" are known to forego any such "foolishness." They pounce quickly, and gobble down their dinner, with thoughts only of "getting fat before others." But in their haste and greed, they are left with a severe case of indigestion, and they may even throw up their meal half-eaten. Such "internal contradictions" leave white cats looking better fed, but in the long run, they are more sickly than their red fellows. Fifteen years ago many Chinese grew impatient with "playing with the mouse," which had left them exhausted, and at times even hungry. With growing fervor, they embraced the goals of "white catism," and with the ideological reassurance that "to get fat is glorious," they have eagerly gobbled up all the mice in their reach ever since. But today they are starting to feel an aching in their guts, and the memory of their sleek youth now haunts them when they look in the mirror. "Older" and wiser, and still hurting from the battles of the past, they neither can nor will return to the foolishness in which they once engaged.

Yet if they want to live secure and healthful in their future old age, they may have to give up the goal of becoming "fat cats" as fast as they can, and take up once more the youthful values that once inspired their lives. Such sentiments were expressed in the Academy of Social Science survey "Mao Zedong in the Hearts of Modern People," by one older person who gave a kind of "warning" from revolutionary age to youth.

> With the lapse of time, in the hearts of the Chinese, what content of Mao's thought still has guiding significance for modern society and political life?
> In answering this question, 60 per cent of middle and old people first mentioned "Serve the People".
> One senior worker said excitedly, "Chairman Mao said to serve the people with whole heart and soul. We dare not say that we should use our whole heart and soul. But it is better to use half heart and soul for the people than use whole heart and soul for oneself. In my opinion, it will be enough if we all learn this from Mao."

Unless this attitude spreads more widely again among the older generations, and is once more taken up in turn by the youth, there can be no hope for socialism in China. But this requires moving away from the "get rich quick" ideology of the market reformers, and returning to revolutionary values as a guide to social practice.

More is at stake here than just the form of the domestic society, however. It is the very national sovereignty of China that will ultimately be determined by which direction the Chinese people choose to follow in their "heart and soul." Thus it is Mao himself who gave the definitive reply to Deng Xiaoping, sarcastically repudiating his "cat remark" line.

> Such persons do not grasp class struggle, and always fail to put forward guiding principles. If it is all the same to them whether it is a white cat or a black cat, they will not mind if it is imperialism or Marxism-Leninism either.[1]

As Mao makes clear, there is a relation between ideology and politics and the form and consequences of economic development. If China does not deepen the revolutionary socialist process, the ultimate alternative is reimposition of imperialist control. Contrary to the apparent "burying" of "Maoism," therefore, the very globalization of capital and growing subordination of the Chinese economy to its power make the lessons of the revolution more, not less, relevant in the present.

The people of China, of course, have no more "responsibility" than those of any other country to undertake social struggle or to help lead the entire world. As the example of such revolutionary nations as Cuba shows, even very small countries can have a leading role if they hold to a principled set of values. It least behooves the semi-somnolent and largely well-fed Western left, in the United States especially, to ask the Chinese to keep "making the revolution" for them. If anything, it is the West which needs to find a revolutionary path, which would help open the "socialist road" everywhere. Nevertheless, if any country still has the potential to stand up to the power of global capitalism, and U.S. imperialism in particular, and force a reexamination of the world system—on every issue from human rights to third world development—it is almost certainly China more than any other nation today which can still play this role. Thus the course chosen by the Chinese people in the next few years will have enormous impact on the entire globe. If they move toward full "marketization," there will no longer be any major alternative pole left in the world to the vast power of global capital. But if they still cling to the basic values which marked their revolutionary socialist system, however qualified and weakened now, and move once again to strengthen the collective principles and institutions of their society, they may yet offer effective opposition to the dominance of capitalism and the United States. For the history of the Chinese revolution still offers many keys to the impasse of how the power of globalized capitalism can be confronted worldwide today.

Thus as the renewed battle against global capital develops, and the peoples of the world grope their way toward a new level of understanding of what socialism means, the experience of China, not only before its Liberation, but after as well, will no doubt again offer valuable lessons. This includes such concepts as that of bottom-up struggle on a mass basis, in which every worker, peasant, and intellectual is encouraged to confront the forces of exploitation and oppression, even if they act alone, and to take a direct role in running society at all levels. This combination of collective control by the masses and the right to rebel against arbitrary authority in the widest variety of circumstances, is a powerful legacy of revolutionary practice. So too, the ability to achieve a moderate rate of growth on a sustainable basis, including ecologically, while strengthening egalitarianism between social strata and economic and geographic regions, may well help provide a guide to the future, as the peoples of the world strive for development without class polarization and environmental disaster.

Yet here too the Chinese experience will have to be revised in light of both past failures and present circumstances, and merged with knowledge gained by people worldwide in every arena of struggle. For though capitalism seems well on the way to triumphing everywhere, its forces are coming to be spread very thin, which allows local struggles to escape effective control, especially if they occur simultaneously throughout the global system. As the examples of Somalia and Bosnia indicate—though they hardly serve themselves as models for progressives—the ability of the United States to impose its will is weakening. From the forests of Chiapas to the streets of Okinawa, a broad array of social forces are organizing to oppose the current structure of the international system. Possibilities for the successful renewal of class struggle and mobilization of the masses of people around the globe may therefore be closer to realization than is apparent at the present time, and the movements of the past may soon become more relevant once again.

The experience of China in partially "delinking" from the dominant world system and developing the methods of popular struggle may thus merge with more recent lessons to help point the way toward a new level of resistance to imperialist power and globalized capital. Yet if the Chinese choose only to pursue their own most narrow interests and the goal of "getting rich before others," they will have little to offer the rest of the world in this regard, except the example of one more predatory nation seeking wealth. In that case, their gain will come only at the cost of displacing the current global powers, and their riches too will in time almost inevitably be built on the exploitation of even poorer lands. But there is an alternative, if China holds to its revolutionary past. The Chinese may thus again play a leading role, but only as an equal among others, and only if their growing national power is used once more to "serve the people" of the world.

The ideological debates of the past, and the very concept of class struggle, may seem "old fashioned" in the new age of computers, faxes, and satellite dishes, which bring the outside world even into remote villages. The glitter of Chinese society today is increasingly blinding, pushing into the background any thoughts of the "bad old days" of socialist revolution. This blindness is compounded by the tendency of the growing influx of visitors to China, especially from the United States, to be drawn from the business and professional classes, with their contacts among the Chinese often similarly limited and mainly found in the burgeoning urban centers, particularly Guangzhou, Shanghai, and Beijing. For those like ourselves as well, it was all too easy to forget that even students like those with whom we mainly associated in Changchun still constitute only the tiniest fraction of the population—a mere 2.8 million nationwide, or .23 percent of its people. The overwhelming majority are workers and peasants living in semipoverty, and with whom virtually no Westerners have contact—except, increasingly, as bosses. Thus China and the world have certainly changed, but they are perhaps not as different from the past as those who today dominate the global system would like to think.

In this respect, it is good to remember that Shanghai and other Chinese cities have glittered before, especially in the 1920s and 1930s, as Communist forces took their Long March to power in the countryside. Given the recentness of its rise to wealth, there is already a strangely of *"après moi le déluge"* frenzy, and a quite literal *"fin de siècle"* quality to China, as it faces the new century without the monumental leaders of the one that is ending. The "princes" are said to be stashing their money in Swiss banks, the universal sign worldwide of a growing uneasiness among the rich and powerful, and businesspeople in Guangdong are buying forged U.S. passports for as much as $20,000, "for ease of travel and protection in case Chinese policy changes."[2] Even as some prepare to flee if necessary, others adopt an almost slavish attitude toward foreign capitalists, bringing the new global relations of China and the brutality of the class attitudes which are inseparable from them literally down to "street" level. Thus,

> American bankers and executives are often treated like Communist royalty when they travel on the mainland. When a group of institutional investors traveled to Guangzhou in October, a police car escorted their bus through red lights, shouting cars out of the way with a megaphone and guiding it down one-way streets the wrong way.[3]

It is not difficult to imagine the anger of the people of China, with their deep historical memories, as they are once again forced to make way in their own cities for the foreign capitalists, so reminiscent of the arrogance and "extra-territoriality" of the old imperialist concessions, when "barbarians" from abroad could ignore local laws at will and exclude "dogs and Chinese" from parks. All those with a sense of national pride must shiver at the future prospects of their country, watching officials like these grovel before and collude with the growing power of global capital in "socialist" China.

Beneath the new glitter, there are thus other and older forces rumbling, less blinded by sudden wealth, since they are excluded from it, and their memories may be a good deal longer than those who are newly enriched. For most Chinese, the "new" capitalist forces penetrating their country offer the same old imperialist subordination, dragging them once again into the most brutal and degrading divisions of the world system from which they had escaped. But they are hardly alone in suffering this condition. Across the globe, from 1970 to 1990, the GNP per capita gap between rich and poor countries doubled, from a ratio of 1:28 to 1:56, usually accompanied by ever greater domestic polarization. Even the divide between the middle and top nations increased by half, from 1:6 to 1:9, and these tendencies are still increasing. Such a growing polarity of the people of the world cannot be sustained much longer, and China is no more immune to the consequences than any other nation. When the inevitable day of reckoning comes, all their beepers and fancy cars will not be enough to save the Chinese "new rich," any more than their counterparts elsewhere, if the workers and peasants of China in their hundreds of millions decide that they have had enough, and return once again to the revolutionary road they followed for so long and on which they gained so much.

NOTES

INTRODUCTION: THE "THIRD WAY"

1. Mao Zedong, "On Coalition Government," in *Selected Works* Vol. III (Peking: Foreign Languages Press, 1967), p. 257.

CHINA AT THE BRINK

1. The common exchange value of the yuan was changed on 1 January 1994, from around 5.7:US$1 to 8.7:US$1. This accounts for the variations in the conversion rates from different time periods.
2. *China Daily*, 6 August 1995.
3. *China Daily Business Weekly*, 19 December 1994.
4. *China Daily Business Weekly*, 19-25 September 1993.
5. *China Daily Business Weekly*, 8 May 1995.
6. *New York Times*, 15 February 1993, p. A6.
7. *China Daily*, 9 October 1994.
8. *China Daily*, 22 November 1993.
9. *China Daily*, 10 March 1994.
10. *China Daily*, 7 February 1994.
11. *China Daily Business Weekly*, 28 November-4 December 1993.
12. Peter M. Lichtenstein, *China at the Brink: The Political Economy of Reform and Retrenchments in the Post-Mao Era* (New York: Praeger, 1991), p. 74.
13. *New York Times*, 3 March 1995, p. A14.
14. *China Daily*, 30 April 1994.
15. *New York Times*, 29 December 1992, p. D17.
16. *New York Times*, 11 May 1993, p. A4.
17. Ibid.
18. *China Daily*, 28 September 1993.
19. *China Daily Business Weekly*, 24-30 October 1993.
20. *China Daily Business Weekly*, 19-25 September 1993.
21. Ibid.
22. *China Daily*, 28 March 1994.

23. *New York Times*, 26 March 1992, p. A14.
24. *New York Times*, 10 April 1994, p. A3.
25. *China Daily*, 31 October 1994.
26. *China Daily*, 28 November 1994.
27. *China Daily*, 26 October 1994.
28. Ibid.
29. *China Daily*, 27 April 1995.
30. *China Daily*, 31 October 1994.
31. *China Daily*, 11 March 1995.
32. *China Daily*, 9 March 1995.
33. *China Daily*, 16 February 1995.
34. *New York Times*, 14 April 1991, p. A8.
35. *China Daily*, 26 October 1994.
36. *New York Times*, 14 April 1991, p. A8.
37. *China Daily*, 3 May 1994.
38. *China Daily*, 27 April 1995.
39. *China Daily*, 20 March 1995.
40. *China Daily*, 27 April 1995.
41. *China Daily Business Weekly*, 20 March 1995.
42. Ibid.
43. *China Daily*, 10 February 1995.
44. *China Daily*, 29 April 1995.
45. *China Daily Business Weekly*, 20 March 1995.
46. *China Daily*, 13 February 1995.
47. *China Daily*, 3 June 1995.
48. Ibid.
49. *China Daily*, 24 November 1994.
50. *China Daily*, 7 June 1995.
51. *China Daily*, 1 November 1993.
52. *China Daily*, 7 June 1995.
53. *China Daily*, 12 May 1994.
54. *China Daily*, 21 February 1995.
55. *China Daily*, 15 February 1995.
56. *China Daily*, 9 March 1995.
57. *China Daily*, 21 February 1995.
58. *China Daily*, 17 February 1995.
59. *China Daily*, 17 June 1995.
60. *China Daily*, 1 March 1995.
61. *China Daily*, March 29 1994.
62. Ibid.
63. *China Daily*, 25 May 1995.
64. *China Daily*, 23 July 1994.
65. *China Daily*, 25 May 1995.
66. *China Daily*, 23 July 1994.
67. Ibid.
68. *New York Times*, 4 August 1991.
69. *China Daily*, 20 December 1994.

70. *China Daily*, 3 June 1995.

71. Ibid.

72. *China Daily*, 28 April 1995.

73. Ibid.

74. *China Daily*, 15 November 1993, 12 November 1993.

75. *New York Times*, 15 August 1993.

76. Ibid.

77. *New York Times*, 15 November 1995, p. A7.

78. *New York Times*, 17 July 1995.

79. Ibid.

80. *New York Times*, 15 November 1995, pp. A1, A7.

81. Ibid.

82. Maria Antonietta Macciocchi, *Daily Life in Revolutionary China* (New York: Monthly Review Press, 1972), p. 106.

83. *China Daily*, 7 June 1995.

84. *China Daily Business Weekly*, 20 February 1995.

85. Ibid.

86. *China Daily*, 5 May 1995.

87. *China Daily*, 16 February 1995.

88. *China Daily*, October 11 1993.

89. *China Daily*, 7 June 1995.

90. *China Daily*, 27 February 1995.

91. *China Daily*, 27 April 1995.

92. *China Daily Business Weekly*, 13 February 1995.

93. Ibid.

94. *China Daily*, 30 April 1994.

95. *China Daily*, 4 November 1994.

96. *New York Times*, 29 December 1992, p. D17.

97. *New York Times*, 11 May 1993, p. A4.

98. *China Daily*, 31 May 1995.

OF TIME AND THE CHANGJIANG:
CHINESE HISTORY PAST, PRESENT, AND FUTURE

1. Elisabeth Croll, *From Heaven to Earth: Images and Experiences of Development in China* (New York: Routledge, 1994), p. 7.

2. Agnes Smedley, *The Great Road* (New York: Monthly Review Press, 1956), pp. 23-34.

3. Han Suyin, *Wind in the Tower: Mao Tsetung and the Chinese Revolution 1949-1975* (Boston: Little, Brown, 1976), p. 222.

4. *China Daily*, 1 February 1994.

5. Ibid.

6. *China Daily*, 13 September 1994.

7. Ibid.

8. *China Daily*, 23 September 1994.

9. *China Daily*, 7 June 1995.

10. *China Daily*, 23 September 1994.

11. *China Daily*, May 8 1995.

12. *China Daily*, 27 February 1995.
13. Ibid.
14. *China Daily*, 23 March 1995.
15. *China Daily*, 3 April 1995.
16. *China Daily*, 5 September 1994.
17. *China Daily*, 3 June 1995.
18. *China Daily*, 27 September 1994.
19. *China Daily*, 28 October 1994.
20. *China Daily*, 25 February 1995.
21. *China Daily*, 2 January 1995.
22. *China Daily*, 26 January 1995.
23. *China Daily*, 4 May 1995.
24. *China Daily*, 3 October 1994.
25. *China Daily*, 8 October 1994.
26. *China Daily*, 25 March 1995.
27. Ibid.
28. *China Daily*, 29 October 1994.
29. *China Daily*, 8 June 1995.
30. *China Daily*, 29 October 1994.
31. *China Daily*, 8 October 1993.
32. *China Daily*, 9 December 1993.
33. *China Daily*, 22 March 1995.
34. *China Daily*, 3 May 1995.
35. *China Daily*, 3 April 1995.
36. *China Daily*, 20 September 1994.
37. *New York Times*, 15 January 1996, p. A4.
38. Middletown (New York) *Times Herald Record*, 3 April 1992.
39. *China Daily*, 31 December 1993.
40. *China Daily*, 21 February 1995.
41. *China Daily*, 31 December 1993.
42. *New York Times*, 14 October 1995, p. A1.
43. *China Daily*, 20 September 1994.
44. Ibid.
45. *New York Times*, 15 January 1996, p. A4.
46. See, inter alia, *Chinese Geography and Environment* 1, nos. 3-4, and *Chinese Environment and Development*, Spring 1993.
47. *New York Times*, 15 January 1996, p. A4.
48. *New York Times*, 21 January 1992, p. C10.
49. *New York Times*, 15 January 1996, p. A4.
50. Ibid.

OF HUMAN RIGHTS AND WRONGS: CHINA AND THE UNITED STATES

1. *New York Times*, 29 January 1990, p. B1.
2. *China Daily*, 27 February 1995.
3. Ibid.
4. *China Daily*, 11 March 1995.

5. *China Daily*, 8 February 1995.
6. *China Daily*, 27 February 1995.
7. Ibid.
8. *China Daily*, 27 February 1994.
9. *China Daily*, 17 February 1995.
10. *China Daily*, 7 March 1995.
11. *China Daily*, 11 March 1995.
12. Ibid.
13. *New York Times*, 23 February 1995, p. A9.
14. James F. Petras and Morris H. Morley, "The New Cold War: Reagan's Policy Toward Europe and the Third World" in James Petras, et al., *Capitalist and Socialist Crises in the Late Twentieth Century* (Totowa NJ: Rowman & Allanheld, 1983), p. 14.
15. *China Daily*, 10 February 1995.
16. *China Daily*, 7 March 1995.
17. *China Daily*, 4 March 1995.
18. *New York Times*, 30 March 1994, p. A10.
19. *New York Times*, 9 March 1995, p. A5.
20. *New York Times*, 29 March 1994, p. B7.

MEIGUO, ZHONGGUO:
"AMERICA THE BEAUTIFUL" VERSUS "CHINA THE CENTRAL"

1. *China Daily*, 6 April 1995.
2. Ibid.
3. Middletown (New York) *Times Herald Record*, 3 January 1995.
4. *China Daily*, 27 October 1993.
5. *New York Times*, 12 March 1995, p. A1.
6. *China Daily Business Weekly*, 30 January 1995.
7. *China Daily*, 13 October 1993.
8. *China Daily*, 4 January 1995.
9. *China Daily*, 2 January 1995.
10. *China Daily*, 7 February 1995.
11. *China Daily Business Weekly*, 3 April 1995.
12. Ibid.
13. Ssu-yu Teng and John K. Fairbank, "China's Response to the West," in Robert T. Dernberger, Kenneth J. DeWoskin, Steven M. Goldstein, Rhoads Murphey, and Martin K. Whyte, eds., *The Chinese: Adapting the Past, Facing the Future* (Ann Arbor: Center for Chinese Studies, University of Michigan, 1991), p. 69.
14. *China Daily*, 5 June 1995.
15. Ibid.
16. *China Daily*, 1 November 1993.
17. *China Daily*, 17 February 1995.
18. Ibid.
19. *New York Times*, 19 June 1991, p. A4.
20. *China Daily*, 24 February 1995.
21. *China Daily*, 4 May 1995.

22. *China Daily*, 9 January 1995.
23. *China Daily Business Weekly*, 9 January 1995.
24. *China Daily*, 25 October 1993.
25. *China Daily*, 19 November 1993.
26. *New York Times*, 27 February 1995, p. D1.
27. *China Daily*, 17 January 1995.
28. *China Daily*, 1 March 1995.
29. *China Daily Business Weekly*, 5 June 1995.
30. Ibid.
31. *China Daily Business Weekly*, 20 March 1995.
32. *China Daily*, 22 February 1995.
33. Ibid.
34. *New York Times*, 17 February 1995, p. A1.
35. Mao Tsetung, *Five Essays on Philosophy* (Peking: Foreign Languages Publishing House, 1977), p. 155.
36. Karl Marx and Friedrich Engels, *The German Ideology* (Moscow: Progress Publishers, 1976), p. 67.
37. *New York Times*, 17 January 1995, p. A18.
38. *China Daily*, 5 January 1995.
39. *China Daily*, 16 January 1995.
40. Ibid.
41. *New York Times*, 17 January 1995, p. A18.
42. *China Daily*, 6 January 1995.
43. *China Daily Business Weekly*, 16 January 1995.
44. *New York Times*, 8 January 1996, p. C3.
45. *China Daily*, 19 December 1994.
46. *New York Times*, 18 February 1995.
47. *China Daily*, 2 December 1994.
48. *New York Times*, 16 February 1995, p. D6.
49. *New York Times*, 8 February 1995, p. D1.
50. *New York Times*, 3 January 1995, p. C10.
51. *China Daily*, 5 December 1994.
52. *China Daily*, 10 December 1993.
53. *China Daily*, 1 March 1995.
54. *China Daily Business Weekly*, 5 December 1994.
55. Ibid.
56. *New York Times*, 27 February 1995, p. D6.
57. *China Daily*, 20 May 1995.
58. *New York Times*, 27 February 1995, p. D1.
59. *New York Times*, 1 December 1995.
60. *China Daily Business Weekly*, 23 January 1995.
61. *China Daily*, 7 November 1994.
62. *San Jose Mercury News*, 18 September 1995, p. 11A.
63. *China Daily*, 3 June 1995.
64. *China Daily*, 2 May 1995.
65. *China Daily*, 10 May 1995.
66. *New York Times*, 26 December 1994.

67. *China Daily Business Weekly*, 22 May 1995.
68. *China Daily*, 2 December 1994.
69. *China Daily*, 13 March 1995.
70. *China Daily*, 24 December 1994.
71. *China Daily Business Weekly*, 16 January 1995.
72. *China Daily*, 29 December 1994.
73. *China Daily Business Weekly*, 5 December 1995.
74. *China Daily*, 17 June 1995.
75. V.I. Lenin, *Imperialism: The Highest Stage of Capitalism* (New York: International, 1969).
76. J.A. Hobson, *Imperialism: a Study* (London: George Allen and Unwin Ltd., 1938), pp. 308-9.
77. *China Daily*, 2 January 1995.
78. *China Daily*, 5 December 1994.
79. *China Daily*, 22 December 1994.
80. *China Daily*, 5 December 1994.
81. *China Daily*, 12 January 1995.
82. Ibid.
83. *China Daily*, 6 January 1995.
84. *China Daily*, 27 December 1994.
85. *China Daily Business Weekly*, 7 November 1994.
86. *China Daily*, 14 December 1994.
87. *Far Eastern Economic Review*, 1 September 1994, p. 48.
88. *China Daily*, 20 May 1995.
89. *China Daily*, 18 February 1995.
90. *China Daily*, 20 May 1995.
91. *China Daily*, 23 November 1994.
92. *China Daily*, 12 January 1995; 30 March 1994.
93. *China Daily*, 30 March 1995.
94. *China Daily*, 25 March 1995.
95. *China Daily*, 25 May 1995.
96. *China Daily*, 5 June 1995.
97. *China Daily*, 31 May 1995.
98. A. Tom Grunfeld, *The Making of Modern Tibet* (London: Zed, 1987), pp. 11, 13.
99. *China Daily*, 9 March 1994.
100. *China Daily*, 16 March 1995.
101. Grunfeld, p. 63.
102. Ibid., p. 55.
103. *China Daily*, 2 February 1995.
104. *China Daily*, 24 May 1995.
105. *China Daily*, 5 June 1995.
106. *China Daily*, 30 March 1995.
107. *New York Times*, 31 January 1996, p. A2.
108. *New York Times*, 10 June 1995, p. A4.
109. *New York Times*, 24 January 1996, p. A3.
110. Rupert Hodder, *The West Pacific Rim: An Introduction* (London: Belhaven Press, 1992), p. 114. Quote from *The Economist*, 16 November 1991, p. 18.

111. *New York Times*, 18 May 1995, p. A25.
112. *New York Times*, 25 October 1995, p. A15.
113. Nicholas D. Kristoff, "The Real Chinese Threat," *New York Times Magazine*, 27 August 1995, p. 50.
114. Middletown (New York) *Times Herald Record*, 10 July 1995.
115. *New York Times*, 11 June 1995.
116. Ibid.
117. *China Daily*, 16 June 1995.
118. *Far Eastern Economic Review*, 1 September 1994, p. 46.
119. *The Defense Monitor* 22, no. 2 (1993): 4; *New York Times*, 1 February 1995, p. A20.
120. *China Daily*, 19 January 1995.
121. *New York Times*, 2 February 1995.
122. *China Daily*, 20 May 1995.
123. *China Daily*, 6 September 1994.
124. Ibid.
125. *New York Times*, 2 January 1995.
126. *China Daily*, 25 March 1995.
127. *New York Times*, 2 January 1995.
128. *China Daily*, 18 November 1994.
129. *New York Times*, 5 May 1995, p. A11.
130. *New York Times*, 2 January 1995.
131. *China Daily Business Weekly*, 24-30 October 1993.
132. Kristoff, "The Real Chinese Threat," p. 50.
133. *New York Times*, 27 February 1995, p. D1.
134. *New York Times*, 30 December 1994, p. A8.
135. *China Daily*, 11 December 1993.
136. *China Daily*, 15 May 1995.
137. *China Daily*, 28 March 1994.
138. *New York Times*, 18 February 1995, p. 4.
139. *China Daily*, 12 November 1994.
140. Kristoff, "The Real Chinese Threat," p. 51.
141. *New York Times*, 23 May 1995, p. A10.
142. *New York Times*, 20 March 1996, p. A9.
143. *New York Times*, 1 August 1995, p. A2.
144. Immanuel Wallerstein, *The Capitalist World-Economy* (New York: Cambridge University Press, 1979), pp. 5-6.
145. *China Daily*, 31 May 1995.
146. *China Daily*, 7 June 1995.
147. Ibid.
148. *New York Times*, 27 August 1995, p. A6.
149. *New York Times*, 1 February 1991.
150. *China Daily*, 25 March 1995.
151. *China Daily*, 15 May 1995.
152. Ibid.
153. *China Daily Business Weekly*, 26 September 1994.
154. *China Daily*, 8 June 1995.

MAO AND DENG:
"ONE-AND-A-HALF-" OR "TWO-LINE" STRUGGLE?

1. *China Daily*, 27 December 1993.
2. *Los Angeles Times*, 21 March 1992, p. A1.
3. *China Daily*, 27 December 1995.
4. *China Daily*, 3 November 1993.
5. Ibid.
6. Mao Tse-tung, *Selected Works*, Vol. I (Peking: Foreign Languages Press, 1967), pp. 26-27.
7. Quoted in Immanuel Wallerstein, *The Capitalist World-Economy* (New York: Cambridge University Press, 1979), p. 11.
8. Han Suyin, *Wind in the Tower: Mao Tsetung and the Chinese Revolution 1949-1975* (Boston: Little, Brown and Co., 1976), p. 246.
9. "Speech at the Rally of People of All Walks of Life in Yenan Held to Celebrate the 60th Birthday of Stalin" (April 1965), quoted in *The Great Proletarian Cultural Revolution in China (10)* (Peking: Foreign Languages Press, 1967), frontispiece.
10. Comments made by Mao at the working conference of the Central Committee of the Communist Party at Peitaiho, August 1992, and the Tenth Plenary Session of the Eighth Central Committee, September 1992, quoted in *Important Documents on the Great Proletarian Cultural Revolution in China* (Peking: Foreign Languages Press, 1970), p. 20.
11. Statement made regarding the "Draft Decision of the Central Committee of the Chinese Communist Party on Certain Problems in Our Present Rural Work," May 1963, quoted in ibid., p. 22.
12. *China Daily*, 25 November 1993.
13. *China Daily*, 5 November 1993.
14. *China Daily*, 6 November 1993.
15. *China Daily*, 15 November 1993.
16. *China Daily*, 12 November 1993.
17. *China Daily*, 28 September 1994.
18. *China Daily*, 15 November 1993.
19. *China Daily*, 13 November 1993.
20. *China Daily*, 8 November 1993.
21. *China Daily*, 6 November 1993.
22. *China Daily*, 5 November 1993.
23. Ibid.
24. *China Daily*, 13 November 1993.
25. Arif Dirlik, *Transforming the Revolution: Waking to Global Capitalism* (Hanover, NH: Wesleyan University Press, 1994), p. 88.
26. *China Daily*, 13 November 1993.
27. *The Nation*, 11 June 1990, p. 811.
28. *China Daily*, 15 November 1993.
29. *China Daily*, 20 May 1995.
30. *China Daily*, 11 March 1995.
31. Carl Riskin, *China's Political Economy: The Quest for Development Since 1949* (Oxford: Oxford University Press, 1987), p. 138.

32. Lowell Ditmer, *Liu Shao-ch'i and the Chinese Cultural Revolution: The Politics of Mass Criticism* (Berkeley: University of California Press, 1979), p. 41.

33. *China Daily*, 5 November 1994.

34. Mao Tsetung, speech at Chengchow, 27 February 1959, in Mark Selden, ed., *The People's Republic of China: A Documentary History of Revolutionary Change* (New York: Monthly Review Press, 1979), pp. 467-74.

35. Jonathan D. Spence, *The Search for Modern China* (New York: W. W. Norton, 1990), p. 670.

36. Susumu Yabuki, *China's New Political Economy: The Giant Awakens*, translated by Stephen M. Harner (Boulder: Westview, 1995), pp. 20-21, figure 3.3.

37. Robert Pollin and Alexander Cockburn, "The World, the Free Market, and the Left," *The Nation*, 25 February 1991, p. 227.

38. Peter M. Lichtenstein, *China at the Brink: The Political Economy of Reform and Retrenchments in the Post-Mao Era* (New York: Praeger, 1991), pp. 51, 53-55, Tables 3.3-3.8.

39. Ibid., p. 28.

40. Judith Banister, *China's Changing Population*, p. 83.

41. Ibid., pp. 83-84.

42. Ibid., p. 87.

43. *New York Times*, 14 May 1991, p. 8.

44. Banister, p. 94.

45. Ibid., p. 92-93.

46. *China Daily*, 26 May 1995; 2 March 1995.

47. George Thomas Kurian, *The New Book of World Rankings* (New York: Facts on File Publications, 1984), pp. 327-329, Tables 256, 257.

48. Ibid., pp. 331-332, Table 259.

49. Banister, p. 116, note.

50. *New York Times*, 14 April 1991, p. 1.

51. Ibid., pp. 1, 8.

52. Ibid., p. 8.

53. *New York Times*, 30 March 1991, p. 2.

54. *New York Times*, 14 April 1991, p. 1.

55. *New York Times*, 17 June 1991, pp. A1, A8.

56. Ibid.

57. *San Jose Mercury News*, 7 March 1996, p. 14E.

58. *San Jose Mercury News*, 23 October 1995, p. 14A.

59. Lichtenstein, *China at the Brink*.

60. Han Dongping, "Cultural Revolution in Villages," unpublished thesis, 1992.

61. Richard Curt Kraus, "Withdrawing from the World-System: Self-Reliance and Class Structure in China," Chap. 10 in Walter L. Goldfrank, ed., *The World-System of Capitalism* (Beverly Hills: Sage Publications, 1979), p. 247.

62. Han Dongping, "Cultural Revolution in Villages."

63. Ibid.

64. Judith Goldman, *New York Times Book Review*, 12 February 1995, p. 16.

65. Orville Schell, *The Nation*, 17-24 July 1995, p. 86.

66. Andrew Nathan, Foreword to Li Zhisui, *The Private Life of Chairman Mao* (New York: Random House, 1995), p. vii.

67. Academy of Social Sciences, "Mao Zedong in the Hearts of Modern People," Beijing, 1993.
68. Ibid.
69. Ibid.
70. Schell, p. 86.
71. "Mao Zedong in the Hearts of Modern People."
72. Han Dongping, "Cultural Revolution in Villages."
73. Ibid.
74. *San Jose Mercury News*, 14 October 1994, p. 23A.
75. Ibid.
76. C.H. Hua et al, "An Open Letter Critiquing the Memoirs of the Private Physician of Mao Zedong," pp. 4-5; Li Zhisui, *The Private Life of Chairman Mao.*
77. *China Daily*, 25 November 1993.

CONCLUSION: THE MOTIVE FORCE OF HISTORY

1. Quoted in Su Ya and Jia Shengzhu, *Bai Mao Hei Mao: Zhongguo Gaige Xianzhuang Toushi* [*White Cat, Black Cat: Chinese Reform—Present Situation and Perspective*] (Changsha: Hunan Art and Literature Publishing House, 1992), p. 1.
2. *New York Times*, 26 March 1992, p. A1.
3. *New York Times*, 15 February 1993, p. A6.

INDEX